You're Not the Boss of Me!

Understanding the Six/Seven-Year-Old Transformation

Ruth Ker, Editor

Editor: Ruth Ker
Cover and Interior Illustrations: Barbara Klocek
Graphic Design: Sheila Harrington
Managing Editor: Lory Widmer
Editorial Support: Lydia Roberson
Administrative Support: Melissa Lyons

© Waldorf Early Childhood Association of North America
First English Edition, 2007
Published in the United States by the
Waldorf Early Childhood Association of North America
285 Hungry Hollow Road
Spring Valley, NY 10977

Grateful acknowledgment is made to Floris Books
for permission to reprint an excerpt from
Freya Jaffke's book *Work and Play in Early Childhood* on pages 77 to 79.

This publication is made possible through a grant from the Waldorf Curriculum Fund.

Library of Congress Cataloging-in-Publication Data

978-0-9722238-8-1

10 9 8 7 6 5 4 3 2 1

Contents

Section Six

Foreword

When we are able as Waldorf early childhood educators to share our experiences and heartfelt questions with our colleagues, wonderful things begin to happen. Carried and nurtured by a larger group, our questions deepen and grow. We receive new intuitions and insights for our work with the children, parents and colleagues. And if we are able to share these questions with one another over time, a mood of research develops, and the fruits of this research become visible and can be shared with others. This book represents the harvest of such collaborative research, carried over the past seven years.

It all began with a question carried in the heart of Ruth Ker from the Sunrise School in Duncan, British Columbia. It was Ruth who in 2001 first expressed to the WECAN Board her concerns about the older children in our kindergartens: were we truly meeting their needs? She noticed that she herself struggled in her encounters with the older children, and that the children themselves seemed to be asking for something more than she was able to provide. With support from WECAN, Ruth surveyed kindergarten teachers throughout North America to see how they viewed their work and then embarked upon a journey, visiting kindergartens throughout North America to experience how the older children and their teachers were faring. During her travels, she encountered others who carried similar questions, all working in very different ways to meet the older children they worked with.

These colleagues joined Ruth in 2003 to form a WECAN Working Group on the Older Child: Barbara Klocek from the Sacramento Waldorf School, Tim Bennett from the Seattle Waldorf School, Louise deForest from the Green Meadow Waldorf School in Chestnut Ridge, New York, and Nancy Blanning from the Denver Waldorf School. Through the generous support of the Norton Foundation, this WECAN Working Group was able to meet in retreats each year for three years, sharing and deepening their questions. Other educators, medical doctors, and parents were invited to join them in their efforts, and the initial intent to share their thoughts in a small *Gateways* collection grew into this major resource on the older child in the kindergarten, *You're Not the Boss of Me!* The fruits of the Working Group's activity have grown beyond what could be encompassed in one volume: a second volume on school readiness is planned for the coming year.

The activity of the WECAN Working Group has also grown beyond our North American borders; the International Association for Steiner/Waldorf Early Childhood Education has recently formed a Working Group on the Six-Year-Old Child, so that these questions can be pursued and deepened on a worldwide basis. As educational reforms in Europe and throughout the world bring pressures on Waldorf Schools to lower school entrance age and introduce school experiences to kindergarten-aged children, the need to understand and advocate for the needs of six-year-olds becomes ever more urgent. We are pleased that our WECAN Working Group is able to make a contribution to this growing need.

And it all began with a question carried in Ruth Ker's heart! We thank her for her loyal pursuit of the question, her deep capacity for listening with respect to the perspectives and different approaches of others, her willingness to develop new capacities in order to serve the work, and her midwifery skills in bringing this publication to birth. Many thanks also to the Working Group members and their colleagues for their excellent contributions to this shared research project, and especially to Barbara Klocek for her artistry, visible on the cover and in the illustrations.

The Waldorf Early Childhood Association is very pleased to publish this collection. We hope that it will offer insights into the growing child, practical support for teaching and parenting, and a stimulus for development.

Susan Howard
WECAN Coordinator

Introduction

Ruth Ker

This is not a book that will tell you the way things ought to be done in a Waldorf kindergarten. Rather, it's a collection of articles written by people who are currently teachers, doctors and parents of kindergarten children. These people, who offer their thoughts in the hopes of strengthening and broadening our understanding for the older child in the kindergarten, carry daily questions themselves. This book is also addressed to parents, and works with the intention of strengthening the bonds between the parent and the teacher. I hope that you will find ideas within the covers of this book that will connect to your own personal endeavors and reinforce your own unique artistry. Maybe a few new inspirations will creep in as you read through the pages as well.

In the 1980s there were a variety of conferences featuring master teachers who were speaking about how they addressed certain early childhood issues. As audiences listened to these colleagues from Europe, Scandinavia and North America, it became obvious that there were many approaches to this blessed work we have undertaken. Once one got over the shock that "there is no manual," comfort could be taken in the fact that there is room for flexibility and personal artistry within the basic tenets of Waldorf early childhood education.

Time and again, Rudolf Steiner speaks about the teacher as an artist. And, it certainly was artistry I encountered when I began my search on behalf of the WECAN Board to find others who could work with me on the Older Child in the Kindergarten project.

The goal of this search was to find teachers who were accomplished and comfortable in their work with the older kindergarten children, and to select a variety of teachers with different approaches so that understanding of this stage of child development could be deepened and expanded. I was excited to make these journeys to Massachusetts, Maine, New York, Washington State and California, but I wasn't prepared for the powerful effect these people would have on my own classroom. As I write this, I feel such gratitude for what these colleagues have taught me and for how the children in my own kindergarten have benefited.

It's important to note why this research group was born in the first place. It arose initially out of a continued perception on the part of our North American kindergarten mentor teachers that many teachers were struggling with the older children in the kindergarten. In 2002, the Waldorf Early Childhood Association of North America responded to these queries by sending out and later publishing the results from a survey on this topic. WECAN wanted to know if the teachers themselves were experiencing frustrations about the work with the older children. What were their struggles? What was going well and what were their burning questions? A copy of this still-pertinent survey can be acquired through WECAN Publications and it contains many astute observations and suggestions from colleagues all across North America.

When it became obvious that it would be of benefit to explore this topic more, advice was sought from the survey respondents and from WECAN Board members about who could be helpful partners to assist in this work. Then funds were sought to make it possible for me to travel to the classrooms of these teachers and search out members to participate with me on a WECAN Older Child in the Kindergarten Project Group. This group was often referred to as the Working Group on the Six-year-old.

The first classroom I visited was that of Barbara Klocek in Fair Oaks, California. There I encountered a balanced indoor/outdoor program with strong routines and lively children who were held with firm, loving limits. Drama, puppetry and creative play, interspersed with work activities. flowed throughout the morning program, intermingled with musical interludes. Here I also witnessed older girls and boys tenderly and creatively playing with their "Little Ones." (You can read more about the Little Ones in Section Three). Barbara had many older boys and girls in her class who were meaningfully engaged throughout the whole session. The presence of the healing forces of love and joy in this kindergarten were palpable.

Visiting Louise deForest in Chestnut Ridge, New York was an opportunity to experience an inter-generational program. Not only did I spend a kindergarten morning with her but, after the session, I went for a meal at the Fellowship Community (a home for the elderly) situated close by her kindergarten. The meal was a delicious main course followed by the apple cobbler that Louise and her kindergarten children had prepared that morning. In

Louise's morning kindergarten program, after some play, circle songs and indoor snack preparation, the rest of the morning was spent outside doing meaningful work for the Fellowship Community. It was delightful to accompany Louise and her students through the fields and blossoming apple orchards to the farm where the kindergarten children do farm maintenance chores each day. I helped as the children picked up rocks on the fields, planted some seeds, cleaned stalls, and fed the cows, horses, and sheep. (You can read more about this program in Section Four.) Louise's work is permeated with great warmth and meaningful work activities.

Tim Bennett's program in Seattle, Washington is located in an enchanting garden oasis situated close by a busy intersection. The morning session began with an outdoor circle that included the parents. Then I marvelled as he and the children confidently crossed this intersection where five roads meet and meandered their way through a vast city park. The park had many movement and play experiences for the children—large climbing hills; cement bunkers for balancing upon; tall trees with overhanging branches on which to swing; rabbit warrens where the bunnies popped out when the children climbed onto the surrounding rocks; green meadows with tiny flowers; and trees with canopies that enabled the children to hide out or build little spaces within their embracing branches. Along the walk there were stopping places and the children launched into activity whenever this happened. Tim whittled quietly or responded to the children in a matter-of-fact, patient, and firm way. We walked back to the classroom, once again crossed the intersection and played in the outdoor play yard while snack was prepared. The play yard also had challenging movement experiences for the older children. Here I saw a child skipping with a chicken in her arms and also two children experimenting with raising and lowering each other up and down with a thick rope hoisted over the limb of a large tree. Tim's presence was quietly capable and the environment inspired the children to meet their needs for challenging movement activities.

Nancy Blanning's developmental movement circles captivated me when I experienced them in a curative training course where I was her student. In her school in Denver, Colorado, where she is a part-time remedial teacher, she is able to visit the kindergarten and share some of her circles. This helps her to work with individual children and the whole group, and to assist the kindergarten teachers with their first-grade-readiness assessments. Nancy's work as a remedial teacher has deepened her insights into child development and the movement needs of the young child, and has heightened her observation skills. She has been a valuable asset to our project group.

Above, I alluded to the changes that developed in my own approach after visiting these colleagues. These adaptations unfolded over time throughout the program that I operate of balanced indoor and outdoor activities. How could I avoid taking along a big rope on our morning walks just in case there was a tree limb close by? How could I resist finding a way to bring the "little ones" to the children; or adapting a much needed quiet rest time to my daily routine; or using movement journeys at circle time; or looking around my environment to discover how we could better serve the community through meaningful work activities? Old Man Trouble (see Section Two) has also been a valuable disciplinary tool for some of my frisky older kindergarten children.

After visiting these colleagues and asking for their interested participation in this working group, grants were applied for and received. Then, we began to gather together once yearly for three years to study Rudolf Steiner's lectures on the nature of early childhood and more specifically, on the change of teeth and the birth of the etheric. Phone and email conversations happened in between, and also research with other colleagues throughout North America and Europe. Consultations with anthroposophical doctors helped us to orient to other reference books and the medical perspectives surrounding this important transition time of the six-year change.

Living meditatively into the words and indications of Rudolf Steiner made all of our work together come alive.

This time of change, which basically reflects the transition time beginning somewhere around five and extending to the time when the child is ready for first grade, has been called many things. In this book you will see it called the six/seven-year transformation, the six-year-old change, the crisis of will and imagination, the birth of the etheric, the seven-year crisis, the six-year crisis, the change of teeth and so on. Part of our retreat time was caught up with reflecting upon the many ways of explaining and naming this potent time of transformation. When the change happens, and the mysteries surrounding what the older child in the kindergarten undergoes, were explored on many different levels.

These concentrated times of retreat and study served to potentize each one of our individual classroom practices. The results of our observations during the year away from one another, along with the fruits of our continuing research, added to our next Working Group retreats.

Living meditatively into the words and indications of Rudolf Steiner made all of our work together come alive in a way that I have never experienced when studying as an individual on my own. What the children were doing in the classroom had even more meaning for me and led me to penetrate the topic of our study even more. We all sampled first hand what Freya Jaffke expresses in On the Play of the Child: "Every teacher who lives intensively with the various indications given by Rudolf Steiner (also meditatively with certain passages) will notice a growing sense of responsibility towards the children."[1] It is safe to say, in this case, that this "responsibility towards the children" expanded to include a genuine desire to

---

1   Freya Jaffke, ed. *On the Play of the Child: Indications by Rudolf Steiner for Working with Young Children*, (Spring Valley, NY: WECAN Publications, 2004), 3.

share the fruits of our labor with parents and teachers. We concluded that to write a book together was the perfect way to serve beyond our individual classrooms and bring a more compassionate understanding for the older children in the kindergarten to others.

As we assembled all of the various contributions for this book, it became apparent that two separate volumes were being formed. *You're Not the Boss of Me!* is the first volume. The second volume, which is scheduled to be published in 2008, will be a collection of articles on the topics of school readiness and the transition into the grade school.

I have never edited nor written a book before and this has been a steep learning curve for me. Many people have put their confidence in my fledgling skills and many people have helped this book to happen, particularly the Working Group; my dear husband, Michael Ker; Susan Howard; and the managing editors of this volume, Lydia Roberson and Lory Widmer. A big heartfelt thank-you to all of these people.

The result of all of this effort is the book that you hold in your hands. We all hope that it will aid you in your work.

May your work be blessed with the life and spirit that serves as a wellspring for the children who carry our future.

—*Ruth Ker, June, 2007*

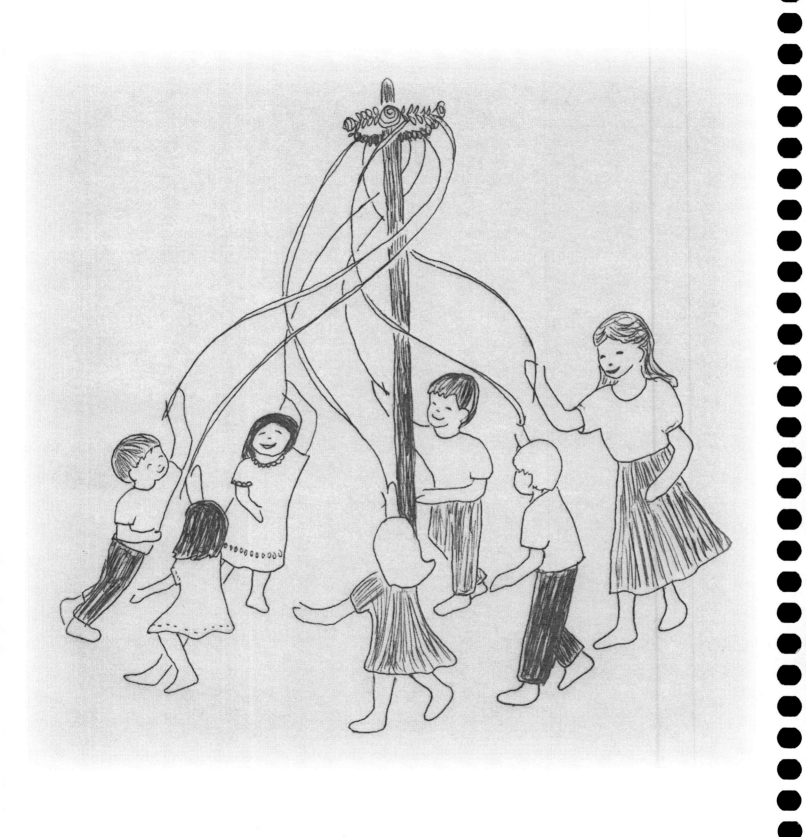

Pictures
of the
Six/Seven-Year
Change

When at the change of teeth the etheric body is loosened and stands alone, then the building up of the memory is separated off from the physical, and remains almost entirely in the element of soul, and this fact can really put the teachers on the right track. For before this change, the soul and spirit formed a unity with the physical and etheric. After this, the physical, which formerly worked together with the soul, is expressed in the form of the second teeth, and what collaborated with the physical in this process is separated off and is revealed as an increase in the power of forming ideas, and in the formation and reliability of the memory.

Rudolf Steiner
The Roots of Education

Observations
of the
Six-Year-Old Change

Ruth Ker

Much has been said in the Waldorf movement about the nine-year change. But what about the six-year change? This transition time, often called "first puberty" or "first adolescence" is a time when children go through an abundance of transformations. These can bring symptoms of chaotic behavior manifesting in even the most well-adjusted children. In many years of working in early childhood classrooms, I have had much to learn from the "sometimes mystifying and formidable" older children in the kindergarten. These experiences have been both humbling and informative.

It is obvious that sometime around the age of six, children begin to undergo many changes. As kindergarten teachers we would do well to awaken to the beckoning needs of the children for our conscious support through this very overwhelming and profound period—the six-year-old change. Rudolf Steiner in *The Essentials of Education* says, "I know that there is a certain amount of awareness these days concerning the changes that occur in the body and soul of children at this stage of life. Nevertheless, it is not sufficient to enable perception of all that happens in the human being at this tender age; we must come to understand this in order to become educators. The appearance of teeth … is merely the most obvious sign of a complete transformation of the whole organism. Much more is happening within the organism, though not as perceptible outwardly."[1]

It would appear that the first challenge we have as teachers is to investigate in more depth the nature of the six-year change. Our colleagues and the children's parents benefit from us doing this research. The change of teeth can be a difficult time for all of us who are accompanying the child on his/her journey, so building understandings of the dynamics of this change and then sharing them with others can be a tremendous support for all.

1   Rudolf Steiner, *The Essentials of Education*, 16.

Joan Almon, in her article "First Grade Readiness,"[2] likens this change to that of the "caterpillar spinning a cocoon and emerging as quite a new creature, a butterfly." She points out that the child at this time of the six-year change does not simply experience a linear growth cycle happening on a continuum but, rather, the child goes through a transformation on many different levels.

This realization alone can enable us to empathize with the child and to respond with the empathic inner attitude of "I see you are undergoing transformations. I love you *and* these new changes and I will help you to find your way." Of course, this would never be spoken to the children directly. However, if we as caregivers can be prepared *inwardly* to see and meet the new behaviors of the children, then the children and their parents are more at ease in our presence. The children can then have a safe place to test out their newfound need to push for boundaries, we are braced to meet them and the parents can have trust that we truly understand their children. Our role, as teachers, of bringing information to the parents about the six-year transformation cannot be overestimated and is discussed later in this article. We can also encourage parents to do their own research and hone their observation skills. After all, they have the closest contact with their child and they can do much to help us round out the picture of what their child is experiencing.

Sometime between the age of five-and-one-half to seven we begin to see that the children are asking for something more from us in addition to our continued working out of imitation. Let's look at some of the developments that naturally occur at this time and discern what it is as caregivers that we can do to meet these children. These new developments lie behind the changes that we see in the child's responses to his/her world. Taking interest in what's happening for the child will help us to know what is the best way to respond. This care-filled attention will also help us, through time, to develop our own organs of perception enabling us to accumulate a wealth of insights into the nature of the change.

There are two helpful diagrams that I share with my colleagues and the parents. The first is the flow line showing the three-year ego incarnation times.

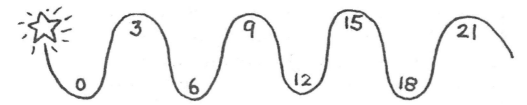

We know that each of these ego incarnation cycles is accompanied by varying degrees of separation on the part of the child. This new state of being can even resemble antipathy, especially as the child grows beyond the nine-year change. For the younger child, we can witness a growing ability to stand apart from activities. This reaction can manifest

2   Joan Almon, "First Grade Readiness," 119.

with the parent, teacher, or with anyone implementing well-known rules. It is a necessary development because it helps the child to separate more and meet the world on his/her own. As well, the six-year cycle marks the time when the etheric of the child begins to separate more from the parent. This is a time when the kindergarten teacher must realize that the parents and the children will be feeling this "pulling apart" whether it is at a conscious or unconscious level. Sometimes parents suddenly want to homeschool as they feel their children separating from them. Sometimes the children react by not wanting to come to school, or they may one day cling to the parents' legs and another day tell their parents that they want to come into the school by themselves. "Please stay in the car, Mommy. I want to go to the gate by myself today."

Our role, as teachers, of bringing information to the parents about the six-year transformation cannot be overestimated.

I'm reminded of the morning that Sally came to school carried in her dad's arms. Sally was a child who had very creative and imaginative play and her love for the kindergarten was obvious. We had begun to see the change in her outwardly for a couple of weeks because her usual calm and elaborately costumed dress-up play had been replaced by a frenzied need for movement. We were pretty sure that she was experiencing some aspects of the change because her limbs and torso were also stretching and growing. But we were not prepared for her appearance one morning in our play yard with her head buried in her dad's shoulders. "I don't want to go to school. Everyone is so mean to me," she said.

At that point, Daddy was prepared to withdraw Sally from school. I winked at him, sent Sally off to pick flowers with a friend and we talked some more about what we both were experiencing with Sally's behaviors. The next time we looked, Sally was playing happily with her many friends, and father went home grateful for the realization that Sally was showing him how she was experiencing some of the new kinds of feelings that were awakening in her as she felt the change coming. It is not uncommon that children will experience a regression before they launch into their new independence. A few days later, I overheard Sally saying to some friends, "You know what? I just pushed my dad away today! I said, Daddy you get out of here."

I want to mention that I begin to talk to the parents about the six-year change at the beginning of every school year. I tell them to expect great changes in their children and I explain this in detail. It is very helpful to have already developed this rapport with the parents before their children begin to show behavior and body changes. I tell them that, although there are many usual body and consciousness changes to look for, each child tends to have his own unique way to display this. It's important to open up the channels of communication with the parents so that both teacher and parent can take comfort in shared observations. In this way, a sense of partnership prevails with the parent. When the children have passed through the change, especially if they have been met with loving firmness, there is the possibility that they can re-enter their surroundings transformed and in a more peaceful state. The children need their teachers to develop this rapport with their parents so that consistent support systems are provided at home and at school.

What children like Sally teach us is that the change happens on many different levels. It is certainly a very profound physical phenomenon, but the effects also ripple into all aspects of the child's development. Another graph that helps us to see this follows.

We know that in each of the seven-year cycles there is a period of more developmental emphasis on willing, feeling and thinking. Within these cycles there are also times where little seeds of willing, feeling and thinking are cultured and developed for future developmental phases. We could create a line graph to show this.

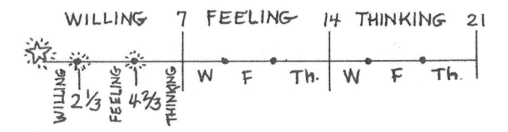

Running the risk of oversimplifying a complex topic, this can help us to see a number of things. If you look at the graph at the place around the period of five-and-a-half to seven, you will see that the child is experiencing a great deal at this time. We see the will of the feeling phase coming from the future (often depicted as chimneys with smoke coming out of them in children's drawings). And we see the awakening of ideas, pictures and burgeoning imaginations is shown by the thinking/willing aspect at the end of the first seven-year cycle. For the first time since birth, thinking and feeling are strong presences in the child's biography at the same time as willing. Of course the nature of these capacities does not yet resemble that of the adults and older siblings in her life. Few of us understand what the young child faces in his experience at this time. It appears that willing, feeling and thinking are operative all at the same time with a double dose of will!

Again, please note that the thinking, feeling and willing capacities do not manifest in the child as we experience them in the adult. There can be the temptation as adults to see these seed forces emerging in the young child and to assume that it is now time to launch in to more complicated responses.

Dr. Michaela Glöckler counsels us, "We can give children a beautiful security of dream consciousness and gently guide them towards awakeness. We need not push them out too quickly, but guide them out. If they have not fully experienced the dream consciousness of early childhood, then as adults they can turn back and seek this lost paradise. They seek the dream experience through drugs, for instance. We all had something similar to drug experience in childhood when colors, pictures, etcetera, were so vivid, and we could fully live within them."[3]

3   Michaela Glöckler, "Forces of Growth and Forces of Fantasy," 82.

Working with the Imagination

As mentioned, many adults are tempted to approach the child using intellectual reasoning, especially at the time of the six-year change, but, instead, what the child really needs is for us to attach to his lively imaginations. In fact, Rudolf Steiner in *The Kingdom of Childhood* goes so far as to say we can "ruin" a child if we speak to him in intellectual ways instead of in pictures at this time.[4] In *The Roots of Education*, Steiner also says, "We are often particularly gratified if we can teach a child something that he can reproduce in the same form several years later. But this is just as though we were to have a pair of shoes made for a child of three and expect him to wear them when he is ten. In reality our task is to give the child living flexible ideas which can grow in his soul… We must ourselves partake in the inward activities of the child's soul, and we must count it a joy to give him something that is inwardly flexible and elastic; and just as he grows with his physical limbs so he can grow up with these ideas, feelings and impulses, and in a short time he himself can make something else out of what we have given him." [5]

Also in *The Kingdom of Childhood*, Steiner advises us that children at the change of teeth need "soul milk" from us now and that we "must take the keenest interest in what is awakening at the change of teeth… You must allow the child's inner nature to decide what you ought to be doing with him." [6] I have reflected on this term "soul milk" for a number of years now and some of my thoughts about the teacher's role in providing soul milk for the older children in the kindergarten are shared in another article in Section Two of this book.

One six-year-old expressed what Steiner refers to as "the awakening at the change of teeth" in this way to her parent, "Mom, everything is different. You and Daddy are different. The trees look different. Even Harlequin, the cat, is different now. And Mom, it's just like I don't even know how to play anymore." Another child expressed, "Everything is boring. It's boring at home. School is boring. I'm going to run away to the Fairy Mother's house." These two expressions show different aspects of what Freya Jaffke calls "the crisis of will and imagination." If we are lucky enough to hear children express themselves in ways like those mentioned above, we can know that the time is at hand when they need extra attentiveness and support. Freya Jaffke explains further by saying, "an obvious crisis can be observed in many children, particularly in those who are actively creative. Further changes occur in the children's development because the formative forces actively structuring the body from within are increasingly freeing themselves from the metabolic and limb system. The will has to re-orientate itself to unite with the ideas which are gradually awakening in children of this age. This takes a while. For a time children will not have so many imaginative ideas, their will appears to be paralyzed and they ask, 'What shall I do?' or say: 'I'm bored.' " [7]

This can be a confusing and very serious time for children and they certainly don't feel in control. Their body is changing, their consciousness is changing and their connection to their world is changing. Let's look more closely at some of these changes.

4   Rudolf Steiner, *The Kingdom of Childhood*, 35.
5   Rudolf Steiner, *The Roots of Education*, 27-28.
6   Rudolf Steiner, *The Kingdom of Childhood*, 30-31.
7   Freya Jaffke, *Work and Play in Early Childhood*, 65.

Physical Changes

Physically, we know that the etheric body is actively working to penetrate and fashion the child's body. The child is trying to make his body his own and to break away from the ties of heredity. When the etheric has penetrated the hardest substance in the body, the bones, then it is free to move on to its new work. Although in the past educators have paid much attention to the release of the milk teeth and second dentition as a signal for this readiness, now we are being advised to pay more attention to the appearance of the six-year-old molars as a sign that readiness is on its way.

The activity of the etheric also shows itself outwardly in the movement of the children. They tend to have more frenzied gestures, race around, and steadfastly seek out movements. We could say that they are doing their best to assist the etheric in its work. As teachers we need to meet these changes with warmth and the attitude that "this too shall pass" and then provide opportunities for the movement expression to happen. For this we must hone our powers of observation and draw on our reserves of patience. The children are like bubbling pots. A child who, from the beginning of the school year, has shown calm and careful eating habits at the snack table all of a sudden is not able to sit still at the meal, and we begin to wonder if she is going to fall off the bench. We also notice that the child's limbs begin to stretch and her waistline, wrists, and neck become more apparent. Baby fat begins to disappear and, along with that, dimples on the hands and face. The older children love to challenge themselves with obstacle courses, long adventure walks, skipping, working with real tools, purposeful work activities, and running games. I have found traditional games to be an ideal tool at this time for helping the children socially and to support their need for organized movement. Doing things for others—helping the farmer to clean out stalls, feeding his chickens, herding the lambs; picking up scraps of litter on Mother Earth on morning walks; taking apart the grain grinder to clean it; cleaning and oiling outdoor tools; building paths, firepits, gardens—all of these things can help to channel the will that we have carefully nourished throughout the early years so that now purposeful moral activity can manifest, not frenzied, erratic behaviors.

We have a responsibility to help the children to find worthy channels for their activities while their etheric completes its task of penetrating their bodies.

I have found it effective to have one or two children every day be the "kings" and lead our morning walk. I begin this practice when the class understands about being "all-together" on our walks. If the leaders run on ahead and leave the others far behind, then I beckon them back to the group with my bell and they wait for another day to lead us on our walk. Giving the children opportunities to work with impulse control when it is obvious that there are repercussions if they "forget" is one way to help them find ways to bring control over their own gestures. At the present time, our morning walks take us through the playground where the older grade school children play. Lately we have undertaken some meaningful work here and the children in my class are spreading "soil that the worms made in our compost pile" on the playground for the lower grades' children. After this, we will cast seeds to help the grass to grow on this playground. "The big children are going to be so glad that we're doing this," is something that the children say over and over again every day. As teachers and parents, we have a responsibility to help the children to find worthy channels for their activities and ways that we can assist them while their etheric completes its task of penetrating their bodies.

As their bodies stretch and grow and their appetites increase, they begin to give us clues in their play that the change is upon them. They often try to build furniture up to the ceiling or, outdoors, they want to climb onto the roof of the shed. A child is fortunate indeed to have an environment where she can be helped to find ways to meet this need to stretch upward while at the same time maintaining healthy boundaries. In one school setting I visited, the children were provided with a sturdy rope which the teacher threw over a strong tree branch. The children played at raising and lowering each other up and down out of the tree while the teacher attentively watched.

We can see this stretching experience in other ways too. In the children's drawings, we can see ladders and zigzag lines. The children are showing us their experience of the change of teeth and the stretching of their torso and limbs. Of course, along with this time come complaints of tummy aches and joint pains. This time of stretching has many accompanying physical sensations which, for the children, can be unconscious. They often don't know that their irritability is associated with these sensations, but we can know this is a possibility and respond more empathically to the children.

At a more invisible level, the children are also working to establish their dominant side and to be able to comfortably cross over the vertical and horizontal midlines. Clapping games like "Hot Cross Buns," "Pease Porridge Hot," "A Sailor Went to Sea Sea Sea," or bringing crossover gestures into circle time can assist the children. Skipping can assist the children rhythmically to bring balance and regularity to their movement as well. A list of skipping verses is provided in Section Five.

Symmetry and balance begin to appear more in the children's drawings as their rhythmic system is more stabilized. The figures in their drawings are also often constructed standing on the earth and there is a well defined difference between the sky and the earth. Sometimes we can see evidence of the beginning of the symmetry that they practice in first grade when they do their form drawings.

One day I watched unnoticed as a child, in a very concentrated way, colored a whole page with bold red color. That evening her mom said she ran a temperature of 104. There seemed to be no illness attached to this fever, but she came back to class a few days later a very different child. Soon thereafter her limbs began to stretch and she had a vivid dream about first grade. Fevers can often accompany the six-year transformation time. There is more information about dealing with fevers in Section Six of this book.

Emotional and Social Changes

Probably the most individual differences are seen in the emotional and social changes that children undergo at this age. Some children respond with more bravado and some inwardly ferment their six-year-old brew.

One of the most common responses I've witnessed is the need of the children to be the boss. Parents, teachers and their peers are no longer safe from being corrected at every mistake. This, coupled with the arrival of a sense of time (before, after, and so on), can show itself at circle time when the child speeds up the verse to be finished before the others or on the morning walk when the child slows down her walking so that she can arrive way behind the others. Going along with what everybody else is doing is no longer an unconscious priority. Some children love to play at being different.

With their friends they have long conversations about who is "first boss." We hear the children say over and over again, "But I want to be the boss!" "I know. You be first boss, you be second boss, you be third boss. I'll be fourth boss and I get to say what we do!" And often their playmates and those who stand as authorities in their life will hear, "You're not the boss of me!" A matter-of-fact response is needed then. "Teacher knows the rules of the land," or, as I have said to my own children, "That is my job. Your angel asked me to be your helper." Children benefit immensely by being met directly at this time, and a neutral, informing tone of voice can reassure them that the boundaries are still in place even though their whole being is in upheaval. What a relief this is for them!

Another aspect of this time of transformation is that the children's consciousness changes from a state where they unite with the objects of their play to a state where they have an imaginative idea about the play and they want to implement it. Freya Jaffke explains this by saying, "the stimulus for play no longer comes so much from external objects, but it comes now more and more from inside. This means that now the child has an inner picture, a picture from her imagination of past events, and she can bring these up in her play independent of place, time or people."[8] As mentioned above, this can be a frustration to the children, and they may become listless or watchers in the play for a while until they can find their way with this new capacity.

This is not necessarily a bad thing. It can be a graceful transition time if the children do not become too anxious. However, if the teacher feels that it has gone on long enough, then bringing the children (hopefully one at a time) to help with the teacher's work can be enough of a jumpstart to propel the child back into the play. From that perspective of helping the teacher and watching other's play, the children can often see something interesting that they want to join. It's often the play of the younger children that encourages the older children to re-enter the play. Sometimes the older children like to help set up the creative activities and arrange props for dramas or puppet plays. They can also be valuable in assisting the younger children—tying shoes, holding hands on walks, threading needles,

8   Freya Jaffke, "Stages of Development in Early Childhood," 11.

helping with handwork projects, etc. It's also a thrill when the older children can get to the point in the course of the year where they can make the bread, prepare the soup, or clean the kindergarten all by themselves.

Tying the fingerknitted ropes into all sorts of lines, cobwebs, or telephone wires is often a signal of the presence of this new "thinking." The arrival of these picture imaginations in their consciousness propels the children into a real need to have the experience of their idea being played out. We need to assist these children to develop useful social skills so that this need can be fulfilled.

As I write this, Samuel comes to mind. Samuel was a capable, hardy, and fiery boy. He had a passion for leading the play but was very able to play co-operatively as well. Somewhere around six-and-three-quarters, he began to grow quite bossy with the children. Daily he would try to organize the whole class into his play. Most of the time the children would ignore his bossy ways, but this did not deter him. I watched him one week desperately trying to herd, cajole, and manipulate the class into his game. Monday to Friday I observed Samuel diligently struggle to be "first boss." Then, on Friday, with great satisfaction, he constructed a corral with a fence that raised and lowered and, one by one, he captured the interest of his peers and he was able to herd the ponies, donkeys, pigs, and cows into his corral. The look of conquest on his face was palpable.

Children benefit immensely by being met directly at this time.

Sometimes, children can become stuck in their play as this new capacity for picture imaginations floods in. They love to play the same game over and over again or take most of the play session to set up scenarios. It warrants careful observation to see when the child is served by the imagination or when it could be helpful to move it on by a simple introduction of a complementary idea. Freya Jaffke explains this very well in an example she gives in her book, *Work and Play in Early Childhood*,[9] where she describes helping the stagnating play of a group of six-year-olds by suggesting that now the animals in the circus need to eat. It took only one sentence well-placed by an observant teacher to transform a stuck play situation into one that could move on with endless possibilities.

Some other common things that we may encounter in the child's play at this time that is often called "first puberty" or "first adolescence" are the tendencies to wrap presents and give them to others; playing at getting married or getting drunk; whispering to others to do naughty things; making up teasing rhymes about others; giggling; being silly; playing at being a "teeeeeenager"; playing dogs on leashes (master and servant); making money; theme play like restaurant, store, hospital, airport; informing their friends about who they hate today; a multitude of bathroom words; and much more. There is also a tendency for the children to want to pair off and choose a special friend. Playing at exclusion becomes a pastime. Of course, it is important to meet all of these behaviors and themes with the matter-

9   Freya Jaffke, *Work and Play in Early Childhood*, 68.

of-fact attitude that the right-way-of-the-world will be upheld. "We'll still be remembering our kindergarten ways." "The teachers in the grade school say that the children need to know their kindergarten ways before they come to first grade." Even though the child has these experiences and impulses flooding into him, he still needs to rest in the security that the world is a safe and moral place and there are others that will help him to make it so. Again and again, I have experienced the gratitude of the children when I have met their pushing of the boundaries with loving firmness. Often they will come and sit on my lap, take my hand or hug me. They want to press up against this comforting boundary and, on some level, they are grateful for its consistency and availability while they are trying out their newfound, confusing state of consciousness.

Awakening Ideas

Sooner or later during the school year the children begin to have conversations about God and infinity. What a privilege it is to overhear these precious communications. If only we could keep alive the power of these wonderings! The most recent conversation I overheard about infinity happened when two children were discussing it around our snack table. "Infinity means 1068!" said one child. "No," said another, "it just means keep on going."

We can begin to see that the children are no longer so bound to the present and they begin to experience the future coming to them. Some children are able to relate their dreams. One mother told me about her daughter's dream. "Valerie dreamed that the kindergarten door opened and everyone in the class, even the teachers, got wings! Then she saw everyone flying down the hallway together, opening up the doors of the grade school and looking around to see what was inside the classrooms."

The past also becomes more retrievable in their memories. They begin to tell their parents the stories they have heard in kindergarten; we see them looking out and away as they imagine the stories at story time or as they imagine what their bedroom looks like when we ask them about it. One child said to her mother, "I don't need to go to Grandma's house anymore. I can see Grandma whenever I want to." Some children can express the arrival of this ability to see things in the "mind's eye." Others find it overwhelming and, as it floods in and initially overwhelms other capacities, they may express, "I'm bored." Another way of interpreting "I'm bored" is "There's something new happening and I don't know how to relate to it yet."

However, once the children begin to take hold of this change in consciousness, one gets the impression that they delight in stretching their capacities in many ways. They tend to play with this just like they play out other areas of their experience. They love to play with some of their favorite games and circle verses by going through the motions silently. It exercises their developing capacity of hearing the words inwardly and letting the pictures dominate. Here is a game centered around the verse "Little Brown Bulb."

A little brown bulb went to sleep in the ground
In his little brown nightie he slept very sound
King Winter he raged and he roared overhead
But that little brown baby stayed snug in its bed
But when Lady Spring came tip-toeing over the lee
With fingers to lips as quiet as could be
That little brown bulb peeked up its head
Threw off its nightie and jumped out of bed. [10]

The children delight in circling around two or three other children covered up in a blanket that represents Mother Earth. We mouth the words to the verse silently, going through the gestures of King Winter roaring and Lady Spring tiptoeing and then we see if our friends hidden under the blanket can "peek up their heads, throw off their nighties and jump out of bed" at the appropriate time. Of course, playing this game many times and saying the verse out loud precedes the time when we can finally say it silently.

One day as we were playing this game, I forgot one of the lines. One little boy looked at me ponderously and said, "That wisdom must be coming up your legs and making your head so big that you can't find those words." I thought, "Does this sound like what we would expect to hear from a six-year-old? Is he describing my condition or his own?" Edmond Schoorel, in his book *The First Seven Years: Physiology of Childhood*, describes very well the process of maturation and how it moves from below upwards. He says, "The process of maturation begins in the lower pole, which is dynamic and prone to change, and ends in the tranquilizing and crystallizing activity of the head."[11] We can learn so much from the children if we develop a relationship with them so that they know that we are interested in what they have to say.

In closing, I'd like to acknowledge again the grandness of this change which happens for the children somewhere between five-and-a-half and seven. It's a time when the child's organism undergoes physical, emotional, social and consciousness transformations. And again I would encourage parents and teachers to truly listen to the children and to cultivate the eyes to see what is happening for them. Please make your own observations and take deep interest in the older children in the kindergarten or at home. As teachers in mixed-age kindergartens we are a bridge for the children when they are passing through this truly amazing transformation. We are a bridge from the age of imitation to the time when the children have a growing need to see the world through the eyes of a beloved authority. If we are able to respond to their activity at the time of "first puberty" with healing deeds and imaginations, then this is one way that we can fulfill our task as educators to work with what Steiner called moral imagination. We can be instruments to help guide the children in

10 Wynstones Press, *Spring*, 20.
11 Edmond Schoorel. *The First Seven Years: Physiology of Childhood*, 113, 123.

building a moral foundation. We must accompany them in such a way that the powerful will that we have nurtured in them throughout early childhood has a proper vessel in which to germinate and grow. It is an honor always and a trial sometimes.

If we can do this, then the interest that we take in the children enables us to connect to their imaginations and their developmental processes. These deeds of deep, loving interest then endorse the children's attempts to stretch into these new horizons. Taking up and embellishing their questions, interests and perceived needs are perhaps the most powerful tools we have. We are doing a great service when we can take the courage to be lovingly present at this threshold for these older children in the kindergarten. ✦

References

Almon, Joan. "First Grade Readiness," in *The Developing Child: The First Seven Years*, edited by Susan Howard. Spring Valley, NY: WECAN, 2004.

Bates Ames, Louise and Frances Ilg. *Your Six-Year-Old*. New York: Delacorte Press, 1981.

Glöckler, Michaela. "Forces of Growth and Forces of Fantasy: Understanding the Dream Consciousness of the Young Child," in *The Developing Child: The First Seven Years*, edited by Susan Howard. Spring Valley, NY: WECAN, 2004.

Jaffke, Freya. "Stages of Development in Early Childhood: Tasks and Goals for Parents and Educators," in *The Developing Child: The First Seven Years*, edited by Susan Howard. Spring Valley, NY: WECAN, 2004.

Jaffke, Freya. *Work and Play in Early Childhood*. Edinburgh: Floris Books, 1996.

Schoorel, Edmond. *The First Seven Years: Physiology of Childhood*. Fair Oaks, CA: Rudolf Steiner College Press, 2004.

Steiner, Rudolf. *The Essentials of Education*. Great Barrington, MA: Anthroposophic Press, 1997.

_____ . *The Kingdom of Childhood*. Great Barrington, MA: Anthroposophic Press, 1995.

_____ . *The Roots of Education*. Great Barrington, MA: Anthroposophic Press, 1997.

Wynstones Press. *Spring*. Stourbridge, England: Wynstones Press, 1999.

Additional information gathered through consultation with Dorothy Olsen, Dr. Johanna Steegmans, and Dr. Claudia McKeen.

The Birth
of the Etheric
Notes from an Interview
with Johanna Steegmans, MD

Nancy Blanning

Dr. Johanna Steegmans, anthroposophical physician and special friend to parents, early childhood educators and young children, met with the Older Child in the Kindergarten working group in February, 2006, when they were preparing for this book. Although the questions and responses were oriented to the work of the kindergarten teacher, there is much in this chapter that pertains to the influences that the parent can have on the child in the first seven years of his life.

The working group came with two fundamental questions. The first was "How does the birth of the etheric body affect the six-to-seven-year-old child in life experience and behavior?" A second question was "How can educators hone their observation skills so that they can see the manifestations of this birth and recognize first grade readiness?"

Dr. Steegmans began by describing the nature of the etheric body in general. She explained that, until just a few days before physical birth, the higher members of the human being still live in the sheaths and have not connected with the physical body yet. "The etheric body lives in the hands of the hierarchies." Its task is to work on the physical body after birth, to penetrate it, and then be freed, at the time of the birth of the etheric—somewhere around six to seven years of age—for other tasks appropriate to the grade school years. It is important to remember that the etheric body is not an undifferentiated substance but a fine filament composed out of the four ethers, each of which has different qualities. The individual ethers were characterized as follows:

The highest of the ethers is the *Life ether*, which is connected with the earth element. Its task is to solidify, making things firm, and it mainly manifests in our skeleton and our skull. It may seem a paradox that this ether, which is the highest, is also the most resistant as it works in the density of the bony system. Yet within the bone is the bone marrow that also brings life. In very young children there is still some bone marrow in the skull. This eventually dies away, as the head should not have life as such within it in that way. If the marrow actively remains, disease and illness will result.

The next is the **_Chemical or Tone ether_**. This ether's gesture is to combine and separate. It is also called the musical ether when referring to the tones. Connected to the physical element of water, in the upper pole the chemical ether creates the spinal fluid. In the lower pole, it creates muscles; muscles are energetically "fluid" in their nature. When we begin to move, it is like a melody. Chemistry provides a picture for us of the muscles in movement —a symphony of motion in which our body goes through a process of attracting and then distancing or repelling.

The **_Light ether_** has its affinity to the earthly element of air. It brings about the brain in its gray and white matter. It has to do with our thinking. We need nerves and the physical brain to enable us to think. While the chemical ether brings muscles, the light ether brings about the brain and nerves to give us a physical foundation for thinking in the upper pole. In the lower pole, the nervous system is the manifestation of the light ether.

Nearest to us of the ethers is that of the **_Warmth ether_**. We experience warmth both as an ether and as an element. The warmth of the metabolism in the lower body is the manifestation of the warmth ether. In the upper pole this ether manifests as the warmth of the ego when truly meeting one another.

The task of the first seven years of life is to overcome the inherited etheric body and make it one's own.

As a child prepares for incarnation and birth, he passes last through the planetary sphere of the Moon. Here the qualities of the four different ethers are collected to compose the individualized etheric body each child will carry into life. It is as though the incarnating child is a magnet creating his own unique etheric body composed out of these four realms. When we speak of the birth of the etheric body, we have to remember that different qualities are being born out of the individual child's etheric weaving because her own unique fabric is woven out of her particular combination of the four ethers. The ether body we attract around us in the Moon sphere will be the blueprint for the ether body we create in the embryo.

When an individual incarnates, two streams come together. One is one's own karmic stream brought from pre-earthly existence and the other is the inherited etheric stream that comes from the parents. The task of the first seven years of life is to overcome the inherited etheric body and make it one's own.

Then Dr. Steegmans continued to explain more about the journey of the human being after birth. For each of the four bodies—physical, etheric, astral, and ego—there is both an inner and an outer birth. The inner birth of the physical body is at conception, even though it is not yet visible. The outer birth occurs when the child is physically born. When this physical birth occurs, then the inner birth of the etheric body happens. The etheric is not visible but unfolds through the next seven years. It lives in functions. These first seven years allow the maturation of a germ and prepare the emancipation of the ether body itself, which occurs in three steps.

Each part of our physical body emancipates part of the ethers. Etheric forces are freed from the region of the head at 2 1/3 years. Then, when the child becomes social and is able to play, this signals the second birth from the trunk. This occurs at around 4 1/2 when the etheric is freed in the social/rhythmic sphere. At this age the teacher acts as a social model and provides nourishment for the child by supplying warmth and reverence. When the limbs are taken hold of by the actively working etheric, then the birth is complete. The ability to jump rope shows this emancipation of the limbs. While we can look to these as generalized markers of the birth-steps of the etheric, we must remember that this process is individualized with each child; there are delays and accelerations. As we observe the children, we will want to see if they have gone through these three steps of setting the etheric free.

When this birthing occurs, according to the temperament of the child, different individuals take the ethers and use them differently. Childhood is by nature a sanguine time and, as well, all the ethers are operative as they intermingle. We do not usually look to temperament in a young child, but sometimes it is so apparent in some children that it would be foolish to ignore what we see. The choleric will use the warmth ether to be where the ego can live. The sanguine temperament will live in the light ether because it is connected to the element of air. The phlegmatic has the element of water and the chemical ether most active. The melancholic lives more in the life ether, mostly in matter, the earth element.

Rather than regarding temperament, it can be more helpful for early childhood educators to look at which system is dominant—nerve/sense, metabolic, or rhythmic. The child with the nerve/sense system dominant tends to manifest melancholic tendencies. When the metabolic system dominates, the individual tends to become phlegmatic. Either a sanguine or choleric temperament may later manifest when the rhythmical system is strongest. As we look at these tendencies, we may recognize an inclination but should just observe it and not respond to it as we would with a first grader. It is a karmic issue as to which of the ethers the individual chooses. We may see the birth of one or two etheric tendencies dominating with the other balancing ethers missing. This is good information to share with parents, especially if the child has a strong inclination toward one temperament or the other.

These ethers are streaming in two directions as well. The light and warmth ethers stream from above downward. The chemical and life ethers stream from below upward. (We can deepen our understanding of this picture by studying *Balance in Teaching*, by Rudolf Steiner.) After the baby is born, the maturing forces have to stream upward from below to the head in order to wake up the consciousness, so the child at age seven can overcome gravity with a new ego intention. To overcome gravity (as demonstrated with jumping rope), the ego needs to have taken hold of the body all the way through, having developed from the head, down through the rhythmic trunk, and finally into the limbs. A child who jumps rope earlier than seven may be accelerating too quickly. The rhythmic area in the middle/trunk section may not have been fully developed before taking this new step. If the lower pole is developed too fast, then the rhythmical part of the human being, where lightness and darkness meet, will be weakened.

Dr. Steegmans quoted Christof Wiechert when he described that with this etheric birth around six or seven the light and warmth ethers are liberated to become free for learning and thinking. In the outward behavior of the child, we may see the mightiness of the light ether releasing demonstrated by the children when they fall off chairs and race around madly.

As we continue to look at the inner and outer births of the other bodies, we see that the inner birth of the astral body happens around age three. The child says "I" and has the realization of separation from her surroundings. She also experiences that she makes an impact on those around her. These mark the first stage of the birth of the astral body, which lives in sympathy and antipathy. The astral rhythm is exemplified in the three-, six-, and nine-year-old awakenings. The inner birth of the ego is at age ten, but the ego is always there behind the veil from the beginning. When unfortunate circumstances prevail for children who have had a terrible shock or live in horrible circumstances, the ego is pulled into the organism much earlier and has to birth prematurely.

An interesting observation Dr. Steegmans shared was from the work of pediatrician Kaspar Appenzeller. In his work, he listened to the heart tones of thousands and thousands of children. He detected three metric patterns that appear within the heartbeat. In the embryo, the rhythm is the *spondee*—two long beats. This is the meter of the will. The developing child in utero is pure will, pure spirit. The spondee lasts through the first two years of life. When the rhythmical part of the child begins to mature, the *iambic* meter takes over—short, long. This is the meter for most of our life and has to do with feelings. Once the head forces awaken, the rhythm changes to *trochee*—long, short. Rudolf Steiner identified this as the rhythm of thinking; it is also a hardening rhythm. Then the iambic reasserts itself. The hardening trochee rhythm returns during adolescence and then disappears again. The trochee is also apparent whenever there is a tumor. With cancer patients who have died, in the days before death the heartbeat returned from the trochee to the iambic. If there is a hardening around six or seven, there is a trochee rhythm, which then disappears again. While these rhythms are not something the teacher can easily witness, it is astounding to realize that even the organ of the heart is affected by the 6/7-year-old transformation. The changes seen physically and rhythmically in the child confirm that transformation is occurring in the physical and etheric life of the child through the birthing stages of the different bodies.

With the background of this developmental picture, Dr. Steegmans then made us aware of important considerations regarding the role of the kindergarten teacher working with the older children in the kindergarten. Of course the parents in the children's lives can benefit from this information too. As all of these momentous changes are occurring, the 6/7-year-old child seems to beg for authority and boundaries. The older children are crossing the bridge from the age of imitation to a time when imitation and authority are important for their progress. They begin to resist imitation in the kindergarten (though they will happily imitate again the next year when they are held by the authority of the first grade teacher.) All teachers have experienced how unruly and challenging the older children can become. This behavior corresponds to the final release of the etheric body. The first release came from the head with the emergence of thinking, the second from the rhythmic system when the child became able to be social, and finally the last through the will in overcoming gravity. This play between gravity and levity, as mentioned before, can manifest as swinging between silliness and opposition.

The children respond rightly to the authority of the adult who shows that he or she is competent with his or her will in living earthly life.

So when the children are craving boundaries, how can the teacher meet their will with the right kind of authority? It is not a disciplinarian authority that they are seeking. Rather, the children respond rightly to the authority of the adult who shows that he or she is competent with his or her will in living earthly life. Authority is demonstrated through knowing how to do something. This is what the little children look for in the older students in the class. The older children look to the adult for this same competence. In a pictorial way, it was suggested that the children are searching for "the straight line" in the teacher rather than "the curve," which is the archetypal kindergarten gesture of embrace and protection. Now the proper gesture exemplifies the ability to direct the will into the world and a capability with practical life. Greeting the will of the child with this type of authority is the healthy response to this last stage of the birth of the etheric.

Related to this came another question—Rudolf Steiner said that when the children are going through the change of teeth, they need "soul milk." What does this actually mean? Dr. Steegmans said she thinks the children want true pictures of life. The "soul milk" they need is authenticity. In this last stage of the kindergarten years, the children need to have confirmed what they unconsciously remember from pre-earthly life. This confirmation happens when they meet living examples in practical life from the adults in their surroundings. They are longing for form while they are in the midst of demanding freedom—a state of being not unlike that of adolescence. The form they need in early childhood is supplied by seeing practical tasks done in an orderly way with competence, skill, and devoted concentration on the part of the adult.

Manners, which provide forms for behaving in social settings in consideration of and for others, are another means for supplying form and boundaries for the children. Dr. Steegmans observed that this is a most relevant concern now, as there is such a lack of manners in our society. It is also the educator's responsibility to impart manners to the children before they leave the kindergarten. This includes all the obvious social situations where appropriate manners are necessary. This can also extend into the realm of sexual curiosity, which typically awakens with the birth of the etheric. This is a normal development for the child. Etheric forces create awareness in the child of the sexual organs. This awakening diminishes and goes to sleep again. However, if proper boundaries are not provided, allowing this interest to go beyond its normal time frame, then this awakening can be prolonged and hardened into the consciousness of the young child. A combination of manners and authority is the vehicle for communicating what is acceptable, what is not, and delineating the boundaries of privacy for conduct for ourselves and for others. One of the teachers present said as an example that in her kindergarten they have a rule that is spoken matter-of-factly: "Pants up and skirts down in the kindergarten."

In the mixed-age class, the older children are still expected to be within the usual responses of the general group of the kindergarten, but they do need to be given extra direction to transform the disruptive behavior arising from their new etheric reorganization. To be direct is a proper response from the ego of the adult to the child's etheric birth. However, the group of younger and older children, as a whole, must still be held in imitation. Yet the older child needs to be met as an *individual* as well with a loving, matter-of-fact authority that says "You may not do that" or "You may do this." Responding to the child in this way acknowledges his individuality and provides a reassuring, discerning authority that guides the child out of premature individualization back to merging into the social fabric of the kindergarten again.

The kindergarten realm is entrusted with nurturing and protecting the etheric of the children, so healthy forces are generally present as the final aspects of the etheric are birthed at six or seven. The health of the etheric and the impact of sensory experience coming toward the children are related. We see children in the kindergarten who come to us with an inability to hold attention and who are overwhelmed by their sensory experiences. Although the sense organs are part of the physical body, what is taken in through the senses goes into the etheric body. Sense impressions make an imprint on the etheric and are then stored. These imprints create the foundation for mental picturing. When the etheric body is prematurely occupied with activities that should come later, such as early intellectualization, it becomes depleted, "tattered." With a tattered etheric, the child cannot hold calmness in the ether body; the senses are chaotic and cannot mature properly. If the quality, intensity, and speed of sensory impressions overwhelm the child, then the etheric cannot sustain its healthy development. Depleting and even destructive forces can invade the ether space through inappropriate sensory experiences. Soul senses and bodily senses are not able to separate and achieve a much-needed independence. For example, senses will cluster, such as vision and movement together, resulting in compulsive behaviors. The effective therapeutic "sensory integration" activities that we have in the Waldorf curriculum for such children are eurythmy and circle work. It is helpful when the adult is doing the

Putting one's ego consciousness into whatever one is doing is therapeutic for the child.

movements alongside the child. To heal, the adult has to be using her/his will to participate with the child in companionship and partnership. One teacher present said that she used the imagination of having angel wings, with which she reached out and surrounded the child and then she would imagine bringing the child along with her while she did the movements of the circle.

As we look for ways to support and promote etheric health, we must be careful to keep connection with the child, rather than separating ourselves, becoming observers and judges. Dr. Steegmans emphasized that the young child must always be surrounded with our inner picturing affirmations of the human being's archetypal perfection. Every child is striving toward this. What are the "therapies" we can provide? We clearly know the importance and powerful influence of adequate, healthy sleep; good quality food; and consistent, predictable rhythms in the child's daily experience. Spending time in nature is also most important and healing for the child—with the quality and quantity of time to explore, so that the child can soak in quiet impressions from the natural environment without being rushed.

Additionally and most importantly, the teacher, through the gesture and quality of speech, thought, and movement provides therapy. Putting one's ego consciousness into whatever one is doing is therapeutic for the child. The ether body is a time body. When one is present in the etheric body, one creates time. Present-mindedness is the key. This is what/when the children are drawn to imitate. If the teacher loves something, the children will love it as well. Truly experiencing love for what one is doing, being immersed in the moment and portraying joy in the activity of doing it are probably the most important healing qualities that one can offer to the children. Taking the time to devote sincere interest toward what one is doing creates health in the etheric body and inspires the interest and devoted imitation of the children.

With the older child in the kindergarten, the educator is striving to observe signs of the etheric birth so first grade readiness can be confirmed. Dr. Steegmans described that the most crucial physical demonstration of liberation of the etheric—which is never fully complete—is the eruption of the six-year-old molars, not necessarily the change of teeth. The molars are new creations confirming that the etheric birth for school readiness has been achieved. The child also gives clues to us by the examples of his behavior through this birthing process. For instance, the ability to jump rope signals the overcoming of gravity associated with the final birthing step for the etheric in the limbs. As we have already mentioned, silliness and opposition are other signs.

As the older child challenges social rules and expectations, he or she is also asking for form and boundaries to help bring order into the new etheric configuration. As already mentioned, the kindergarten teacher has to take the step from working primarily out of imitation to guiding the older child through authority. How can one operate out of both at the same time? Present-mindedness is again the key. The teacher has to observe what is needed in the present moment with these children, breathing in an alternation between point and periphery as each situation demands. Standing on the periphery, the teacher creates an etheric bubble that holds the children. But the older child needs to be led individually toward establishing his own relationship with the world etheric, not relying too much upon nor being held too tightly in this realm that the teacher has created. The teacher then steps into the point with the child, using appropriate authority to guide the child's emerging individuality toward its own healthy independence and appropriate relationship with the world. To go from imitation to authority is to pass between periphery and point. This passage from one to the other is warmed by the teacher as it passes through the realm of the heart—the great balancer, strengthener, and mediator.

As a concluding picture, Dr. Steegmans described the birth of the etheric body as a process of clothing oneself for life. We can picture this by seeing the child poking her head through a sweater and then gradually pulling the rest of the garment down to her feet. First the head forces are addressed, then the trunk and finally the limbs. When the birth of the etheric is complete, the sweater will have slipped down until it fits comfortably over the length of the whole body. But if the dressing is rushed or if the child is made to go out before everything is properly pulled down and tucked in, the child may be clothed in a shirt that is too short or is haphazard. Giving the etheric enough time to have a healthy and complete birth is one of the greatest gifts we can give a child. The parent's and teacher's attention, observations, and appropriate responses to the birthing moments will assure that the child's wardrobe is functional and complete. ✦

Reference Note

Extensive discussion and further explanation of the birth of the etheric as described in this article is the content of *The First Seven Years*, by Dr. Edmond Schoorel, published by Rudolf Steiner College Press, Fair Oaks, CA, 2004.

Dentition: A Mirror of the Child's Development

Helge Ruof, MD and Jörg Ruof, MD
with thanks to David Sloan for his editing support

Introduction

Teeth are the only part of the body where the skeletal system becomes visible and accessible from the outside. They guard the entrance to the digestive system and, in addition to serving as a speech organ, a key function of the teeth is to take nutrition apart and thus start the digestion process. In animals teeth are powerful weapons—a snarling dog usually shows its teeth, and predators use the teeth to kill their prey.[1] In poisonous snakes, the teeth (fangs) have a venomous channel with an aperture close to the tip of the teeth, so that the venom can pass through. So, in one respect, teeth are closely related to death; on the other hand, dental tissue—in particular the visible part of the teeth, the enamel—is the most durable and the hardest tissue in the human body.

In Waldorf education, the commencement of the permanent dentition is usually considered a sign of school readiness. In that time period the child undergoes important physical changes including: lengthening of the limbs; disappearance of the round belly; development of the typical S-shaped vertebrae and others. The start of the second dentition, therefore, characterizes the transition to the second seven-year cycle of child development that goes until puberty. The aim of this article is to provide an overview of the threefold anatomy of the teeth, the developmental dynamic of dentition, and the soul activities in relation to dentition. We end with a discussion of recent changes in patterns of dentition and suggest some daily observations that might be useful for kindergarten teachers.

Each individual tooth is composed of three parts (Fig 1). The visible part is the enamel, the hardest tissue in the human body. It consists of 96% inorganic mineral and like a crown

---

1   Birds of prey don't have teeth and usually kill their prey using their "tooth-like" claws.

covers the next layer—the dentin. Dentin, like bone, is composed of a mix of organic collagen fibers (20%), the same inorganic mineral (hydroxyapatite) that occurs in enamel (70%), and water (10%). Dentin has the capability to regenerate to some degree and is sensitive to external stimuli such as heat or cold. In adults, when the periodontal structures and the gingiva gradually withdraw, the dentin directly accesses the oral cavity, which often causes temporary hypersensitivity to temperature or sweetness. The central part of each tooth consists of the *dental pulp*, a soft organic connective tissue containing thin-walled blood vessels, nerves, and nerve endings enclosed with dentin. Root channel procedures in dentistry usually include cleaning and sealing the pulp cavity (i.e., a tooth is considered dead after the root canal procedure occurs). While enamel represents the dead, inorganic part of each tooth, the intact pulp cavity represents the part that is alive and sensitive. Dentin contains characteristics of both—the enamel and the pulp cavity.

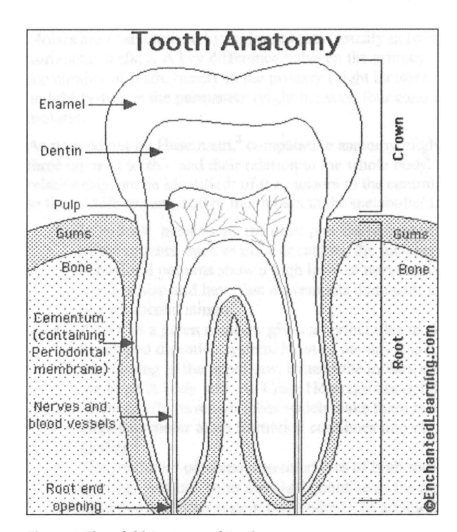

Figure 1: Threefold Anatomy of Teeth

In addition to the three parts that each individual tooth is composed of, three different types of teeth may be differentiated: the *incisors,* the *canines,* and the *molars*. The four front teeth in the upper and lower jaw are considered incisors, which are characterized by a sharp surface and a single root. Next to the incisors are the canines, one on each side of the upper and lower jaw. Finally the premolars and molars are located next to the canines. Molars are characterized by multiple roots (usually between two and three) and a horizontal surface. A key difference between the primary and the permanent dentition is the number of teeth, twenty in the primary (eight incisors, four canines, eight molars), and thirty-two in the permanent (eight incisors, four canines, twenty premolars and molars).

As pointed out by Husemann,[2] comparative anatomy might be helpful to characterize the three types of teeth—and their relation to the whole body.[3] Specifically an intimate relationship can be identified: of the incisors to the central nervous system, of the canines to the middle system, and of the molars to the metabolic/ limb system.

In *rodents*, incisors are the most prominent type of teeth to the extent that in many of the rodents, such as mice or rabbits, the incisors never stop growing. Rodents' behavioral patterns show a high level of nerve activity. Usually rodents are rather small in size and have fast movements that occur as immediate reactions to environmental stimuli.

A cow in a green meadow gives a perfect idea of an animal with a highly developed digestive system. Most of the day it is ruminating. Incisors and canines are missing in the upper jaw. Instead the molars are dominant. Usually *ruminators* are large in body size. As Craig Holdrege has pointed out, the lower jaw canines in the giraffe have two lobes which make them more "molar like,"[4] and in elephants molar tooth formation continues into old age, which indicates ongoing vitality.[5]

The *predators* combine characteristics of both rodents and ruminants. When hunting, they can be as alert and attentive as the rodents, but they have a stronger digestive and limb system than rodents. In addition, they are mid-sized compared to the two other groups. The canines are most prominently developed in predators. For example, in dogs, the strongest and most developed teeth are the canines. Often it can be observed that even the molars become canine-like. They don't possess the horizontal surface that is typical for the molars. Instead, they have sharp cusps.

In humans, the distribution of nerve endings in the oral cavity is greatest in the lips and the front part of the mouth and least in the more posterior regions of the oral cavity. This further underlines the dominance of the nervous system and the related soul activity of tasting in

2   A.J. Husemann, *Der Zahnwechsel des Kindes*.
3   In holistic medicine multiple relationships between teeth and the body organs are stated, for example, in acupuncture. A discussion of these concepts is beyond the scope of this article.
4   Craig Holdrege, "The Giraffe's Long Neck."
5   Craig Holdrege, "The Flexible Giant."

the front part of the mouth. In the back part of the oral cavity where the molars are located, the soul is in a kind of a "sleep-mode" which occurs all throughout the digestive system.

Developmental Dynamic of Dentition

*I*n embryology it is a well-known fact that during the early phase (e.g. sixth week) of the intra-uterine period, the central nervous system is way ahead of the development of the other organs; over time the other systems catch up. Around the twelfth week, we clearly find the rib cage area growing rapidly. In the final intrauterine weeks, the abdominal organs and the limbs develop and grow. Karl König repeatedly refers to this developmental pattern: "Just as in birth the head is the first part of the body to emerge and is gradually followed by the rest of the body…"[6] A similar dynamic can be found when reviewing the facial development. Bath-Balog, et al.[7] discriminate three centers of facial growth: "The growth of the upper face is initially the most rapid, in keeping with its association with the developing brain. The forehead then ceases to grow significantly after age twelve. In contrast, the middle and lower portions of the face grow more slowly over a prolonged period of time and finally cease to grow late in puberty."

The pattern of both primary and permanent dentition follows the same scheme: the incisors, so closely related to the nervous system, are leading, then, step by step, the canines and the molars are developed, with the eruption of the permanent third molars occurring at approximately seventeen to twenty-one years of age. While both the overall embryological and facial development are initially focused on the central nervous system and then steadily move to the middle and lower parts of the respective body systems, the dynamic during primary and permanent dentition starts with the incisors in the front part of the upper and lower jaw and then steadily moves backwards. The back part of the jaw keeps active life and growth forces longer and is therefore able to develop new teeth in a later phase of the child development.

A similar pattern can be found in the development of each individual tooth. Figure 2 shows the "mixed dentition period" which is the time a child has both primary and permanent teeth. A couple of key characteristics of dentition may be explained with this illustration:

- The enamel crown is the first part of the permanent tooth that is being developed.
- The dentin and the dental pulp of the permanent teeth are still developing while the enamel crown is already visible in the oral cavity, i.e. they keep their formative forces longer than the enamel crown.
- Active reabsorption of the primary root dentin is going on while the permanent tooth is developing; while dentin and dental pulp can be re-integrated in the general life processes of the body, the enamel cannot. Together with the upper part of the dentin, it

6   Karl König, *The First Three Years of the Child*.
7   M. Bath-Balogh and M. J. Fehrenbach, *Dental Embryology, Histology, and Anatomy*.

becomes the wiggling tooth. (If you have a chance to observe a tooth that has just been shed focus on the root—and you may see that the lower part of the root is missing, i.e., it underwent active reabsorption.)

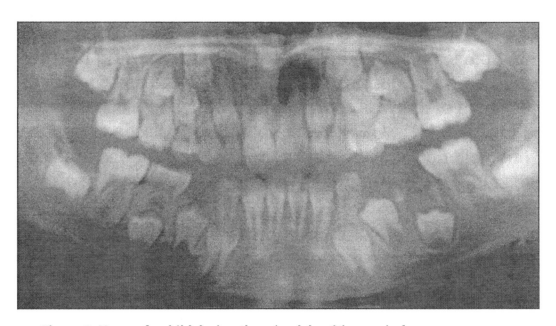

Figure 2: X-ray of a child during the mixed dentition period

Soul Activities in Relation to Dentition

The commencement of permanent dentition is usually characterized by major changes in the child's approach to the environment. Up to this age the child was sitting in the parent's boat, living their rhythms and being part of the immediate family surroundings. Now the social circle widens and the child is exposed to a host of new challenges. The emotional upheaval during this time is considerable and can express itself in various ways.[8] Our own child was eagerly waiting for the change of teeth and almost celebrated the first shed tooth. It gave us the impression that she was relieved from a kind of "damming up" and an enormous satisfaction and excitement of having a visible sign of growing up and moving on.

Primary dentition usually is a very painful procedure for both children and parents. Almost all parents can describe the sleepless nights that the eruption of the first incisor in the lower jaw causes when the child was six to eight months old. The appearance of permanent teeth is experienced differently. Usually no pain is involved and the child appreciates the loss of the primary teeth. This difference already indicates the increased level of freedom the soul has achieved in its relationship to the body. Pain can be described as increased presence of the soul (i.e. consciousness) in a certain bodily area. While in primary dentition the soul is

8   M. Kiel-Hinrichsen and R. Kviske, *Wackeln die Zähne—Wackelt die Seele.*

deeply involved with that process (which is experienced as pain), the consciousness during the secondary dentition is not as involved in the physical body. Steiner describes how, up to the change of teeth, through first learning to speak, the child dreamily follows all that is to become fundamental for its later life, and how only after the second dentition the child wakes up.[9] Waking up may be described as availability of "free consciousness," soul activity that is not involved in and attached to the body process. It has to be noted, though, that permanent dentition is a process that goes on for many years; therefore the mentioned "waking up" is a gradual and not a sudden process.

Steiner further points out that the availability of memory function is a key soul activity that is activated with the change of teeth. He indicates that "when taking in the spoken word, a refined inner habit is formed in the child, who absorbs everything by way of imitation. Out of this earlier specially developed habit—which is still of a more physical nature—a soul habit is formed when the child begins the second dentition. It is this habit, formed in the realm of the soul, which is called memory." Observations with our own children might help to better understand what is meant. No doubt, even our three-year-old child already has some kind of memory. He recognizes names, locations, and much more. However, typically this memory is attached to the environment; it imitates the environment. When we pick our older child up from school and pass by her previous kindergarten the three-year-old child always says: "Here is the kindergarten." His memory therefore is mostly triggered by environmental stimuli and not by internal activity of the soul. A very different kind of memory occurs in the seven-year-old child. The memory function comes from inside; and events are recalled that are not stimulated by the immediate environment.

Trends and Suggested Practical Observations

An increasing body of scientific evidence suggests that dental development in children has been *accelerating*.[10] In addition, epidemic diseases such as childhood obesity are linked to further acceleration of dental development.[11] Furthermore, the pattern of permanent dentition changes; the canines reveal a significant advancement relative to the formation of the first molars.[12] Considering the threefold body structure, this acceleration might result from the prevailing cultural trend that places the nervous system under high stress already in early childhood. This is in sharp contrast to what Verhulst describes as the principle of *retardation*. He refers to it as a key developmental dynamic in humans.[13] In particular he mentions that the human teeth permanently retain the generalized developmental patterns; i.e., all three types of teeth (incisors, canines, molars) are homogeneously (under-)developed. No single type is dominating and developed to its extreme. In addition the dental arch (i.e. the size of the lower jaw) in humans is considerably shorter relative to the length of the skull

9   Rudolf Steiner, *The Child's Changing Consciousness and Waldorf Education*.
10 Holtgrave, Kretschmer, and Muller, "Acceleration in Dental Development: Fact or Fiction."
11 Hilgers, Akridge, Scheetz, and Kinane, "Childhood Obesity and Dental Development."
12 Liversidge and Speechly, "Growth of Permanent Mandibular Teeth of British Children aged 4 to 9 Years."
13 J. Verhulst, *Developmental Dynamics in Humans and Other Primates*.

than it is in other primates. However, from a practical point of view, the most important aspect of retardation is the late onset of permanent dentition in humans. Most primates lose their primary teeth very early in their lives.

A key task of Waldorf education in that context is to focus on a balanced development of all three parts of the body system and provide a platform for a healthy development of bodily movements as well as rhythmical activities. The risk of the current trend towards "fast development" is that it may cause an intense but short-termed development and will diminish the long-term capability to maintain a steady and active development throughout one's whole lifetime. Fast development might be compared to a fruit that is injected with a substance promoting early ripeness. While ripeness is a desirable condition, it should not be achieved prematurely. Otherwise, important long-term developmental opportunities are lost.

A couple of suggested observations might provide the kindergarten teacher with a better understanding of the children and their environment:

- An initial observation a kindergarten teacher might find useful is the *oral hygiene* and appropriate dental care that a child and their parents practice. Lack of oral hygiene may have a variety of reasons. However, in line with the Buddhist saying, "The body is the temple of the soul," appropriate body care should be a key element of child care. Any indicator of inappropriate body care should always be followed through and an understanding should be developed of what is going on.

- The *onset and the pattern of the permanent dentition* as well as the *shape of the permanent teeth* is another area worthy of observation. This might give some insights about whether a child tends towards early or late development, and whether all three systems (central nervous system/rhythmical system/metabolic-limb system) are equally developed or one system is dominating. Observation of the teeth in that context is only part of a more comprehensive approach and should be complemented by observations of the child's movements and others. If a major tooth malformation or pathological positioning of teeth is observed, the teacher should reach out to the parents in order to refer the child to professional care.

- There are two typical *movements of the jaws*: the incisor-like vertical, top-down movement that is used to bite and separate, e.g., a piece of an apple from the whole apple, and the horizontal movement, that is used to further break down the food and extract nutrients. While the first movement is "rodent-like" (and dominated by the front part of the mouth and the incisors), the latter one is "ruminator-like" (and dominated by the molars). In animals, a ruminating cow demonstrates the horizontal jaw movement to an extreme. For a kindergarten teacher, it might be interesting to observe what kind of jaw movement dominates in a child and how long the nutrition stays in the mouth before the child swallows it. Multiple patterns exist: some children ruminate, keep their nutrition in the mouth for a long time, and almost fall asleep while eating. Others are eating fast, biting and swallowing without any real profound interaction with the food. Based on those observations a teacher might start to develop behavioral scenarios to balance the extremes in a child.

- Finally, the teacher should carefully observe the ***transition of the memory function*** in a child. The two different types of memories (imitation triggered by environmental stimuli versus internalized memory function as habit of the soul) should be identified. While the first type of memory requires a "leading-by-example" type of approach, teaching should more and more focus on "leading by images" as soon as the internalized memory function becomes available.

Summary

Among other indicators, the commencement of permanent dentition is an important sign of school readiness. We reviewed the threefold structure of each tooth, as well as the three types of teeth and their relationship to the whole body (incisors—central nervous system, canines—rhythmical system, molars—metabolic and limb system). The developmental dynamic in human beings usually starts with the nervous system and then gradually moves down through the other parts of the body. Similarly, the incisors lead the permanent dentition followed by the canines and the molars. The involvement of the soul in primary and secondary dentition differs. In addition, a new, internal quality of memory occurs at about the time when permanent dentition starts. The current trend of accelerated dental development and the need to provide balanced education that covers all three body systems has been discussed. Four observations that might provide the kindergarten teacher with additional insight were suggested (oral hygiene; pattern of permanent dentition; jaw movement and eating habits; and the transition of memory function). ✦

References

Bath-Balogh, M, Fehrenbach, M. J. *Dental Embryology, Histology, and Anatomy*. St. Louis, Missouri: Elsevier Saunders, 2006.

Hilgers, K. K., Akridge, M., Scheetz, J. P., Kinane, D. E. "Childhood Obesity and Dental Development." *AAPD Journal 28* (2006), 18-22.

Holdrege, Craig. "The Giraffe's Long Neck: From Evolutionary Fable to Whole Organism." *Nature Institute Perspectives 4* (2005).

Holdrege, Craig. "The Flexible Giant: Seeing the Elephant Whole." *Nature Institute Perspectives 4* (2005).

Holtgrave, E. A., Kretschmer, R., Muller, R. "Acceleration in Dental Development: Fact or Fiction." *European Journal of Orthodontics 19* (1997), 703-10.

Husemann, A.J. *Der Zahnwechsel des Kindes: Ein Spiegel seiner seelischen Entwicklung*. Stuttgart: Verlag Freies Geistesleben, 1996.

Kiel-Hinrichsen, M., Kviske, R. *Wackeln die Zähne—Wackelt die Seele. Der Zahnwechsel. Ein Handbuch für Eltern und Erziehende*. Stuttgart: Urachhaus, 2002.

König, Karl. *The First Three Years of the Child*. New York: Anthroposophic Press, 1969.

Liversidge, H. M., Speechly, T. "Growth of Permanent Mandibular Teeth of British Children aged 4 to 9 Years." *Annals of Human Biology 28* (2001), 256-62.

Steiner, Rudolf. Lecture of April 17, 1923, in *The Child's Changing Consciousness and Waldorf Education*. Hudson, New York: Anthroposophic Press, 1988.

Verhulst, J. *Developmental Dynamics in Humans and Other Primates*. Ghent, New York: Adonis Press, 2003.

Seeing the Wholeness of the Child

Nancy Blanning

*K*nock, knock, knock. May I come in? Is there room in the mitten for me?

In the story of "The Mitten," a mitten lost in the forest is discovered by one small animal after another. First comes the mouse, then the hare, each seeking shelter in the mitten from the outside winter blasts. One by one, more animals move in together, each getting larger than the previous one. Will there be room in the mitten for the fox, for the bear as well? How far can the mitten stretch to hold them all? Can the nature of the fox or the bear be understood/trusted/embraced so that they can be admitted into the company and live in harmony with the others?

Our Waldorf kindergartens have always tried to be very big "mittens" and stand as a haven for children. The education strives to honor and respect each individual with his or her differences. We trust in the developmental process, noting that children have different timetables for their maturation. We decline to follow the cultural panic of forcing early developmental expectations and academic tasks upon the children. We know that early childhood has unique tasks to complete that can be accomplished only in the first seven or so years of life. When the child is allowed to grow a strong physical body and strengthen the foundational senses, the tasks of the grade school years will be accomplished more successfully. The kindergarten supports this growth through rhythm, seasonal celebrations, play, work, child-like exploration, and protection from inappropriate and excessive sensory stimulation.

But the children knocking to enter this haven today are often difficult to understand and not easy to embrace. More "foxes," "bears," and even "squawking crows" are asking for acceptance into the mitten. Many are mysteries to us. There is the nervous, pale, anxious child who can be either excessively meek or wild and hysterical in reacting to whatever comes toward him. There is the clumsy child who constantly bumps into others, falls over her own feet, drops things, dribbles food all about as she falls off her chair at the snack table . There is the loud child who vocalizes at the quietest moments, disrupting the mood that the teacher has tried so hard to create. There is the distracting and inattentive child who does not imitate or become engaged in the story. There are children who cannot tolerate being touched and those who hang on everyone, especially the teacher.

While we might wish for less challenging, less complicated children, the fact is that these are the children of our modern age. Whether they are termed "millennial children," "star children," "Christopher children," learning disabled, autistic, sensory integration challenged, or whatever, they are the children who stand before us. And their numbers increase each year in schools everywhere. They present us with a dual challenge. We need to train our observation to see from where the difficulties arise, to recognize indicators that point to sensory disturbance or immaturity that can explain some behaviors. Yet as we develop this "diagnostic" vision, we must also see the strengths the child carries to be celebrated and built upon. We also need to school ourselves in remembering what is typical for each age group; the six- or seven-year-old can confuse our observation because some developmental progress seems to fall apart at this time. We want to keep alive and healthy our Waldorf commitment to seeing and honoring the wholeness of the child within his age context, without ignoring or denying challenges.

This article will give some indications to help us develop a mode of looking at this vast subject.

Looking at the *twelve senses*, as described by Rudolf Steiner, can be a gateway into understanding what we are seeing with the children. Of these twelve—*touch, life or well-being, self-movement, balance, smell, taste, sight, warmth, hearing, word, thought*, and *sensing the ego of the other*—the first four are deeply related to the young child. Steiner identified touch, life/well-being, self-movement, and balance as the foundational senses the young child works to strengthen during the first seven years of life. These are also characterized as the "will" senses through which the human being has inner experience of him/herself. The next group includes the more familiar senses of smell, taste, sight, and warmth (the ability to sense temperature being something different from touch). These are often denoted as the "feeling" senses which lead us into experience of the world around us. The final group Steiner sometimes called the "social" or "spiritualized" senses of hearing, word, thought, and sense for the ego of the other human being. Through these last four we have the possibility to interact with our fellow human beings and to move into realms of thought and ideas that reach beyond our strictly personal experiences. These first senses build the foundation to support development of the higher ones. How well the child may be able to encounter and enjoy other human beings and creatively participate in social life has its seeds planted in the first seven years of life.

While we might wish for less challenging, less complicated children, the fact is that these are the children of our modern age.

When we look at a young child, we can see how absorbed the child is in strengthening and utilizing these senses. Babies love to be touched and held. They gradually gain regulation of their body rhythms for sleeping and eating, becoming increasingly comfortable in the metabolic and organic life of the physical body. They are soothed by movement, liking to be rocked, bounced about, and carried. They work ceaselessly to gain control of the limbs and bring them into intentional, coordinated movement. They struggle into uprightness and maintain balance for standing. Ultimately, they put all these together to take their first steps into the world. When uprightness and walking are achieved, the highest senses of word, thought, and sensing the other ego can begin to birth themselves. The child can now continue to strengthen and mature these senses. They run, spin, jump, climb, push, pull, swing, and dance through their first years. Through doing so, they explore and interact with the world environment and the words, thoughts, and presence of other human beings.

The challenging behaviors we see in young children often arise from problems with these foundational senses. We can understand why these problems are increasing if we look at our life style. Western societies have changed so much with modern conveniences that there is less opportunity for the senses to easily develop. Possibilities for free exploration and unrestricted movement are limited. Practical chores and work tasks common in the past are no longer required of us. The culture is increasingly entertainment-based with the children passively watching or interacting with movement only with the eyes and hands. Children are wisely protected in car seats but with the consequence that they may be held immobile for significant parts of their day. And premature and stressful birth experiences add to the strain on sensory development. Each of these factors can limit healthy development and result in inaccurate perception of and response to the world around us. This is often what is happening with the perplexing and mystifying things we see children do.

In mainstream diagnosis and therapy, sensory integration work emerged in the 1960's through the pioneering work of A. Jean Ayres, a researcher and occupational therapist. She identified that there were dysfunctions in sensory experiencing of the world. She brought forth clinical, mainstream observation of the foundational senses Rudolf Steiner had already described in the early 1900's. If we inform and humanize these observations through the anthroposophical understanding of the human being, they can become a useful tool for us. We can use these perspectives in understanding some of the mysteries we encounter in the children.

The first is **touch** or the **tactile** sense, as the mainstream defines it. Our skin is the organ for touch. Steiner described that it is through touch that we experience boundary. Touch tells us where we stop and where the world begins. Difficulties with touch have long been observed. Our language describes someone as "touchy," by which we mean too sensitive, over-reacting to what most people tolerate as acceptable or normal. When we have a touch-sensitive child, we may see refusal to hold hands; distaste for getting hands dirty or sticky, such as with kneading bread; fussiness about clothing, tags, sock seams; over-reaction to another child coming too near or brushing by; extreme reaction to pain or injury; picky eating and strong reactions to food textures, and so on. On the other extreme is the child who is under-responsive to touch. He may seem uncaring that his hands are dirty, perhaps even crusted with mud or snow; be undeterred or unresponsive to an injury that should cause painful response; wear shoes on the wrong feet; be undisturbed that clothes and socks are twisted; physically touch or bump other children and innocently deny that it has happened; eat sloppily; need to feel and touch whatever is in the environment, almost compulsively. These children often exhibit social difficulties as well. Their sense of boundary perception is either too sharp or too diffuse. Others cannot get close enough to them to develop relationship or the child is too intrusive into the domain of others. Without a healthy sense of touch, it is difficult to have trust in the world or to be trusted by others.

The **sense of life** is the second in this group. This refers to our organic life and how well our metabolic and rhythmic life is functioning. When things are going well, we are unconscious of this sense. When we become tired or hungry, ill, or if our rhythmic life in breathing, sleeping, or digestion is disordered, then the life sense rises to consciousness. The health of the life sense is visible to us in the children's vitality. Often the children are pale, sluggish, under-rested, and may have dark circles under their eyes. They may be fussy eaters, wanting mostly foods easy to digest (pasta being a favorite). They may have allergies and food sensitivities as well. When this sense is healthy, one has the experience of inner comfort and well-being. When it is disordered, there is a tension, an inability to relax.

Self-movement is known in mainstream terminology as **proprioception**. Steiner described that through this sense we experience the body as a whole. Through self-movement, we know where the limbs are in relation to each other and the rest of the body. Because of self-movement, we can know when we move and coordinate and control what we intend. Each joint has small sensors, called proprioceptors, that register movement, position, and tension in the limb, telling us where each body part is. The experience of body geography is possible because of self-movement. The child with inefficient self-movement or proprioception often appears clumsy, is a "crasher and basher" with other children; likes to be on the bottom of a pile of children; slaps feet on the floor when walking; pushes against other children or objects; chews on objects, shirt sleeves, or collars; has difficulty with self-help skills of dressing, putting on shoes; needs to see what he is doing rather than feeling where the body should go; knocks over or spills things; has difficulty with rhythmic movement; applies too much or too little tension to muscles to direct and control movement. With healthy self-movement or proprioception, Steiner describes that one can experience freedom of soul. Without it, one stumbles around in the body, following wherever it goes rather than directing it.

The last of this group is **balance** or the **vestibular** sense. We know where our bodies are, particularly our uprightness, in relation to the earth and its gravity through balance. The vestibular sensory organ is composed of the three semi-circular canals of the inner ear. Set at right angles to each other, they correspond to the directions of the three planes of space—right/left, front/back, and above/below. Tiny calcium carbonate crystals floating in viscous fluid within the canals move to stimulate sensation of position in these planes. If we experience disequilibrium in position, we can adjust our posture to feel secure again. One's sense of security and stability, both physically and emotionally, depend on correctly functioning balance. This system is particularly threatened by childhood ear infections, which can cause damage to the balance mechanism and/or hearing. Infections can also affect speech development, as well as processing and understanding of the spoken word (known as auditory and language processing.) Children with vestibular immaturity or damage are often ones who seek constant motion. They wiggle in their chairs, rock, bounce, have difficulty sitting still. They may love to spin and seldom or never feel dizzy. They may be nimble as cats when moving quickly but have challenge balancing on one foot or holding balance when walking a beam slowly. These children have under-responsive vestibular systems that need a constant inflow of stimulus to give balance information. On the other extreme are those children whose vestibular system is so sensitive that they avoid movement. They will likely stay away from anything to do with swinging or spinning. They avoid heights, cannot learn to ride a bike. Such a child may stake out a quiet and secure corner of the classroom, content to stay there all morning during free play time. The vestibular system does not only perform its own task. Many other sensory experiences are processed through it—vision, posture, muscle tone, and spatial orientation, to name a few. The foundational health of this system is critically important because so many things depend upon it. In the soul realm, balance also allows us to develop equilibrium and, says Steiner, a feeling of inner rest.

The chance for experiencing wholeness of oneself depends upon the integration and mutual support of these senses.

The healthy development of these four senses creates the foundation for a firm and secure footing in the world—physically, quite literally, and also emotionally and socially as well. The chance for experiencing wholeness of oneself depends upon the integration and mutual support of these senses one to another. It is essential that the guardian adults caring for and guiding the children be able to observe healthy or challenged sensory development. Looking to the "symptoms" noted above is a starting place. As we educate ourselves toward what kinds of movements and sensory experiences that will help to strengthen a weak system, we can guide the children toward these healing activities.

Yet determining when something calls for special attention depends on context—the child's age and developmental history. A mixed-age classroom setting offers an advantage. When a teacher and child have been together for two or three years, the teacher has seen the degree of progress over time. She or he can observe whether balance, for instance, has been a challenge consistently, whether the child has always been "wiggly" or "touchy," and so on. Having this context will be especially important when looking at the six- or seven-year-olds when many things seem to fall apart. Children at this age often display behaviors that could be perceived as sensory problems. *Your Six-Year-Old*, by Louise Bates Ames and Frances Ilg of the Gesell Institute of Human Development, gives a very helpful summary of common six-year-old behaviors. In the social realm, the six-year-old can be both verbally and physically aggressive, even belligerent, quarrelsome, boisterous, argumentative, excitable, and emotional. He can too often be rough in play and sometimes mean to younger children. Are these signs of a diagnosable "syndrome" or of being six?

In the physical/movement realm, the six-year old may eat sloppily, stuffing his mouth and dribble food. She may knock over milk and grab for food, which could suggest tactile and proprioceptive difficulty. The six-year-old may wriggle and kick her legs, rock and tip her chair, bite or tear at fingernails, scratch, grimace, grind teeth, chew on hair or pencils. He may be restless when sitting, kicking the chair, even falling off onto the floor. Hands are always

More and more children are seeking haven in the Waldorf kindergarten "mitten."

busy, especially around the face. Facial grimaces are frequent, seeming almost tic-like in nature. Irritating throaty noises or throat clearing are common as well. The child may be clumsy, "falling over a piece of string." In the touch realm, the child may express extra sensitivity, disliking hair combing. Physically the child may be full of complaints. These can be indicators of long-term difficulty with the senses of touch, self-movement/proprioception, or balance/vestibular or may be short-term expressions of the disequilibrium that the six-year-old is passing through. We must ask whether what is being seen has been typical for the child over time or is a recent phenomenon coinciding with this transitional age.

Several dangers can present themselves here. One is that we are tempted to jump to conclusions about what we are seeing, forming a diagnosis rather than participating in a process. Even when we have watched long and observed well, accurately seeing a sensory difficulty, there is the temptation to define the child as a "vestibular problem" or the child with "proprioceptive difficulty" or the "tactile sensitive" one. We can lose the archetypal image of the wholeness of the child in the fragmented details. The more we can observe the child with warm interest and let the picture stand open by asking questions rather than forming answers, the more teachers can become servants of healing. We can inwardly carry the intention about the child, "The picture of who you can become is still being filled in. As your teacher, I will hold the wholeness of who you truly are as my guide."

More and more children are seeking haven in the Waldorf kindergarten "mitten." Their challenges are increasingly complex and the behaviors they bring to us challenging to meet. More "foxes" and "bears" are knocking. To make room for them, we need to develop new tools of observation and understanding of the burdens and gifts these children carry. We need to expand our picturing of what the children need to achieve health, with extra awareness of foundational sensory development. Even if we do not know what to do, appreciating what the child is struggling with opens up our sympathetic tolerance to difficulties. Educating ourselves to know what is developmentally typical of different ages, especially the six-year-old, is also essential to have the right context for what we see. The children's needs are calling upon us to develop this type of looking. This means both learning to look carefully and to hold the picture of wholeness the child is struggling to fulfill. The archetypal wholeness already exists. It is our task to perceive it permeating and radiating from each child. To see this wholeness is perhaps the most healing deed we can perform. ✦

References and Suggested Reading

Ayres, A. Jean. *Sensory Integration and the Child*. Los Angeles: Western Psychological Services, 1979.

Bates Ames, Louise and Frances Ilg. *Your Six-Year-Old*. New York: Delacorte Press, 1981.

Bluestone, Judith. Workshop training handouts. Seattle: The HANDLE Institute Int., 2003.

Goddard-Blythe, Sally. *The Well-Balanced Child*. Stroud, UK: Hawthorn Press, 2004.

Kranowitz, Carol. *The Out-of-Sync Child*. New York: Penguin, 1998.

Steiner, Rudolf. *Anthroposophy, A Fragment*. New York: Anthroposophic Press, 1996.

Steiner, Rudolf. "Man's Twelve Senses in Their Relation to Imagination, Inspiration, Intuition." Lecture given in Dornach, August 8, 1920.

Steiner, Rudolf. *The Study of Man*. London: Rudolf Steiner Press, 1966.

Steiner, Rudolf. *A Psychology of Body, Soul, and Spirit*. New York: Anthroposophic Press, 1999.

Is Our Educational System Contributing to Attentional and Learning Difficulties in Our Children?

Susan R. Johnson, MD

I have great concerns about teaching preschool and kindergarten children to read and write. Developmentally and neurologically it doesn't make sense. There is a developmental progression of sensory-motor skills that a young child needs to master in the first seven years of life. Despite what we think, learning is not "all from our head." It is the movements of our body in utero, through infancy and childhood, and even adulthood that form the neural pathways in our mind that we later use to read, write, spell, do math, and think in an imaginative and creative way. I see countless numbers of children in my practice who have been diagnosed with "ADD" or "learning disabilities" who miraculously improve when they are taken out of an "academic" kindergarten or given an extra year in a developmental kindergarten that emphasizes movement and the integration of their sensory-motor systems.

My seventeen years of experience as a developmental and behavioral pediatrician have shown me that children who have difficulties reading and writing usually have a poorly developed sense of balance, have difficulty making eye contact, have difficulty tracking or following with their eyes, can't easily distinguish the right side of the body from the left, have difficulty sitting still in a chair and locating their body in space. Many of these children who have difficulties reading and writing also have poor muscle tone exemplified by a slumped posture, a tense or fisted pencil grip, and "flat feet" (collapsed arches). Sometimes these children are overly sensitive to touch and have difficulties in their peer relationships because they are using their minds and eyes to help their bodies navigate in space and thus miss the social, non-verbal cues from their playmates. These children also have an overactive sympathetic nervous system ("fight or flight" reaction) and are therefore very sensitive to the stimulant effects of sugar, chocolate, lack of sleep, changes in routines, television, and playing video and computer games.

Children who are ready to read and write should be able to pay attention and sit still in a chair for at least twenty minutes (without needing to wiggle or sit on their feet or wrap their feet around the legs of the chair as a way to locate their bodies in space by muscle movement or activation of pressure receptors). They need to be able to balance on one foot, without their knees touching, and in stillness, with both arms extended out to their sides while they count backwards without losing their balance. They need to be able to stand on one foot, with arms stretched out in front of them (palms facing up) with both eyes closed for ten seconds without falling. They need to be able to reproduce patterns of abstract lines and curves (e.g., various geometric shapes, numbers, or letters) on a piece of paper with a pencil when someone else draws these shapes, numbers or letters on their backs. Finally, a child needs to be able to walk slowly on a balance beam, skip and jump rope before attempting to teach that child to read and write.

If children can't do these tasks easily, then they haven't integrated their vestibular and proprioceptive (sensory-motor) systems, and they will have difficulty sitting still, listening, focusing their eyes, focusing their attention, and remembering numbers and letters in the classroom. Children integrate their sensory-motor system through body movements and not through flash cards or playing electronic games. Physical movements such as skipping, hopping, rolling down hills, playing catch with a ball, jumping rope, running, walking, clapping games and circle games, as well as doing lots of fine motor activities with their fingers—cutting with scissors, digging in the garden, kneading bread dough, pulling weeds, painting, beading, drawing, sewing, finger knitting—build and strengthen neural pathways. In contrast, watching television or videos and playing computer games are extremely poor sources of stimulation for their sensory-motor development and actually prevent the integration of their nervous systems by keeping children in a state of stress, activating their sympathetic nervous systems of "fight or flight."

I have great concerns about teaching preschool and kindergarten children to read and write.

Finally, the ability to print and match a particular sound to a specific letter (phonics) in children is predominately a left-sided (analytic) brain activity. Developmentally, the left side of the brain doesn't fully start to develop or myelinate until ages seven to nine years (especially true for boys). When we teach children to read or write at an earlier age, we stress their minds and their bodies and force them to use only the right side of their brains for reading (sight memory). The right brain is more intuitive and looks at the whole picture rather than at details, so the child usually looks at only the first and last letter and the length of the word and then makes a guess at what the word could be without being able to sound it out. Some children can easily switch from the right hemisphere to the left as they get older, but many children (especially the ones who can't skip) haven't developed the pathway (corpus callosum) to quickly travel from the right side of the brain to the left side and thus end up being stuck trying to read and spell with the right hemisphere. These children often write letters backwards, can't spell, and can't seem to remember what sounds go with which letters. The effort required to write is also tremendous.

In addition to our American diet which is high in simple sugars, high in partially hydrogenated ("bad") fats and so low in omega-3 fatty acids, I wonder if much of our current epidemic in attentional and learning problems comes from our children watching too much television, playing too many video games, spending too much time in front of a computer screen, and being pushed to read and write too early. We need to surround the young child with what I call the "Buddha" state. This is regulated by the nervous system referred to as the parasympathetic, which is supported by adequate sleep, predictable rhythms and routines, wholesome nutrition, warmth, harmonious non-competitive rhythmic movements, and most importantly, our love. Children's brains develop and integrate when they are in the "Buddha" state. Their brains can't fully integrate or develop when they are in a state of stress or survival mode, i.e. "fight or flight."

Therefore, I support preschools and kindergartens that emphasize healthy movements, promote daily living skills (e.g., sweeping, stirring), as well as encourage creative "pretend" play. If preschools and kindergartens, and the governmental laws that set the standards for education, can support these healthy movement activities and stop trying to teach our very young children to read and write, then I believe we will start seeing healthier eight- and nine-year-olds who can listen, focus, sit still, write, read, pay attention, and learn with ease.   ✦

Section Two

Meeting the Challenge— The Role of the Teacher

Our being, as adults, enters a child's being just as the candlelight enters the eye. Whatever we are around a child spreads its influence so that the child's blood circulates differently in the sense organs and in the nerves; since these operate differently in the muscles and vascular liquids that nourish them, the entire being of the child is transformed according to the external sense impressions received. One can notice the effect that the moral and religious environment of childhood has had on an old person, including the physical constitution. A child's future condition of health and illness depends on our ability to realize deeply enough that everything in the child's environment is mirrored in the child. The physical and moral elements are reflected and affect a person's health or illness later.

Rudolf Steiner
Waldorf Education and Anthroposophy 2

Old Man Trouble

Tim Bennett

A friend of mine once said to me, "The bigger you are, the harder you fall," and I think that there is some truth to this, especially with the older child in the kindergarten. We all fall down sometime or hurt another; that is part of human nature. The six-year-olds are the big ones of the kindergarten and most definitely take the hard falls.

Thornton Burgess, the great children's writer, has a character in his books who always comes around when things go from bad to worse. His name is Old Man Trouble, and he likes nothing more than to have a good fight or a good laugh at someone else's misfortune. So over the years, I have made Old Man Trouble a part of my kindergarten. He has become a faithful companion, especially when mischief, mayhem and any form of trouble arise.

How does this work? Well, picture two boys having a great time outside, using sticks to swordfight. One child gets a little carried away and the other child gets hurt. Then I usually hear a call for help. When I get there, I make sure everyone is okay. Then we sit down, and the first words I speak are, "Looks like Old Man Trouble's been around these parts." At the beginning of the year, the children look around to see where he is. Usually, he has already gone by the time I show up. We talk about being careful with our sticks and then the boys go off, usually merry and with smiles on there faces.

What I find is that Old Man Trouble helps the children to breathe and slow down. It gives the situation at hand a name, i.e. "trouble." The children see that when I come into the situation, Old Man Trouble disappears. After a few weeks, all the children know or have heard me speak about Old Man Trouble. When a situation arises where the children can sense that things are not as they should be, some child often comes to me and says, "I think that Old Man Trouble is over there, Tim. You better come look." I find that some children actually "see" Old Man Trouble and I am again reminded that what I build up as an image in my own thoughts is taken up in the thought life and fantasy of the children.

I also use Old Man Trouble when working with verbal conflict. It truly frees up the children when they are not directly blamed. Old Man Trouble is the one who takes the blame, if he has whispered in your ear, telling you to do some unkind deed. This helps to resolve most conflicts in a much simpler manner. Usually humor can come in and brighten the situation, so the conflict can be seen in a more objective and flexible perspective. The conflict doesn't need to be seen as personal and fixed when dealing with six-year-olds. Everyone can feel honored and heard. You are part of the drama, but other forces are at work too, as we grownups know all too well.

So, as a ninety-one-year-old farmer friend recently told me, "It is best to get up early before the devil puts his shirt on." Now, getting up early may help you to stay ahead of the devil, but if you are anything like me, Old Man Trouble will still find his way into the kindergarten. So when you next find trouble arising in your classroom, why not bring the children the wonderful image of my friend, Old Man Trouble?

Now, what makes Old Man Trouble disappear? Love, respect and understanding. As the social climate of your class ebbs and flows, so can the presence of Old Man Trouble. When those six-year-olds fall hard, Old Man Trouble can be there to help them get up. ✦

Our Role in Meeting the Children

Barbara Klocek

How can we meet the different children in the kindergarten? Some children are four years old, some are six, and what a difference that makes! As well, even at this young age, they bring their home environments, their incarnating bodies and their individualities. We multiply that times the number of children in the class and it can indeed be a challenging task for the teacher.

Early in the year, the challenge lies in getting to know the children. As one little girl entered in with a firm step and a social smile, I thought, here is a strong, solid girl. This was confirmed a few days later when I saw her pinch the child next to her. Firmly I said her name. She looked at me, surprised, and burst into tears. I had spoken too firmly to her, for there was another very sensitive side that I had not yet seen. I had jumped too quickly to the conclusion of who I thought she was. I have taken that event into each school year as it starts and try to keep my thoughts of the child as open as possible. I also have a page for each child in my yearly notebook in which I write observations starting with the first day. I try to write in it at least every few weeks. It is amazing to see what I had observed the first week and then a few months later, for the picture deepens and reveals many layers as the year progresses. I have also found it invaluable in parent conferences to bring up specific incidents that might otherwise disappear in my memory. I find the ebb and flow of time in the kindergarten and the dreamy consciousness of the children create a mood that is not conducive to observation. The recording of my observations over time awakens me to my perceptions as well as to who the child is becoming.

What about meeting the different ages? This is a whole dance in itself. How gently and tenderly we need to meet the younger children. We are like a wave to them, and sometimes we can be so overpowering. Often before they know us, even our looking at them is perceived as painful. I have come to see how sensitive they are even to my mood, which I had thought was only being experienced in my inner landscape. Several little boys were becoming more and more rambunctious in the classroom, and I felt my irritation growing. As I began to move towards them, the sensitive children began to draw back. Not all children are so sensitive, for at the other end of the spectrum, some of them are surrounded by a kind of dream aura, unaware of my movement and my mood. This has led me to being more active outwardly when I sense something is not going well so that I do not get to the point of becoming irritated, disturbing everyone's inner landscape. This has also led me inwardly to strive to be very peaceful and calm in the classroom so that I am perceived by the sensitive children as a safe and easy energy to be around.

What a joy it is to have a child for a second year. The foundation of trust and understanding has already begun. They return with joy to the rhythm of the kindergarten and help the new children find their way through the day. With these children, there is an opportunity to go deeper in the relationship. A group of three boys comes to mind concerning this. The first year, they came in already knowing each other, and paying attention to the teacher was not a skill that was in place. They initially would not let any other new children play with them and rudely turned them away. I tried drawing out one of the group by helping me with a task but met with little long-term success because the call of the pack was so strong. I suggested to the parents to have play dates with the new children, which was nice, but did not change the dynamic when the three were together in the class. They all had summer birthdays and were five years old before starting their first year. I finally decided that they needed a vacation from each other for a while. They remained in my class but were told gently that they needed to have a vacation so that they could make new friends. At first, they were at a loss for what to do, but before long they each began to find new friends. A new lightness came into each of the boys. After about a month, they asked if they could play together. I said they could if they included the other children. What a difference it made to the whole class dynamic, for they became much more joyful and inclusive. When they returned for their second year, they welcomed the new children, both older and younger, and the mood of inclusiveness and acceptance carried through the year. I have also used the vacation with social relationships where I thought the children could not resolve the issues on their own. I had two very strong, choleric girls who were drawn together and had wonderful times. However, sometimes they would get in a pattern when they were only able to quarrel with each other. With a vacation time, they both could relax, relate to other children and come back to each other in a different gesture. I see the vacation as an opportunity for the child to be allowed time away from a difficult or unhealthy relationship. This allows a breathing in relationships that sometimes I have found that children are not able to create on their own.

As the child becomes six years old, a new dynamic can appear. Instead of the adult (parent or teacher) being the center of his world, which is a lovely characteristic of the five-year-old, the child becomes the center of his world. New capacities of inner awareness in imaginations, memory and feelings are developing. Out of this, play becomes more planned. Often they don't even need to play but would rather sit and talk. This time is often referred to as the adolescence of childhood, for the teenager also often considers himself the center of the world and has a strong inner life. With this shift, there can begin a challenging of the teacher in subtle ways. Indeed, this is the beginning of the consciousness change when, instead of learning through imitation, the child learns through the loving authority of the teacher. This is usually a tumultuous time at home as well, and the phrase, "You're not the boss of me!" echoes around them. We need to meet them with a different gesture. The same child who, a year earlier, was an eager helper now doesn't want to help at all. This is the time for loving firmness and the gentle but firm words: "You may help."

The child at six is much more awakened to his or her feelings and identifies with them in a new way. Sympathy and antipathy become more pronounced. I have found one of the tasks with these children is to help them begin to do things that they do not want to do. We all have this as part of our life task that returns again and again to us. It has shown itself earlier in the child at two, but at that point is more related to the will. We can help them overcome their antipathy with our warmth and enthusiasm. As we enter into the activity, from washing dishes or cleaning up the outside toys, we bring joy into our mood and movements. Often this is enough to help them, for they are still under the mantle of imitation as well.

Perhaps they need some one-on-one time to help them enter into activity. Our love and attention is healing. This time, one-on-one, may also reveal a challenge that they are having with an activity. One six-year-old girl was not drawn into our enthusiastic activity of jumping rope outside. For a while, I let it be, but then, one day, said, "All the six-year-olds get to practice now." How self-consciously she tried, for it was not easy for her to get off the ground even though she was tiny. What a wonderful teaching moment it was as we all watched her try, and I consistently told her how well she was doing. There was an unkind comment from one of the skilled children, and another teaching opportunity presented itself as I reminded everyone how hard it was when they were first learning, and how we have to help each other as we practice. The tiny six-year-old took it to heart and every day wanted to practice. We all happily followed her progress.

Kindergarten teaching requires a great mobility of soul.

I was once asked by a new teacher if our gesture should be Michaelic (a straight line) or Gabrielic (a curved line) in the kindergarten. What a wonderful question. I have found I need to be both depending on the child and his or her age. Often there comes a point in the year where we are called to be a clear straight line as an older child challenges us. Sometimes the young children need the safe enclosure of the curved line of our arms around them.

Kindergarten teaching requires a great mobility of soul. With the children, as we turn our attention on them, we need to change our inner tone or landscape. One child needs to sense a quiet valley for his soul. Another child needs a warming fire to be near. Another child longs for a clear fence that holds her boundless energy. It is through deepening our understanding of child development and by practicing both our outer observation and our inner calm that we can sense what each child needs and reflect it. ✦

Soul Milk

Ruth Ker

To prepare for this book, five North American colleagues gathered once a year over a period of three years to study, do research and discuss the nature of the six-year-old change. As I write this, our work is still ongoing with further outreach involving anthroposophical doctors and conversations with international colleagues who are doing similar research. During our retreats we studied many of Rudolf Steiner's lectures. Rudolf Steiner had much to say about this time that he called the change of teeth and this article is punctuated with many of his wise words.

During one of our studies together an indication of Steiner's affected me so deeply that I have been carrying a question about it since that time. In the book *The Kingdom of Childhood*, Rudolf Steiner, while explaining what teachers need to draw upon within themselves to meet the children at the transformation time of the change of teeth, says that this time in their development is often heralded by many questions from the children. Steiner goes on to say "The child is curious but not with an intellectual curiosity… The child has fantasy, and this fantasy is what we must engage. It is really a question of developing the concept of a kind of 'milk of the soul.' For you see, after birth, the child must be given bodily milk… And when children come to school at the age of the changing of teeth it is again milk that you must give them, but now, milk for the soul… all that the children receive must be unity; after the change of teeth children must have 'soul milk.' "[1]

"Soul milk? What did Steiner mean by soul milk?" For years now this question has accompanied me. And, a subsequent question has arisen out of this pondering. "What is it that I need to do in the kindergarten and within my own self development that will

---

1   Rudolf Steiner, *The Kingdom of Childhood*, 14.

enable me to meet the children at the change of teeth with "soul milk"? Needless to say, this contemplation has given rise to many conversations and, with gratitude to all who have been willing to take the time to focus on this with me, I'd love to share some thoughts with you.

As early childhood educators, we are familiar with the idea that we work as priests/ priestesses and strive to be worthy models so that children have proper gestures, speech and attitudes to imitate. Joan Almon, in her article "The Healing Power of Play," comments on this role of the priest/priestess. She writes, "Normally the priest is at the altar, looking up to the spiritual world and guiding the congregation toward the divine. Young children, however, have just left the world of the divine and are finding their way to the earth. Our task is to help them find their way while recognizing that the divine world works strongly into the earthly. We stand not at the usual altar, but at the work table, baking the bread of life, sewing, gardening and much more." She goes on to say "There is a difference for the children in whether we experience the earth merely in its most external materialistic way or whether we recognize the hand of the divine in the creation of all that is earthly."[2] I think, for instance, of the many times that a child has brought me a freshly-picked flower. What is wanted from me in that moment? Can I be so present with the child that I can see the hidden heart in the snowdrop or the star in the primrose? Can I also be conscious enough in that moment so that some elements of the child's experience become available to me?

Rudolf Steiner said, "We must learn to listen to the remarks of those who are in some way inferior to us, suppressing every feeling of superiority or knowing better. Listening to children in this way is especially useful, and even the wisest of us can learn a great deal from them."[3] Surely this kind of attentiveness is a prerequisite for understanding the children's life of fantasy and how we can meet their experiences with soul milk.

In addition to taking up this role of the priest/priestess in the kindergarten classroom, we also hear that the class teacher's role is that of an artist working out of benevolent authority. This artist eventually passes the children on to the high school teacher, a true scientist who works to meet the adolescent's quest for truth. For each of these periods Steiner says the students progress through a need, first, for bodily milk, then soul milk, and finally, spiritual milk.[4] Of course, the parent's daily close contacts with their children provide many opportunities to nourish their children with these substances of physical, soul and spiritual milk.

As teachers in a mixed-age kindergarten we accompany the children to the threshold of their entrance into the grade school. Often, however, the children go through their change of teeth and the consolidation time after the birth of the etheric while they are still in the kindergarten. This puts us in the position of being a bridge for these children at a time when they need to be met by both imitation and authority. We walk the dual path of being

---

2   Joan Almon, "The Healing Power of Play," 14.
3   Rudolf Steiner, *How to Know Higher Worlds*, 47.
4   Rudolf Steiner, *The Essentials of Education*, Lecture five.

the priest/priestess and the artist/beloved authority. Not only are the older children in the kindergarten requiring us to live in these two worlds, but also we can experience the disparity between the needs of the imitative youngest children and those older ones who are reaching out for direct and firm boundaries. At this time it is our task to be the priestly role model anchoring the purposeful, meaningful work for the older children, and also to be the loving, interested bridge-maker who cares enough to say "Yes" to their new changes while responding with reassuring boundaries. The children need to feel acceptance from us about these changes bubbling up in them, not alarm, and they need to experience that we know how to meet them with strength. Also, the younger children in the mixed-age group are visibly relieved when the teacher can set firm limits with their older peers who seem to be disturbing the peace and order of the kindergarten.

What are the boundaries, rules and limits that we carry for the children during the six-year transformation when they show us that they are overcome with changes in their consciousness, physical body, emotional stability and social capabilities? Can we adults who earlier inspired them with our gestures and attitude toward life and real work now re-inspire the same children with proper responses to their testing of the world?

This summer, at a teacher's conference entitled "The Joys and Challenges of Working with the Older Child in the Kindergarten," many kindergarten teachers expressed the difficulties they were experiencing with the older children in their kindergarten classes. There was a visible sigh of relief when the teachers present heard that it is all right to relate to these older children with firm, clear expectations. Some teachers expressed that they received lots of permission in their early childhood trainings to work out of imitation with the older children but they felt guilty that they might not be pedagogically correct if they addressed the older ones directly with firm limits. As we practised ways of bringing form directly and lovingly to the older children through clear statements and picture ideas, it became obvious how these clear directives could be freeing for the older children and their teachers too. It's better for the children to have the "right way-of-the-world" affirmed to them at this six-year-old transition time than it is to allow them to become entangled in constantly testing-out boundaries. I often remind parents and colleagues that the limits that we bring to the children now provide the inner voices that they will hear inside themselves later on. We want them to have these wellsprings inside themselves during adolescence when we hope that they will be able to say "No" to even stronger temptations. The six-year-old change, often called first puberty, can be a foreshadowing of things to come. Let us take part in the child's biography now in such a way that we provide strength for their future.

So, in the face of encountering these changes in the children, how can we provide the soul milk that Steiner talks about?

The children need to feel acceptance from us about these changes bubbling up in them, not alarm.

I began pondering this question by reflecting on the word "soul" and realizing that in many places Rudolf Steiner speaks about the three different aspects of the soul—the thinking, the feeling and the willing. And then I looked at what I could do in my gestures and inner work to transform these three different qualities of the soul.

When I first began to teach, focusing on working out of imitation, I realized how many of my gestures needed transformation. I remember a master teacher coming to observe one of my circles. She later encouraged me to study and practice some of the archetypal gestures—planting seeds, scything, sewing etc. For a while I became hyper-aware of how I was moving and speaking and it took painstaking and patient practice to let go of some of my previous habits. However, when I began to experience the children's quickened interest in me, I realized that my striving was paying off in more focus from them during circles, handwork and work activities. The children are truly inspired by real work. One example of this is the daily work we do in our kindergarten garden. One of our oldest boys approached me the other day, swinging his shovel and whistling. "So," he said, "we have a lot of work to do in this garden. We'd better get going!" A quiet peace settled over this usually frisky boy as he turned the soil and talked about "helping the worms" and "being careful not to step into the garden in case he might squish the bugs." His sense of well-being became visibly heightened when he was allowed to work on his own in one area of the garden.

Giving extra responsibility to these older children who are capable of carrying more is another way to meet their need for stretching boundaries. We can step in and respond to their need to play with the limits by honoring them as capable helpers in the land who can do appropriate other tasks. We can ask the older children to help the younger ones with knot tying, dressing, threading needles, fingerknitting and finding things. Margret Meyerkort tells an anecdote about asking an older child to sort out a small dispute in the class when one child had taken something from another. The older child went to the perpetrator and firmly said, "Give that back!" The child immediately gave the toy back and the play went on undisturbed. Of course, one would have to be assured that the child chosen to do the task is able to set the right example. Sending the older children on missions away from the kindergarten room also creates valuable forays for them where they can stretch a boundary—perhaps a note needs to go to the office, a tool be procured from the tool shed, some laundry delivered to the other kindergarten class, etc. These are all ways that we can show the children that there are appropriate ways to flex their newfound strengths.

Let's assume that, through our presence and appropriate outer and inner responses to the children we are indeed dispensing soul milk. If so, then, since the soul has three different components, what does it mean to nurture the child with soul milk from our own willing, feeling and thinking capacities? Let's explore these questions a little further.

Willing

So much happens to young children when they go through this change. Please refer to Section One for further explanations of these changes. We are witnesses to a time in the children's development when their bodies seem out of control, their limbs are flailing out, often accidentally hitting other people or items. Sometimes we see them racing around the playground, stumbling and accidentally bumping into people and things or, if we're inside, we see them toppling over benches or losing balance easily. Often they will blurt out true but hurtful things—"Look at that fat lady's hat." "She can't even tie her own shoes." Of course, it's important to set a limit (with a picture, of course) when we see the child in these experiences. For instance, "Let's remember the speed limit" (when a child is racing out of control), or "Momma Bird helps her friends to do things when they don't know how. She even helps them build a nest" (when the children are ridiculing another because he or she doesn't know how to do something), or "Can you show me where the switch is to turn down that loud siren" (when the sounds get too noisy). It is much more effective to bring a boundary to the children by connecting to their play and then providing a suggestion which carries them into a next step in their play scenario. The older children can become stuck in their play and their insistence on playing the same scenario every day with themselves in the position of the "first boss" can be limiting for everyone. The teacher or parent must take the initiative to step into the play, connect to it and help it move forward in a fair and equitable way. Sometimes this requires only a sentence, or sometimes it requires being present for a while so that cooperative play can once again prevail.

But, is there something else that we can do to shepherd the actions of the older child in the kindergarten and dispense the much needed soul milk of which Steiner speaks? A hint came to me in another shared study.

In Lecture Five of *The Essentials of Education*, Steiner is speaking again of this transition time at the change of teeth. He talks about the child at this time developing a new relationship to the teacher. Now it becomes important who the teacher is as well as what the teacher does. He says the child will model the teacher because he loves her/him and if the teacher loves something, then the child will also love this thing. Rudolf Steiner speaks of the "hidden forces between the child's heart and that of the teacher" and the need of the teacher to "plan education so that the (child's) natural need to take pleasure in goodness can develop." He says, "Children do not ask (questions) intellectually with words, but deep in their hearts." [5] He goes on to say, "We get close to children during this stage of life only by placing them in the context of natural authority. Children see what lives in the teacher's gestures, and they hear something revealed in how the teacher's words are spoken."[6]

Reading this made me realize what an impact we could have on the children if we, as parents or Early Childhood teachers, could strongly model the healing deed. So I began to work even more steadfastly at repairing the outcomes of the children's reckless deeds. The following examples are some of the ways that we uphold the healing deed in our classroom. When

5   Rudolf Steiner, *The Essentials of Education*, 71.
6   Ibid., 70.

someone gets hurt, it is the (often unaware) perpetrator who runs to get the healing basket and administers the bump cream. When things get broken the six-year-old who broke them sits with me while we repair them with loving gestures. When things are spilled the child tidies them or wipes them clean. When the children criticize another child, I ask the child who is being criticized, "Do you want to play that way?" The same question is asked when the sometimes robust six- and seven-year-olds are infringing on the younger children in a mixed-age group. The answer on the part of those who are the offended is often "No." I then say, matter-of-factly and decisively, "They don't want to play that way." This can be quickly followed by "Let's… " and then a redirection for the game can follow. Some other ideas are: when a child is "budging" in line, we take her aside and have her watch how the other children are doing it; when something gets ripped, if it's a simple repair then the child sews it himself; if something is used inappropriately, then the child who "forgot" remedies this by fixing, replacing or undoing the gesture in some way. For instance, sand is shovelled back into the sandbox when it has been tossed outside of it.

Now it becomes important who the teacher is as well as what the teacher does.

This winter in our region we have had a particularly wet and muddy environment. I asked the parents permission to allow the children to "mine" the clay on our clay hill because I knew it would result in some muddy outdoor clothes going home each day. They all agreed and, needless to say, many of the children delved into this exploration wholeheartedly. We had many days of blissful and productive "mining" and many mud balls adorned the entranceway to our kindergarten room. However, one day, some of the older boys and girls decided to smear the clay on themselves instead of just getting inadvertently muddy in the process of focused play. When I spoke with my colleague about this new turn of events, we both agreed that the children weren't much dirtier when they purposefully spread the clay on themselves then when they unconsciously played solely with the elements. However, the gesture and the inappropriateness of their motive were very different when they were purposefully smearing themselves.

We decided on a consequence that was not intended to be a punishment. When we arrived back at the classroom after our morning outdoor playtime, we had the children who had been smearing themselves leave their outdoor clothes outside. Then when indoor playtime started, these children, one by one, washed their outdoor clothes. This took quite a bit of time out of their own personal indoor playtime and they were alone while they did this chore. I thought this solitary activity, when the children would probably be wanting to enter free play instead, would bring an organic lesson to them and an end to the clay smearing play. However, I wasn't quite prepared for the results. At first the children responded with pure delight. Water play! Yeah! Some of the children were even singing and joyful as they individually washed their clothes. After three days of summoning my strength to bring this extra task into our normal routine (it required extra work from me as well as maintaining our regular program—filling tubs with warm water which quickly became muddy and had to be dumped and filled again, then wringing clothes etc. etc. etc.), I was exhausted and ready to give up this idea of providing a natural consequence. Then, on the fourth day, I heard one of the older girls say, " I'm not going to put it on my clothes today. I want to build a house at play time." Then, one by one, over the course of the next few days, similar responses happened. The consequence had worked (not without an inordinate amount of willpower on my part)! Now we could legitimately abandon the clothes washing. Every day now, the children still are captivated by the play at the mud hill but the clay that gets on their clothes now happens accidentally during the course of healthy play.

It is always good to remember that when the older children are going through the six-year change many of them respond to the encroaching chaos in the same way that they have become accustomed to approaching life…they play at it indefatigably! The will that it takes on the part of the parent or teacher to meet each one of these moments of "playing with the boundaries" is tantamount to pushing a huge boulder up a hill. However, if the adult is able to kindly and matter-of-factly meet each situation with strength, then peace often settles upon the scene.

The older children often express their gratitude after a limit has been set by bestowing their respect and affection upon the adult. As one of the children in my class said last week, "The teachers and the office are the boss of the whole world." What a relief for a young child to feel that someone is in charge! This same child embraced me as he went home that day. What precipitated this statement and this hug? That day, one of the older kindergarten children, his friend, had told him while we all sat around the snack table that the kindergarten teachers "are just in kindergarten. They have stupid rules. They're not the boss of me. They don't know anything about the big school." My kind but firm response was " Oh yes, I AM the boss of this land. The angels and your Mom and Dad asked me to be your helper too while you are in this land."

Each year, one or more of the older children display the tendency to lag behind when we go on our walks to and from the garden. This often happens around the same time that I begin to hear the same children expressing causal thinking (if I do X, then Y will happen). When these incidents happen, I shepherd the rest of the group, as I always have done, in the proper direction without stopping. At first the child who is staying behind is often horrified that we are leaving without her. Then when she catches up with us, this is often one of those times that I receive a big hug. To me, this seems like an affirmation and an indication that the child is relieved that there is regularity and reliability in her world.

To be in the life of a child going through the six-year-old change is an honor. It is also a time when the teacher/parent must be prepared for unpredictability in the behavior of the children, challenges to authority and upsets in routines. It takes strength of will to stand as a loving authority at this time. Balance and nurturing in our own personal routines of self-care, study and health-giving play can support us to be present with strength for these children.

Feeling

Often, children's drawings at this time show houses with chimneys that have smoke curling out of them. Audrey McAllen out of her wealth of research and practice says that "When there is no smoke emerging from the chimney, [there is a possibility] that the will is not sufficiently active: there is apathy in the will forces."[7] Another way that these active will forces work is in the awakening of stronger forces of feeling. Indeed, the children do seem to display many more criticisms and disparaging remarks and tend to be more sensitive to the actions and words of others. Whereas the younger child in the kindergarten tends to be resilient in fending off rejections, the older child can harbor grudges and have lingering reactions. Often the whispering that the older children love to do is accompanied by pointing at other children or, in the case of many of the girls, outright playing at excluding others. Some boys also play this exclusion game. It is when these inner fires are awakening that the adults in the children's lives may become more challenged by their behavior. Many adults are still dealing with their own wounds caused by similar past events. These kinds of anti-social feeling reactions that the older children in the kindergarten are trying out have left us speechless and wounded too in the past. Of course, we run into trouble if we assume that these events are being absorbed by the children in the same way that they impacted us. Generally our wounds come from a period of time that is much later in life in our own personal biographies. Most older children in the kindergarten are involved in a preliminary developmental phase.

These new inwardly-impelled ways that the older kindergarten children are testing, if properly addressed, can be opportunities for reminders to them that there are rules of respect and order in this world. Of course these reminders are best delivered if they can be in picture images. "Mama bird helps the little baby birds to remember not to peck each other." Most older children will easily transition out of their misguided way of relating if we are able to guide them in a matter-of-fact, calm and appropriate way. The children need repetitive reminders to use their kind ways at this time. For after all, "we have to know all about our kind ways in the kindergarten and then we can go into first grade." Dr. Johanna Steegmans states that "one of the most important things that the children learn in the kindergarten is manners." Recently I was present at a lecture by Jack Petrash where he spoke about delivering these reminders with brightness and warmth. These inner, non-judgmental, sunny attitudes on the part of the teachers assure that the children are able to openly receive them.

In the same way that we work actively with the children's tendencies to exclude one another, we must also work with other anti-social behaviors—taunting, pushing, hitting, racing to

7   Audrey E. McAllen, *Reading Children's Drawings*, 36.

get things first, bossiness, stubborn insistence on getting their own way and many more. Regression is one of the symptoms that six-year-olds can demonstrate. Behaviors that were overcome as younger children can resurface again. Matter-of-fact reminders can go a long way to remind them. "You may join us now." "We'll be helping our friend." "You weren't interrupting, were you?" "Is it better to say 'GIVE THAT TO ME RIGHT NOW' or 'Please may I have it when you're finished?' " It can be a great comfort to the older children that there is a reliable someone present who is taking care of the order of things even though the children's own organisms are in upheaval.

To assist us in this work, as teachers and parents, we have to take care of our own inner life. To work well with the willing aspect of our soul we had to practise new gestures, gain strength and ignite the impulse to do the healing deed, but now we are called upon to look inside and figure out how to respond to these feeling impulses that are coming from the children. Barbara Klocek, in her article "You Can't Play with Me" in Section Three, talks about working with the excluding behaviors of the older child, but how do we deal with the disparaging and critical behaviors that the children are showing?

In *How to Know Higher Worlds*, Rudolf Steiner talks about the importance of adults "bringing devotion into our thought life." He says, "Each moment that we spend becoming aware of whatever derogatory, judgmental, and critical opinions are still remaining in our

> *It can be a great comfort to the older children that there is a reliable someone present who is taking care of the order of things.*

consciousness brings us closer to higher knowledge. We advance even more quickly if, in such moments we fill our consciousness with admiration, respect and reverence for the world and life."[8] He goes on to say, "At first glance it is not easy to believe that feelings of reverence and respect are in any way connected with knowledge. This is because we tend to see cognition as an isolated faculty that has no connection whatsoever with anything else going on in our souls. Thus we forget that it is the soul that cognizes. What food is to the body, feelings are to the soul. If we feed the body stones instead of bread, it will cease to function. It is the same with the soul. We nourish it with reverence, respect and devotion. These make the soul healthy and strong, particularly for the activity of knowing. Disrespect, antipathy, and disparaging admirable things, on the other hand, paralyze and slay our cognitive activities."[9] What more needs to be said about the tremendous service we can do for the children if the adults in their lives are able to model ways of transforming criticism into respect and admiration? We provide them with worthy examples that may be wellsprings for their present and future soul development. Stories where the hero/heroine is able to meet criticism or menacing forces and transform the situation can be food for the child's soul as well. In Section Five, "The Magic Lake at the End of the World" is such a story.

8   Rudolf Steiner, *How to Know Higher Worlds*, 20.
9   Ibid., 21.

What do the six- and seven-year-olds want more than to believe that the adults in their lives are genuine, authentic and really know what they're talking about? The children often say, "Is that true or real?" It is such a disappointment to them if we show them what they must do and then we ourselves are not able to do this. They begin to separate themselves from us and look on with a penetrating and sometimes sceptical glance. They try out new ways of responding to us to see if they can stretch the classroom boundaries or they try to catch us out in a limit that we can't uphold. How delightful it is for them when they are able to correct the teacher about a word in the story or say, "That's not true, yesterday you said… " It is a time when we need to stand in front of them with strength as well as reverence, respect and devotion.

Steiner goes on to say, if we read further in this chapter of *How to Know Higher Worlds*, that the "soul that learns feelings of devotion and reverence changes its aura. Certain spiritual yellow-red or brown-red colors disappear and are replaced by tones of blue-red."[10] This brings to mind the painting of the Sistine Madonna by Raphael. This painting portrays a picture of a child coming to birth carried by a figure dressed in red and blue. In our work of assisting the child's etheric and sharing our own etheric forces during the developmental period that Steiner called the change of teeth, are we not standing, as teachers and parents of the six-year-old, at another threshold where we are delivering the child through another birth? As midwives for the birth of the etheric we would do well to don our blue and red gowns. Working actively with the natural antipathies that the child displays during the 6/7-year transformation is a tremendous opportunity for all of us to grow.

Joan Almon writes, "For the young child, our inner mood and gesture speak much louder than our words. If we hold the divine in our heart and if our own inner practices are directed toward the spiritual, then the children feel at home on the earth in a way that they never can if they are surrounded by a purely materialistic view." [11]

Thinking

In all that has been said it becomes obvious how willing, feeling and thinking are qualities of our soul life that are interwoven and inseparable from one another. A healthy soul/spiritual life is the basis for a healthy society, a healthy kindergarten and a healthy child. The ability to monitor our inner dialogue and to work with positivity and inspired pictures requires hard work on our part but it has a direct impact on the child and the kindergarten environment.

One cannot aspire to providing pictures for the children without understanding that this deed requires the **will** to create within us, the **feeling** sense of what is appropriate and the **thinking** ability to form an appropriate image. In the article "Observations of the Six-Year-Old Change" in Section One of this book, there is a graph that shows the interplay of willing,

10   Rudolf Steiner, *How to Know Higher Worlds*, 22.
11   Joan Almon, "The Healing Power of Play," 14.

feeling and thinking in the first seven years. The end of the first seven-year cycle is a time, especially, when seed forces for the later thinking processes are established. Hopefully these forces will be given the opportunity to sleep in the child's being until they can later awaken in full strength manifesting as the quest for truth in adolescence.

As stated in the quotation at the beginning of this article, Steiner stresses that the enlivening of thinking at the change of teeth is *not* indicative of intellectual curiosity but rather of forces of fantasy. Steiner encourages us to engage these forces of fantasy. In another lecture, Steiner says, "In reality our task is to give the child living flexible ideas which can grow in his soul."[12] He goes on to say that "we must ourselves partake in the inward activities of the child's soul, and we must count it a joy to give him something that is flexible and elastic; and, just as he grows with his physical limbs so he can grow up with these ideas, feelings and impulses… and can make something else out of what we have given him."

I find that providing these picture-ideas, these wellsprings for the child's soul, takes practice. It is not something that comes easily or naturally for me. Even though I know it is not healthy for the child, I recognize that it is easier for me to just intellectually state what and why we must do something. However, it becomes very evident in the unfolding of the kindergarten day just how effective these imaginative, "flexible and elastic images" are. "Come little squirrels and gather up all the nuts" is much more effective then "Now we'll tidy up." Or "Let's hear brother Robin's voice instead of the squawking parrot" is met with compliance much more easily than "Please use a softer voice."

In order to assist myself in building a repertoire of these images for the children, I spend time collecting material—songs, stories, circles and picture-images that are appropriate for the mixed-age kindergarten. Duplicating them sometimes and filing them in ways that make sense to me helps me to retrieve them during different seasons of the year. Then, when I am "in the moment" with a child, I can listen deeply to his or her offerings and connect to them as best I can with pictures. Then, later I can do my research and find tried-and-true images that have served other children in the past. Perhaps it's a story or circle that deals with the theme or a picture-image recorded and used in the past that can again serve at this moment with a different child. As I repeat these steps each year, my repertoire builds and I begin to retain more. The result is that I can become more fluid and capable in the present to connect to the children's questions, imaginings and play scenarios. Therefore the ability to dispense soul milk in the form of picture-ideas can develop and grow through time.

As mentioned above, sometimes children just need to hear, "You're not managing so I have a job for you," or a similar clear directive. This delivery of the clear expectation also has its place when we have already tried connecting imaginatively to the child's play and the older child is not responding to an image provided. It's important that we always follow through with the limit that we have set even if we think "I wish I hadn't said that." It's also important that we

12 Rudolf Steiner, *The Roots of Education*, 27-28.

involve the parents. We might say lightly at the end of the day in the presence of the child, "We have had a good day and tomorrow I will be happy to see Andrew again. I'm sure it will be a lovely day too" (not "a better day"). It's important that the child knows that his parents and his teachers are working together.

The art of finding the right story for a group of children cannot be overestimated. Sometimes children who have been in the kindergarten for more than one year will inform us about what story needs to come next. "When do we get to hear about the rooster with the golden comb?" When telling a story, if we can see the inner pictures ourselves, then the children are deeply nourished. The children are also able to absorb the meaning of the story more deeply if the teller has penetrated the true meaning of the story. This is true soul milk! Some teachers consider it their meditative path to read or ponder a particular story for months or years. This can be a very fruitful path and this practice can also stimulate the forming of rich inner pictures that become useful in our daily work in the classroom.

I experimented with this idea with a group of teacher-trainees during a course on fairy tales. Each day we made stand-up puppets for "Mother Holle" and we sampled the story in several forms—as a story, as a puppet play and as a play. Then each night before sleep for two weeks we read the story to ourselves. Never once during class did we discuss the meaning of the images. Then, on the last day of class, we talked about what had been revealed to us when we took the story into our sleep and pondered the images during the day. On the day when we finally got to share the results, I had come to class prepared with the research gleaned from others and myself about the deeper meaning of the Mother Holle story. It was all unnecessary. The students, through their own spiritual research, were able to take us through the story and share the deeper meaning of the images. Since this first attempt to penetrate the story in this way I have used this technique repeatedly with student teachers and we have been rewarded with many fruitful results.

When telling a story, if we can see the inner pictures ourselves, then the children are deeply nourished.

Circle themes with strong images also speak to the children and, because they are able to take these images into their movement then the pictures and lessons can sink more deeply into them. The Briar Rose (mood of the fifth) circle in Section Five is such a circle.

Thinking ahead and making daily, weekly and yearly plans can also help us to provide what Steiner refers to when he says, "all that the children receive must be unity." How can we orchestrate our days so that they flow together like a well-woven tapestry and are not segmented or stilted? It is possible to think through the day ahead, having listened well to the children beforehand, and create a story, work activity and a circle theme that blend together as part of this tapestry. As an example, the story of "The Queen Bee" relates well to a circle about adventuring and encountering the creatures on dear old Mother Earth. On morning walks, this theme of respect for all the creatures can be taken up into our gestures.

Later a puppet play of "The Queen Bee" can be shared and then the puppets can be made available at playtime. In this way the children can be held in a unity that results in many days of focused play, activity and adventure.

The children grow and change over the two or three years that they are with us in the mixed-age kindergarten and we must grow with them. It needn't be seen as a burden for the priest/priestess to become an artist/benevolent authority when the children reach the six-year-old transformation time. It can be an adventure that takes us to new landscapes within ourselves. If we are really able to meet the older children, something wonderful happens. Our relationship to them changes. It becomes a mixture of companionship tempered with respect and clear understandings. An easy authority arises where both parties accept who is the boss. We can incorporate their newfound capacities and their desire to expand into our kindergarten day. They really do have the capability of helping to run the kindergarten and they take pride in this. Enlisting their enthusiasm will fortify them for their next steps into first grade.

Here are a few suggestions that I would like to underline:

- Stand uprightly and firmly in the presence of the older child. Uncertainty on the part of the teacher easily loses the respect of the older child.

- Carry the inner attitude that you know what's going on (even if you are stumped). The child is going through so many confusing changes that he needs a reliable boundary against which he can safely push.

- If you ask a child to do something then you must make sure that the child follows through with your request. Consequently, be conscious that what you ask for must be achievable by the child.

- Try first to connect to the child's images in his play if you are trying to transform a play scenario.

- If the child is playing imaginatively and constructively then do not disturb her. If not, it's time to work! After the children have done some purposeful work, they are often able to go back into play with fresh forces to play imaginatively and constructively. Their will has been engaged in their work and it flows on into the play. Here is a list of some possible six-year-old activities: helping the teacher with handwork, cooking, cleaning, washing out the cubbies, dusting shelves (everything off shelves, dust and then put it all back on again), digging, sawing, sewing, setting the table, setting up for drawing or painting time, carding, washing wool, sanding wooden toys, oiling toys, dumping the compost, sweeping, fetching supplies for the teacher and running errands, washing napkins and doll clothes, polishing, delivering messages, scrubbing pots, picking herbs for the soup, washing benches and chairs, repairing toys. If the child re-enters the play after his work is complete and he is still not able to play, then bring him back to work. This needs to be done in the gesture of "I need your help now," not the punitive gesture of "You can't play." If the child says, "But I want to play now," we can respond, "Oh yes, you will when you are ready to play well."

Appeal to the older children to be helpers of the younger ones. "Pretend you are tidying up and help little Sally." "Let's use our quiet ways when we eat to show our younger friends (in my classroom we call them the "sun children") how we give our mouths and ears a rest." "We can help the sun children to know what we do here" (when an older child may be noticing that a younger one is not knowing how to do something).

Celebrate the older children. They need to take their place in the group, be recognized and respected. Take joy in their newfound skills and capacities. Give them privileges and extra responsibilities. The younger children can aspire to this when they get older.

In conclusion, here is one last quotation from Rudolf Steiner: "Our task, therefore, is to work around children—to the degree that we control our very thoughts and feelings—so that children may become beings who imitate goodness, truth, beauty and wisdom."[13] Taking up the responsibility of being purveyors of "soul milk" may seem like an onerous task but this challenge can also be a joyful journey. Not only will it provide blessed wellsprings for the child's future development, but it is also a path of development for ourselves.　　✦

References

Almon, Joan. "The Healing Power of Play." *WECAN Gateways* (Fall/Winter 2006).

McAllen, Audrey. *Reading Children's Drawings*. Fair Oaks, CA: Rudolf Steiner College Press, 2004.

Steiner, Rudolf. *The Essentials of Education*. New York: Anthroposophic Press, 1997.

_____ . *How to Know Higher Worlds*. New York: Anthroposophic Press, 1994.

_____ . *The Kingdom of Childhood*. New York: Anthroposophic Press, 1995.

_____ . *The Roots of Education*. New York: Anthroposophic Press, 1997.

13　Rudolf Steiner, *The Essentials of Education* (Anthroposophic Press, 1997), 69.

Essential Oil Baths

Louise deForest

first heard about oil dispersion baths more than a decade ago in a workshop offered for caregivers. I found it interesting, but since no one in my family was suffering from any chronic illness, I didn't see that I would ever be using it and put the information aside. Several years later, while I was taking part in a three-year course for remedial teachers, I was again introduced to oil baths and this time the healing potential of these baths really caught my attention.

I hasten to add that the baths I recommend and use cannot be called oil dispersion baths. Oil dispersion baths are unique anthroposophical therapeutic tools, making use of predetermined essential oils to promote the strengthening of ego activity in the individual receiving the bath. Doctors (anthroposophical, naturopathic, hydrotherapists), after a thorough examination of the patient, prescribe the specific oil to be used in the bath, based on their profound knowledge of the character of each oil and the nature of the human being before them. A true oil dispersion bath is used to overcome illness and is always prepared using the specifically designed glass apparatus (created by Werner Jung and his wife in 1937) that dispenses the oil into the bath as micro-droplets that remain suspended in the bath water. This potentizes the oil and allows it to work directly into the individual's warmth organization and circulatory system. The baths I recommend could be called Essential Oil Baths, instead of Oil Dispersion baths, because their function is not to cure but to promote well-being and balance in the whole organism. It's a bit like the difference between hygienic or pedagogical eurythmy, done once a week with our children in Waldorf Schools, and the far deeper therapeutic eurythmy, which uses specific movements designed to address specific, individual difficulties and is done with a specially trained therapeutic eurythmist.

Over the years I became aware that, as a kindergarten teacher, teaching was only one of the many things I was called to do with the children and parents in my classroom. All of us who work as teachers know that we are also called upon to be marriage counselors, therapists, movement specialists, godmothers and godfathers, nurses, confidants and mediators. Indeed, it seems that today the borders between professions, especially in the realm of human care and development, are overlapping. We are called upon to educate ourselves, collaborate with others, and stretch our skill level. Repeatedly, at the end of a difficult morning in the classroom, after reviewing the breathing of the morning, my interactions with the children, the play and the activities offered, I would ask myself what more could I offer to a particular child. Could I really help him or her overcome the obstacles that seemed to be impeding the fullness of his/her healthy development? "What does this child need?" I wondered, and it seemed that the longer I taught, the more I felt I had to learn.

Beginning my exploration of essential oil baths was a step forward on my journey to understanding more about what I could do to help. I can't remember now when I gave the first few baths; perhaps they were to two of my own boys or to one of my godchildren or a friend, but I do remember hearing from those who had the baths about how refreshed they felt and how well they slept afterwards. And I remember how much I, myself, benefited from preparing the bath for someone else.

Holding the clear intention of serving someone else, I would clean the bathroom and prepare a space in the bedroom where they could rest. Then I would draw the bath, light a candle and fill the room with calm, loving thoughts, all the while trusting in this process. While this is what we all strive to do in our classrooms, I was delighted to find another way (outside of the classroom) to physically and spiritually offer a healing balm to someone in need.

About six or seven years ago, I began to recommend these baths for some of the children in my class. These were suggested not as therapeutic interventions, for I am not a doctor, but more in the spirit of hoping to offer a balm to the senses of the child. I knew the physical caring gesture of these baths would also strengthen the bond between parent and child. While I think everyone can benefit from occasional oil baths, in the following descriptions, I will share some of the situations that have summoned the recommendation for an essential oil bath.

I knew the physical caring gesture of these baths would also strengthen the bond between parent and child.

Carmen, the oldest of two children, is an extremely bright, perhaps even gifted, verbal five-year-old, who has been in our early childhood programs since nursery. She is a large-headed child, a deep sleeper and is slow to wake up. She often comes into the classroom pale and grumpy, only to gain color and interest after our morning tea has been served. She is an imaginative and active player who is slow and clumsy in her movements and often on her tiptoes. The rhythms of our morning, week and year live so strongly in her that I have no doubt that, should the need ever arise, she could lead the class and carry circle, story time and puppetry without me. She is the child of two very loving, young parents who are struggling to establish themselves in their professions while carrying a mortgage and a private school tuition. Family life is chaotic and fast paced each morning while everyone scatters to jobs, daycare and school. Even when Carmen is sick, her parents cannot stay home from their jobs to care for her, so she is given a few Tylenol and sent to school (where she quietly rests in a cozy spot that has become known as "Carmen's bed"). She is rushed as soon as she awakes, forced to eat a breakfast for which she does not have the appetite, hurried into the car and eventually dropped off at school in a whirlwind of conversation, impatience, and breathless sighs by her mother. As a result, Carmen often throws huge tantrums at home and is known to be very moody and deeply sensitive to any comment that could be perceived by her as a slight.

I suggested to the parents that this child should receive essential oil baths, both to soothe and protect this child who has been pushed way beyond her tolerance level and to help establish scheduled quality time where the parents can actively nurture their child. Both the child and the parents needed to have non-rushed time together where the mother/father could quietly observe the child and where the child could bask in this loving attention. She received the baths and looked noticeably more relaxed the next day. The mother also said that giving the baths helped her make the shift from job to home in a relaxed, timeless way and allowed her to have the opportunity to pay undistracted attention to her oldest child.

Doug is an intense, forceful six-year-old in his second year of kindergarten. He is an only child and his parents express frustration and confusion about his aggressive and unpredictable behavior. He is a charming and charismatic boy but his social skills are poor and, coupled with his erratic mood swings, this makes life with him in the classroom full of seemingly never-ending conflicts. He is well loved by the other children in spite of his often-belligerent attitudes. The children seem to recognize that Doug is different and that life is harder for him. Before Doug can play, he often has adorned himself with a cloth around his waist and then he asks for a cape to put around his shoulders. His play usually consists of building a kind of fortress around himself and playing within its confines, occasionally making plundering forays into the classroom to "rob" toys or push over someone else's house. He is surprisingly gentle and loving towards animals. My dog, who used to spend each day with us in the kindergarten, is his best friend. Doug's behavior indicates to me sensory integration issues, especially with his tactile sense. When I see him lashing out at others I know he's feeling vulnerable and assaulted by the closeness and movements of others. It must be terribly frustrating and frightening when he is unable to trust the information streaming into him from his senses. When I ponder this, his outbursts take on a deeper meaning for me.

With Doug, too, I suggested regular essential oil baths, again with the hope of accomplishing several things at once. The oil, I believed, would provide this deeply sensitive child with an extra layer of skin so he could feel more protected, safer and held. The bath preparation and quiet time during and after the bath could provide Doug and his parents with a time together lacking in frustration, tension and punishment. I hoped this precious time together could support the building of understanding, rapport and sympathy for his ongoing difficulties. The morning after his first bath, Doug came into the classroom with rosy cheeks and bright eyes and he ran straight to me to give me a hug. Although we were devoted to each other this is something that he did not often do. His parents reassured me that they had not said anything to him about my bath recommendation, but we all know that when we carry the well-being of a child deeply within us, whether we are doing a child study, preparing for a parent-teacher conference or in our meditative practice, on some level the child always knows and is grateful for our efforts.

The last example I want to share is of little Oscar, an intelligent, precociously awake six-year-old who was in his first year of kindergarten. Although Oscar had a younger sister, he was very innocent and naive about all childhood activities. This was a child who resided exclusively in his thoughts and ideas, full of questions and facts, very logical in all his responses and very ill at ease with all the give-and-take needed for successful social relationships with his peers. He tired easily on our walks, had little upper-body strength, did not imitate and did not know how to play. Not only did he not have a clue as to *how* to play, he also couldn't figure out *why* anyone would want to play. Instead, he stayed by my side, full of questions and comments, often curious as he watched me sew or knit, all the while shunning any child who tried to engage him in play.

He, too, received a series of essential oil baths to help soften the sclerotic physical body he was already forming and to provide his parents with an activity where they could silently accompany him in a healing process. So often parents keep company with their children by using a running monologue or they shower their children with questions. With this bath I hoped Oscar's parents could provide him with quiet, attentive companionship, and that the bath would also help him sleep so that he was not burdened by the usual hours of time that it took him each night to digest his day.

Much to the credit of all of these parents, they embarked on an unknown journey, proceeding only with my suggestions. They faithfully and rhythmically gave their children these baths and shared with me their experience. All of the parents found it to be relaxing for themselves. They remarked with gratitude that their children fell into a deep, relaxed sleep immediately after the first bath. Many parents experienced the value of being with their child in a no-stress, no-hurry and no-agenda environment, some of them for the first time. All of the parents expressed gratitude for the opportunity to practically and effectively (not to mention easily) help their child.

When I first suggest oil baths, I speak to the parents about what I see in their child and how I think he or she might benefit (protection, loosening and softening, etc.) and then I speak about my own experience with these baths, both as a teacher and on a more personal level. I then give them the handout[1] which I received (and altered) when I was a student in the

---

1   This handout is reproduced following this article, as well as a description of another kind of therapeutic bath, the nutritional bath.

Gradalis therapeutic training program. I describe to the parents how to prepare the bath, how important a quiet and healing inner state is to the process and also how to mix the oils. I cannot prescribe, nor would I know how to ascertain, what is the exact oil for each child, as a doctor would with an oil dispersion bath. Instead, I suggest they use what is likely to be on hand: olive oil for the fatty oil and a rose or lavender essence for the essential oil. I choose olive oil because most people have it on hand and because it has a long history of service to humanity. The rose or lavender essences are often used for protection and warmth: just what children need today. I also tell parents that I am willing to prepare the bath and the bedroom for the child for the first bath, if they feel hesitant to do so themselves. I have assisted several parents initially to get started with this process but I never stay for the bath and, for subsequent baths, the parents do it themselves.

In Chapter 15 of his book, *Spiritual Science and Medicine*, Rudolf Steiner states that in the future it is essential that we bring the oil forming processes of plants into a relationship with the human ego or I. We are seeing today what Steiner refers to as a "cooling of the soul,"[2] when the ego forces can no longer maintain the warmth organism. One of the main reasons we give any type of oil bath is to engage the warmth organism. In the past, most illnesses were inflammatory in nature, illnesses having to do with warmth, while today, ninety percent of all illnesses are sclerotic in nature. Even our body temperatures are slightly lower than in the past. We see this cooling in many other ways too—children in nurseries and kindergartens are thin, pale, talkative and anxious. Their lower senses are underdeveloped while their upper senses seem to predominate with cold logic and little social understanding. The physical body is often listless or chaotic, there is little stamina and the will-to-do has not yet been developed. Engaging in play and imitation are increasingly difficult for the child and one is struck by the lack of enthusiasm and the difficulty that children are having in connecting with the world around them.

Also, among adults, we have all witnessed and been guilty of lack of interest. How many times in our conversations and meetings do we busy ourselves formulating our answers or arguments instead of listening to the other person? How many times do we refuse to see the other? I commute long hours every week and am always a bit shocked to see people walking around or sitting on the train, living in their own little worlds while plugged into their iPods or talking on their cell phones. And we know the impact that modern technology has had on our ability to engender warmth in our relationships.

I remember a conversation I had many years ago with my next-door neighbor in Vermont. He had been a dairy farmer all his life and at the time of our conversation he was 89 years old. I asked him what major changes he had witnessed in the world during his lifetime so far. His answer was sad and sobering. "The biggest difference I can see," he said, "is that people are less human than they used to be." My friend lived in the times when people, while giving each other tremendous independence—this was New England, after all—were also keenly

2   Rudolf Steiner, *Spiritual Science and Medicine*.

aware of how each family was managing. Wordlessly, they would show up during haying season, once my friend was in his late sixties, to lend a hand. Burned-down barns were raised in a weekend by the whole community and sick neighbors were watched over by all. While these acts of kindness are still found in all of our communities, Harold, for that was his name, felt that people are too hurried today to really listen, and that when they speak they do not take the time to pass the words through their souls, as he would put it. Faces are harder and there is less interest in people's eyes when they look at you, if indeed they make the effort to do so. He felt that people are so busy today trying to keep up that we have forgotten how to live and he saw little joy or gratitude in our modern lives, two attributes that for him were truly human.

Oil baths work directly on the ego organization, or, better said, challenge the I to work through the warmth organism. Oils are basically created in the plant kingdom through the plant's leaves interaction with the warmth and light of the sun forces. Only ten percent of all plants produce ethereal oils. During the day, the sun, through heat and light, lightly touches matter (the plant), and, through the interaction of these two substances, an oil is produced. Essential oils are formed by the combination of carbon (an earthly substance) and hydrogen (connected to the sun) and are formed during the daytime. In the evening these oils travel to other parts of the plant, especially the seed, though some of the oil stays in the leaves. Astral forces, always present when there are excretory processes, such as seed formation, change these oils into essential oils. If one asks oneself, "Where is the soul in the plant?" any biodynamic farmer would tell you that it is hovering above the plant and is active in the seed formation of the plant. Indeed, Novalis asks, "Can we not say the essential oil of the plant is the soul?"[3]

> *There is no limit to the benefits of these baths. People of any age can benefit from them, including the early childhood teacher*

It is interesting to note that, while essential oils are formed by the interaction of carbon and hydrogen, the fatty oils have a chemical relationship to oxygen, which makes them more earthly in nature. The plants that grow closest to the equator have more of a relationship to oxygen than those grown further north; coconut oil is more earthy than, say, safflower oil. Olive oil has the least relationship to oxygen, making it the fatty oil most closely connected to essential oils. Another interesting aspect of olive oil is that its melting temperature is 98.6 degrees Fahrenheit, so that one could say this oil also has a very close relationship to the human being.

There is no limit to the benefits of these baths. People of any age can benefit from them, including the early childhood teacher him- or herself. The baths can be given once a week, though I often suggest a pause in the baths after six to seven weeks to reassess and allow the body to actively carry the impulse of the baths. Only one essential oil is used at a time but the oil can be changed for each bath. Rhythm, as a support for our life forces, is extremely important. The baths should happen at the same time of day and the same day of the week.

---

3   Quoted in Gerhard Schmidt, "Oil Forming Process," 16.

This then has the added effect of bringing the will into the healing impulse of the bath. It is important to have a rest lasting at least one hour afterwards. I recommend that parents give this bath just before bedtime, so that their child can enjoy a deep, healing sleep after the bath. I also encourage parents not to dry their child after the bath, thereby rubbing the oils off the skin, but, rather to swaddle the child and tuck him or her into a warm bed. Pajamas can be put on once the child is asleep and dry.

My experience has been that preparing these baths for the friends, family and children in my care has given many blessings—especially the gift of being truly present in the moment. Letting go of everyday distractions and concerns in order to wholeheartedly enter into a purposeful relationship with earthly and cosmic elements/forces has many healing effects. Just as a doctor-and-patient relationship has the potential of elevating and deepening both doctor and patient, so, too, these baths are healing for both the receiver and the giver. It is in the act of true service to the other that our souls become warmed and that we can say and experience, "Not I, but the Christ in me."

References

Schmidt, Gerhard. "The Oil-Forming Process: The Basis in Nature for Oil-Dispersion Bath Therapy." Spring Valley, NY: Mercury Press, 1983.

Steiner, Rudolf. *Spiritual Science and Medicine*. London: Rudolf Steiner Press, 1948. Recently republished as *Introducing Anthroposophical Medicine*. Hudson, NY: Anthroposophic Press, 1999.

Essential Oil Bath Recipe

Supplies:

1. Prescribed bath oil (usually a ten or twenty percent mixture of essential oil in a fatty oil): one part essential oil (gives a sense picture to the skin) to nine parts fatty oil (provides a sheath).
2. A jar with a cap.
3. Warm towels and/or nightclothes.

Procedure:

Prepare bed, warm room and close all windows to avoid a draft.

The temperature of the bath should be measured by suspending a thermometer in the tub. For cardiovascular and nervous disorders, temperatures should be from 89.6–93° F (32–34° C). For metabolic problems, the temperature should be higher. The person should be comfortable, neither shivering nor perspiring. Do not change the bath temperature in the middle of the bath. You may need to begin the treatments with the bath temperature closer to body temperature and to work it down to the prescribed level in subsequent baths.

Draw the bath. Maintain a quiet, healing mood in the room, lighting a candle or saying a quiet prayer. Do not have your child with you as you do this.

While you are drawing the bath, put the prescribed oil in a mason jar one-quarter to one-third full of warm water. Shake the jar with the water and oil for ten to fifteen minutes to suspend the oil in the water. While you are shaking it, you may change hands but do not stop shaking the jar. "Lighten" the bath water by moving it slowly in a lemniscate; the water must be moving for the oil to disperse properly. Without ceasing to shake the jar, pour the oil/water mixture into the bath. Do not touch the water after adding the oil. Have person lie in the bath, covered to the neck if possible. She should lie very still. If you are giving this to a young child, perhaps you could tell or read her a story. With a pure oil bath, there should be as little movement as possible and no rubbing or washing. After the bath, wrap person in a warm towel, do not dry, and have her rest quietly. Quiet rest leads to a particularly strong effect. Touching or rubbing the body causes the effect of the oil to diminish. Give the person a hot water bottle for the feet, if needed for warmth. She should not perspire.

The initial bath should not exceed seven minutes and may often be as short as three to five minutes. With subsequent baths, one may build up to fifteen to twenty minutes.

Give the bath twice a week for six to seven weeks, always on the same day and at the same time. Rhythm is extremely important.

I have found this bath to be useful for children with sensory-integration difficulties, especially tactile defensiveness and for children who are anxious and nervous. This bath is extremely helpful in consolidating the warmth organism.

Nutritional Bath Recipe

Many children in our time have added stresses in their lifestyle. They travel long distances, have irregular rhythms and routines, suffer from poor nutrition and lack of sleep, are inundated with input to their senses and nervous systems and are susceptible to other interruptions that our accelerated times present. Nutritional baths can be a positive healing tool that may strengthen and counteract some of the repercussions of our challenging times. —*Ruth Ker*

Indications:

1. Convalescence, especially from a wasting illness.
2. Nutritional disorders.

3. Addictions and withdrawal.

4. Child who is not "herself" after an experience or an illness.

5. Detoxification after exposure to chemicals, use of antibiotics, etc.

6. Hyperactivity and chaos.

Do not administer this bath if there is a fever or evidence of a local inflammation (cold, flu, otitis, inflamed cut, etc.).

Temperature:

This is a substance bath. Temperature should preferably not be above 98—100° F (37—38° C), but the patient must be comfortable. Warm the bathroom and the bedroom.

Ingredients:

1. Free-range or organic egg (yolk only): addresses metabolic system.

2. 1 cup raw (or at least non-homogenized with no additives) milk: addresses rhythmic system.

3. 1 organic lemon: addresses nervous system.

Supplies:

1. Small bowl

2. Sharp knife

3. Fork

4. Container for compost

Draw the bath water slightly above the desired temperature. Break the egg, separate the yolk and gently stir the yolk. Add milk to the yolk and stir gently. Cut the lemon UNDER the bath water, score the skin and express the juice. Add milk and egg to the tub water. Mix the ingredients and lighten the water by gently moving it in a lemniscate. Think of drawing two opposite poles together, a picture of the rhythmic system. If your movements are mechanical, if the water splashes against the ends of the tub or if your attention wanders, it will hinder the effects of the bath. The hand should not cut through the water but should rather draw the water along with it… move with the water.

The water is allowed to become quiet. Then the patient lies in the water, submerged to the neck for five to fifteen minutes. After the bath, wrap the patient in a towel without drying her off. The rest period should ideally be an hour. Young children can be put in their pyjamas wet (pure cotton is best) and allowed to sleep through the night. Adjust their wrappings after a short time so they do not perspire.

Do twice a week on the same day and at the same time for seven weeks. Rhythm is very important.

Extract from Work and Play in Early Childhood

Freya Jaffke

Freya Jaffke, in her book, *Work and Play in Early Childhood*, (Edinburgh: Floris Books, 1996), has some valuable information for teachers and parents regarding the transition time leading up to the final freeing of the etheric and, consequently, the child's readiness for the grade school experience. The first excerpt below is from pages 65-67.   —*Ruth Ker*

The Crisis of Will and Imagination Around the Age of Five

At around the age of five, an obvious crisis can be observed in many children, particularly in those who are actively creative. Further changes occur in children's development because the formative forces actively structuring the body from within are increasingly freeing themselves from the metabolic and limb system. The will has to re-orientate itself to unite itself with the ideas which are gradually awakening in children of this age. This takes a while. For a time children will not have so many imaginative ideas, their will appears to be paralysed and they ask "What shall I do?" or say: "I'm bored." We should not appeal to the imagination at this point as it needs to be treated with care and should be left in peace. We can let the children do small, straightforward activities which they will see as being related to what adults do. For example:

* cutting out, sewing, drawing small picture books;

* making needle cases, arranging needles into them;

* sandpapering a letter opener which has been quickly carved by an adult;

* *requesting* help, *without making demands*!

- threading a ribbon or a piece of elastic;

- Drying up, sweeping;

- Sawing wood in the garden place

This kind of work should take place near an adult as the children want and need such proximity. They are still going through a period of imitation even if they are genuinely beginning to work. For the first time there is a hint of obligation but entirely within the context of imitative activity. After a certain period of "work" they will want to play again. The imagination recalls pictures of real life situations, for example a hairdresser, a hospital with an ambulance, a fishing boat, a shop, a family, a fire brigade, a space ship, and turns them into impulses for play.

The Will Unites with the Power of Ideas

It is important to remember that while the environment and the toys have not changed, the relationship to them has. If the will wants to act on an impulse to play, it must now unite with the idea. With the aid of the imagination which has been so richly practiced in the past, it finds or transforms objects into what the idea demands. This is a key process.

Imagination, patience, perseverance and enthusiasm are all necessary to put an idea for play into practice, as is the readiness to overcome problems. The will is strongly involved in all these qualities but in a way which is determined by activities.

For example, a child under the age of five might see a bent stick, pick it up, and say, "I'm a chimney sweep." After the age of five the child first has the idea of wanting to be a chimney sweep and then says: "To be a chimney sweep I need a long rolled up brush." The child looks for one and finally makes one by tying a feather duster to a long piece of string and then fixing the string to a stick.

Before the age of five, the will took hold of an object which, after an external prompt, took on life in the imagination. Now the will has to work from within itself to establish a purposeful connection between the idea and the imagination. Children who have plenty of opportunities to practise this internal work are lucky! It requires effort and may be difficult. However, if the objective is achieved, it is cause for deep satisfaction or even noisy celebration.

If children are not given any opportunity for this kind of internal work, they can easily become unruly. This makes us think that they should be put to work—for example, sandpapering, sawing, nailing—and that they simply need to perform some strenuous task in which they can really work their muscles. They certainly should be allowed to do this when it is required in the normal course of events. An attentive and forward-thinking educator will find enough opportunities for this throughout the year. For example:

- sawing up branches left in the garden after the trees have been pruned;
- renewing the borders of flower beds and moving large stones in the summer;
- attaching logs to boards to make steam rollers;
- excavating lakes and rivers with a spade;
- playing games involving running, calling, catching, rolling tires, skipping

These are all important activities, and children and teachers may work or play in this way with great enthusiasm. However, we should not forget that the forces of the will should not only be practised in physical activity, but also, particularly at this age, internally, in the handling of living ideas. If children grow strong in this sphere as well, they are more likely to become balanced individuals. Nevertheless, if children do not have the opportunity to exercise their imagination, it is better for them to engage in physical work rather than to go racing wildly around.

On page 70 of the same book, Freya Jaffke offers this advice to the adults who care for the older children in the kindergarten:

In the final year of the kindergarten, another crisis in the way children play may occur. The children suddenly no longer feel themselves to be kindergarten children and say, "From now on we only want to work!" Children who feel this can be included in the work of the adult and allowed to help properly. After a short time they will begin to play again. ✦

Building the Social Fabric of a Mixed-Age Kindergarten

When a person comes up against serious things in terms of what works and does not work in life: when faced with matters of usefulness and practicality: in those circumstances we can see a reemerging of an attitude which showed itself in free play earlier on.

Just think what this means. We want to educate effectively and know: you observe a characteristic disposition in the play of a child: you guide and direct it now and this will bear fruit twenty years from now, when this person will be coming to terms with the world, a world which should be useful to him and in which he should find his proper place. Just think what feelings arise in the soul of the early childhood educator, who realizes: what I accomplish with this child, I accomplish for the grown-up person in his twenties.

Rudolf Steiner
Education in the Face of the Present-Day World Situation

Earlier in the same excerpt, Steiner talks about the "consequences of the children's play" in the first seven years showing their "outcome" later because of "what it leads to later on in life… between the ages of twenty-one and twenty-eight, the time of life during which people find their way into the world and have to grapple with real-life experience." —*Ruth Ker*

You Can't Play with Me

Barbara Klocek

When I first began teaching, I thought my main goals were to create a wonderful environment for the children, to create a harmonious breathing in the morning and to give the children an opportunity to experience through their head, heart and hands. I still feel these are important elements in our work; however, over the years I have come to see that there are other more subtle but equally important aspects to our work.

These lie in the social realm. Many questions come to mind. Is it part of the teacher's role to enter into the social realm or do we "let the children work it out"? Do the children feel safe in our classroom? Are the children free to play with whomever they want or can they reject other children? Do we step in when the play becomes exclusive or too rough? Is the role of the teacher to create the social mood, or is this mood set by the children? How do we meet the children who at the age of six are saying, "You are not the boss of me"? What do we do when we are met with outright defiance from a child?

Each year these questions are brought to light with different children. This year I had several situations that needed my attention. One comes to mind when I think of the six-year-old children who have a tendency to exclude other children. Over the years I have come to the rule that all children get to play together. If two children are longing for time alone, I suggest a play date with the families so that the children can enjoy each other's company in that way. This year a six-year-old girl, with a summer birthday, returned as one of our oldest children. Two other returning girls were her best friends and she loved to be the leader. This year, instead of being the mellow trio of last year, they started competing for each other's friendship and were not at all inclusive of the new children. I tried gentle diversions such as having one bake bread while the other two played, but they were like magnets to each other. So around the middle of October my co-teacher and I decided to tell them that they were on vacation from each other so that they could make new friends. The first day or two they were at a loss, but soon they were found happily playing with other children. How delighted the new children were to make friends with them. After a month, we said that we had noticed how many new friends they had and that they could play together if they would include the other children. This worked well for a while but a few weeks later they were in their intensive trio again. So we gave them a week together or a week on vacation depending on the mood of their play and it seemed to work well. There is much more breathing between them now and their circle of friends is much larger. In order to implement this with support, I had a short phone conversation with the involved parents so they would understand how I was working. I was unsure how these parents would feel about these "vacations," but one mother put me at ease, saying how grateful she was and how it was similar to her sending her two daughters to their own rooms until they could play nicely together.

*"You can't say you
can't play."*
"We all play together."
*"We're all together
in this land."*

This brings up the question of whether children should be able to exclude other children. Sometimes this will manifest as children forming a trio, groups with only boys or girls, or various combinations. I have struggled with this question over the years and was delighted to come across the book, *You Can't Say You Can't Play*, by Vivian Paley. She is a kindergarten teacher and storyteller who also struggled with this question and held many discussions with different-aged children about it. She also came to the rule, "You can't say you can't play," and found it created a much more harmonious classroom. I try to put a positive slant on it by saying "we all play together." A colleague told me that she says, "We're all together in this land."

Often preschool is one of the first steps out of the home and into a classroom. One of the main skills children learn is how to get along in a group and this is often learned from the classroom rules of that first experience away from home. The arrows of exclusion and the pain of rejection are hard at any age. We, as teachers, have a unique opportunity to help children develop new social skills. Even at the age of four, and more strongly by the age of six, the children experience sympathies and antipathies toward other children. How can we help them move beyond this reaction and begin to play and work together at another level? I personally have come to see this as an important part of my work toward world peace, in this tiny kingdom called the Red Rose Kindergarten. It doesn't happen magically that the children get along and include everyone, but over time, they open up their play to everyone and indeed welcome new friends. I am fairly active initially, by supporting the children to be included if other children have just said they cannot play, by helping them extend the house, dress up or bring some wooden "cookies" as a segue into the other children's play. As the year progresses, these skills have been learned by the children and I am not so actively involved but watch and listen from an interested distance. Peace does begin to flow in the kindergarten.

Do the children feel safe in our classroom? This, for me, is an important gauge as to whether I am disciplining in the right way. If we as the teachers are not in charge, usually some of the older, choleric children will be in charge. We can see them shouting commands, directing the play, putting themselves first and even challenging the teacher's authority. These children are often the leaders of the class and it is our responsibility to see that they are kind and benevolent kings and queens and not tyrants. So one of my main tasks is to listen with sensitive ears as to when the play is too rough or chaotic. Listening from the periphery I am always sensing the tone in the classroom. If it is not harmonious but has a tinge of pain, anger or fear, quietly I move into that space, sometimes just sitting with my work, or sometimes entering into the play and redirecting it with appropriate interventions. This provides an opportunity to work with the six-year-olds directly, for this is a time when their feeling life is becoming stronger and often they find themselves nearly overwhelmed by their inner storms. New tools are needed to meet these phenomena that the children are experiencing. Here I can help soothe the storm and create a space in which each child can speak and be heard. I can help find a middle path if necessary. With this assistance, I see the feelings of relief on the children's faces and things settle down. Everyone is safe in this kingdom.

Every year as the children turn six they begin to jostle together in a new way. They each want to "be the boss" of the game and voices begin to rise in anger. For example, once all of the boys wanted to be the captain of the boat. I gently and quickly interjected that "on this boat everyone is captain."

I waited too long one year to help temper the power struggle and a pattern of arguing had become established during outdoor play time. Often if the children are given work to do they can happily cooperate together. In one case I bought a bag of six-penny nails and two choleric boys were delighted to be allowed to hammer them into the fence for the first part of recess. Then they were able to settle into play.

I had an opportunity this fall to deal with the outright defiant child. Usually I find this attitude begins later in the year, generally in early spring when the six-year-olds are moving out of imitating and are beginning to find their relation to the world in terms of who is in charge. Rudolf Steiner speaks about the seven-year-old child learning out of a respect for authority as well as out of imitation (as the younger child does). So we as teachers of the six-year-olds are being met with this transition time every year. It is not an easy transition for either the child or the teacher and how we cope with it influences the mood of the whole class. I find that by living and breathing our rhythms and stories so deeply together, the class becomes a living organism around the beginning of December. If, then, in early spring, the six-year-olds are resisting cleanup or circle, the class already is a cohesive whole and my firm but gentle hand will bring a new respect from these children as they experience the teacher as an authority.

However, the child mentioned above came in September with a defiant attitude. Only with much coaxing would he participate in circle. He was rude to the other children in his play as he insisted on his own way. He did not respect the quiet times and would be disruptive at other times. I have in my classroom a "watching chair." This is any convenient chair where a child can sit and watch how other children are doing a task correctly. I find this very helpful early in the year if the children are in line and one is pushing, or at cleanup time when all the children are helping except for one who is spinning out. These children often need to come out of movement into stillness (sitting), to simply notice what is going on. I often will sit down beside the child in the watching chair and point out what the other children are doing and then I will invite him or her to participate in that same way. I do not see this as a punitive redirection but rather as an instructive way to help the child become centered. The children who are being cooperative and gentle, meanwhile, are being noticed for their kind behavior.

I had had this same boy the previous year. His birthday was in June so he was already five during his first year with us. He had some challenges in sensory integration, and had adopted many difficult social patterns from previous daycare situations. His parents were aware of the problems and followed through on my suggestions to give him some extra help through sensory integration therapy. We saw improvement at the end of the year; however, when he returned the following September he was even more defiant. The first year it was difficult for him because sometimes he *couldn't* do what was asked. This year I felt his resistance was because he *wouldn't*. This is a difficult but very important distinction to perceive, but over time, with observation, it usually becomes ascertainable.

His defiance began to spread with his classmates as well as with the teacher. Other children either did not like him or began to imitate him, and I felt the mood of the class was being shaped by his attitude. We had a conference with his parents and I was clear about how serious this problem was. I told them I could not see him succeeding in a larger class in first grade with this defiant attitude. I asked the parents to be stricter in response to his defiance. I felt he needed a wake-up call as to the effects of his behavior. We arranged that when he was defiant in school, his parents would be called to come and get him. When he was taken home it was not to be a time of fun but rather an experience of time-out.

When he returned from a weekend of his parents being more consequent, he was better. However, before long he was refusing to come down from a tree at school when it was time to go inside. I told him I was calling his father. He was startled and said no. I said I needed to phone them because he was not listening. He sat contritely until his father came and I, in front of him, said to the father that I was very sad that he would not listen, and tomorrow we would give him another chance. Coming to school is a privilege.

What a change this brought about. He became much more responsive and began new patterns of cooperation with the teachers. He learned to play much better with the children, although he is still working out issues of "who is the boss." This was the first time in over fifteen years of teaching that I have sent a child home in this way.

I am finding that parents have increasingly more difficulties in setting boundaries and following through on them with their lively children. I have two copies of John Rosemond's book, *Six Steps for Raising Healthy, Happy Children*, in my parent library. This is a wonderful mainstream resource for parents, which supports their relationship with each other, their role as authorities within the family, and the importance of no media for their children.

Our involvement as teachers in the social realm can create an opportunity for many social skills to be learned, for many rough edges to be smoothed and for many friendships to blossom. The children can relax and play and learn because they feel safe and can experience harmony as a reality in our classroom. I like to think of my contribution to world peace as the children pass over my threshold on to their next destination. The six-year-old transformation gives all of us, as teachers and parents, an opportunity to make a difference for the future. ✦

References

Paley, Vivian. *You Can't Say You Can't Play*. Cambridge, MA: Harvard University Press, 1992,

Rosemond, John. *Six Steps for Raising Healthy, Happy Children*. Kansas City: Andrews and McMead, 1989.

The Six-Year-Old in a Mixed-Age Kindergarten

Laurie Clark

For the many years that I have had the privilege of working in a Waldorf kindergarten, I have preferred a mixed-age setting. I repeatedly see that the three-and-a-half-year-olds are pouring out fantasy into play and the older children are organizing this fantasy by putting their newfound capacity for ideas into action. It has been delightful to be part of this mixture. Over the years, I have often witnessed the dilemma of children in the second half of the kindergarten year when the door into the fantasy world tends to close and the door into their new consciousness has not yet opened. I have searched for new ways to serve the needs the children bring at this critical time. Certainly, each year every group of children brings various needs and gifts to the class and every teacher is challenged to respond with what is needed to balance the situation at hand.

One of the best ways to begin to understand the six-year-olds is to listen to the very interesting things they have to say. There is usually an abundant and creative quality in their wonderful questions and conversations. While we were sitting down for snack one day, Kieran, a six-year-old boy, suddenly announced, "Yesterday, I was looking up at the clouds and one of them fell right into my pocket, and here it is!" To the astonishment of the mixed-age group of children, Kieran proceeded to pull out a wad of white cotton. While the younger children looked on in awe, one of the other six-year-old girls in the class broke the spell by replying, "That is not a cloud. That is cotton from a vitamin bottle!" Kieran did not miss a beat, however, and calmly said, "Yes, part of it is from a vitamin bottle and the other part is from a cloud."

What I saw in this situation was that Kieran was protectively pulling the world of early childhood around him with the cloud image while taking a step into the world of reality by agreeing that part of the cotton came from the vitamin bottle. The six-year-old begins to have an increasing ability to distinguish fantasy from reality, though magic keeps a strong hold in the core of the child's being.

Another story told by a six-year-old in our class went something like this: "Did you know, Mrs. Clark, that the world is round? In the North Pole, the people and the polar bears have to put a lot of maple syrup on themselves so that they get sticky enough not to fall off of the earth. They have to have a lot of maple syrup, at least eight hundred gallons for everyone because they are at the bottom of the world." The consciousness of the child at this stage is waking up and trying to comprehend certain facts but continues to weave this reason into their own world view in a constant and creative way.

These comments are a beautiful example of the inner situation of the six-year-old children. They are in the process of bridging two worlds, leaving early childhood behind and beginning to take steps towards the world of the grade school child, ready to learn about the world with a new and awakening awareness that is being flooded with picture imaginations.

The six-year-old begins to have an increasing ability to distinguish fantasy from reality.

The gap in the mouth that appears because of missing teeth is also a picture in the very physiognomy of the six-year-old child's dilemma. The baby teeth have fallen out but the permanent teeth have not yet revealed themselves; a mysterious gap awaits the arrival of its new larger inhabitant. Meanwhile, the child must endure this emptiness. The emptiness in the mouth becomes a metaphor for the state of the child's being. This emptiness can be painful; the child can be extremely sensitive and vulnerable emotionally. Laughter and tears can come streaming in side by side. Restlessness can creep into the child's gestures as she tries to find her footing between two worlds. A major developmental transformation is in process.

On the other hand, the six-year-old children can be the flames of enthusiasm who delight their fellow classmates with ideas for new adventures and new games. During playtime, they are often the ones who orchestrate creative scenarios, becoming so involved in the process that they are completely detached from the outcome and often move on to another idea before the first one can actually happen. At other times, the well of their fantasy life becomes quite dry and teachers can help them to re-engage in the play by drawing them temporarily into some kind of meaningful work. The children are often grateful for this opportunity, and it is soothing to them to have guidance from the teacher to find appropriate activities during this time.

How can the teacher meet the needs and provide activities in the kindergarten to help the child in these extreme situations? How can we as teachers create possibilities for the many new impulses that the six-year-old child reveals and is longing to put into action? Years ago, at our school, Colette Green, a colleague, friend and longtime Waldorf kindergarten teacher, began a Golden Knights Club once a week for about one-and-a-half hours. Some of our older children go home at noon, and some stay longer in the afternoons. Colette had her assistant put the younger children to rest while she took the older ones to another room or outside to do special activities. Since then, all three of the other kindergartens in Denver have adapted this idea in various ways. I have spoken to other teachers around the country that have also done similar things. I am not sure where this inspiration first began. Below are a few suggestions that belong to this idea.

The Golden Knights Club

The very word "club" could denote exclusivity and, at a time when the older children like to play at excluding others, it is important that this is presented appropriately. Of course great care is taken to approach this in a matter-of-fact way and the children soon adapt to the idea that it is just another kindergarten activity that is available for everyone eventually. The younger children can also benefit by looking forward to things in which they can partake another year.

There are many possibilities for activities in the Golden Knights Club. Fairy tales and nature stories that suit the six-year-old but are not appropriate for a mixed-age group can be considered. This is especially helpful when the morning fairy tale is a simple one. The six-year-olds are often ready to expand their attention for longer stories and more complex images. This creates a satisfying mood and atmosphere around the children.

Community Service

Community service of some kind that serves the class or the larger school can be accomplished by these very capable six-year-olds. Great satisfaction is experienced by the children as they do meaningful, real work that is helpful to others. It's even more joyous if the chore that's done is a surprise for the recipient(s)! One of the satisfying service projects that we accomplished was baking and delivering cookies to an older class in the school that had previously served us by performing music at one of our festivals. Sweeping the sidewalk in front of the school, picking up trash and cleaning all the cubbies in the hallway were fine projects. Planting bulbs and flowers in designated areas is a great spring community service. In general, all projects that beautify the school and the grounds for the whole school community can grow into a satisfying social awakening for everyone.

The knights assist inside the classroom as well and are often asked to help with various jobs. Fixing and gluing broken toys and sewing torn doll clothes and aprons are wonderful jobs for these children. They sort all of the crayons into the correct rainbow color families after drawing time. They almost always are asked to help wash the dishes and put them away after snack. The knights are the great organizers during cleanup time and often help the younger children find just where all of the toys need to go. When aprons need tying at baking time or shoes need tying to go outside, the knights are there to help! They sometimes help to finish certain projects for the younger children, such as sewing buttons onto the felted eggs that we made just before Easter time. After watching the teacher set up an obstacle course a few times, the knights enjoy setting it up for the class. Feeling needed to be true helpers in the classroom with their new capacities instills confidence, security and joy in these six-year-olds.

Knights Club Artistic Activities

There is also often (but not every time) an artistic activity. One of the first activities in Knights Club this year was that each child made his or her own jump rope. The children each dyed a soft rope in rainbow shades and then fingerknitted them into fine jump ropes. The children were very happy to put to work the refined independent movement developing in their hands by doing the finger knitting. After finishing, the challenge of learning to jump the rope addressed the coordination and rhythm needed in gross motor movement. Each day at Knights Club, we practiced jumping rope. Obstacle courses were also set up to challenge the six-year-olds' need for ever more challenging gross motor movements. Many other activities that have been done include sewing, handwork, and using scissors to cut out snowflakes, valentines and cutouts for moveable pictures. These creations challenge the fingers of the six-year-olds as they try to coordinate and refine their hand movements.

There can also be a drawing time in a bound book that is used only for Knights Club. The six-year-old tends to naturally create more intricate and detailed drawings and they enjoy the privilege of having their own special book.

Snack

Knights Club also enjoys its own special snack. Often, there are organic cookies or popcorn to eat and a beverage. This sharing of food provides a festive feeling each week. It is a mini-celebration of the qualities and abilities that are unfolding in the upcoming first-graders.

End-of-year Project and Presentation

Sometime in the spring, around April, the Knights begin a project. With a group of children a few years ago, the project that we did was to make simple marionettes. The children each sewed a hem around a square cloth that was then made into a marionette that later became a character in the fairy tale of Briar Rose. I chose this particular story because I had a little girl in the class who had been with us for two years and who had developmental delay challenges. She had truly been "asleep" in the tower and had awoken in so many incredible ways on her journey with us so far. Her marionette became Briar Rose. We practiced the marionette play several times and then did it for the children and parents of the class. Needless to say, for those of us who knew this child and all she had been through, there was not a dry eye in the house!

The previous year, I had a group of six-year-olds who loved to dramatize, or "play" the stories. In the late spring, I told the Grimms' story "The Queen Bee." With the capes and silks used at playtime, they dressed up as the various characters. We practiced the story a few times and on the last day of school we "played" the story for the rest of the class. It was a satisfying experience for all.

Conclusions and Beginnings

Please remember that all of the above are only suggestions for the older children in their last year in the kindergarten. Some teachers may feel that their current group of children would be better served by an environment of simple play. This is also a very valid and rich choice. The programs we create for our own particular groups depend on the children themselves, the circumstances surrounding our kindergarten communities, and the approach the teacher feels would be healthiest for that particular group. The children will flourish in an environment where the warm, sincere and deep interest of the teacher meets the growing needs of the children. ✦

The Raft

Louise deForest

It all started ten years ago. I had been a lead teacher at an established Waldorf school for six or seven years and that year I received an interesting class. (My mother always used the word "interesting" to describe something about which she did not want to say anything negative and so I will call this particular class "interesting.") It was a mixed-age class but the majority of the children were older boys, whom I always enjoy. It was one of those classes that we all get occasionally, where everything that has otherwise always worked, in this case did *not* work. It was a class that came along to wake me up and to shake me out of complacency in my work. In later years, it was discovered that many of these dear children had severe learning disabilities, something that at the time I knew nothing about. What I did know was that they could not sit still for story, they were wonderful players but they quickly fell into chaos, transitions were excruciating for them and they expressed very little interest in all the standard artistic and craft activities offered in a Waldorf classroom. They were doers, this class, but what was there to do? The farm program that I eventually established was still seven years away, though I am convinced that the seeds for that program were planted way back with this class.

One thing they always loved to do was to go for walks and every walk had an adventure. Although the school where I worked was close to New York City, we were blessed with meadows, ponds, forests, farms and hills and there was no shortage of adventure material. To meet their need for movement, we often started our mornings outside, either on our playground or, more often, taking walks, and it was on such a walk that our year-long adventure started.

Close to the school there was a swimming pond where all the children in the school spent long hours with their parents during our hot, humid summers. Behind this swimming pond there was what we call a nature pond, where great blue herons stopped to rest on their flight south, where Canada geese raised their young in the spring and in which snapping turtles, water rats, and countless frogs and fish called home. Wild berries grew along the shore and angelica, wormwood, and wild rose hips formed thickets along the woodland paths. In short, it was a place full of possibilities.

This is where we walked one early fall morning and we all ran to the nature pond to see what new sights the day had for us. We had been watching the water rats' hole and our vigil was rewarded by seeing one of them swim out into the middle of the pond. We all found long branches for fishing or poking into the mucky bottom and waited to see what would surface. In the middle of the pond there was a board, or series of boards, that looked intriguing, so we rallied our forces and with sticks pulling from one side and branches pushing from the other, we brought it close enough to the shore to have a look. One of the children noticed a frayed rope tied to the side and it wasn't long before the whole class was pulling on the rope. Whatever we had at the end of that rope was heavy and BIG. Finally, enough of it surfaced to allow us guesses as to what it had been. It was obviously something made by someone; there were parts of boards nailed together and ropes intertwined through the boards. The cry went out: "It's a ship!" and the thought of pirates living in our woods sent shivers of delight and apprehension through the group. I took a closer look and mentioned that it looked like a raft to me and immediately the children begged to pull it out and use it. Finally, here was something that truly interested them!

As we carried our project through the year, I began to notice that the children were more at peace in the classroom.

In spite of all the force of determination that six-year-old children can muster, we still could not pull it free of the muck and branches in the water and the disappointment was palpable. Before I realized what I was saying, I mentioned that perhaps we should build a new raft. The response was deafening and they were ready to start on this new project immediately. We walked back to the kindergarten and the rest of the day was spent reliving the excitement of our morning.

That evening I went home and wondered what I had gotten myself into. We all know that once we have said something, we are bound to do it, but I found myself hoping that in the next few days something else would come along that would distract them from their project. No such luck! So it was a week or so later that I found myself sharing this story with the parents in a class meeting, feeling more than a bit overwhelmed at the enormity of what I had said I would do. I love to work and am quite handy at most things, but boat building went far beyond my skills and I was sincerely regretting speaking before thinking. Luckily for me and the children, the parents became very excited about this new experience and immediately one mother volunteered to help us one day a week. A father donated logs and one of my colleagues had a shallow pond next to her house, within walking distance of the school, where we could both build and (hopefully) float this raft.

So the planning began. I decided that we would devote one morning a week to this project, Wednesdays, and we would spend most of our morning at the site, having snack there while the weather was still warm. The logs were dropped off and it was up to us to craft, out of these different-length logs, a sea-worthy vessel. On our first working morning, many of the boys showed up with saws, screwdrivers and hammers, and it wasn't many weeks before every child, even the most delicate girl, showed up with tool belts strapped to their waists and boots on their feet, ready for their day's work. My adult helper, Eve Sheridan, a sculptor and artist, was full of enthusiasm, and together we decided on our course of action. First, the logs needed to be cut to size. Then we would lash them together and peg them to boards underneath, holding the logs to each other and to the planks beneath them. We brought saw horses for the hand sawing and collected thick branches for making the pegs. Each workday would find some children sitting on logs in the scant shade of the trees, whittling away at a branch to make the needed pegs; others would be sawing with great concentration on the large logs and others cutting branches to size for the pegs. Once a log was cut to size, we then needed to drill holes for the pegs, so we used a hand drill to make the holes. There was more than enough for everyone to do but, when they tired, and for the inevitable few who could not engage totally in the work aspects, there was lots to do with a large field and pond to explore.

We worked on this raft almost every week for the entire year. It was a long walk for us but we had been granted permission to take a shortcut through a neighbor's garden and backyard and we always stopped for a short rest as we admired her garden. I realize now what a gift that was for us; week by week and month by month we had the opportunity to live the cycle of the year through experiencing her garden. When we started, the asters and mums were in full bloom; then one cold day the garden was covered in straw, a blanket for the winter, and all lay still until one early spring morning we could see little green noses poking up through the straw. On the cold days we would hear the blue jays and chickadees and on some of the days we heard not a sound. Then suddenly there was our dear robin redbreast and sap buckets on the trees and the very air seemed filled with the hum of life again. Watching the subtle changes in this garden became as pleasant a project as our raft, and the children were always eager to look for "garden news."

As we carried our project through the year, I began to notice that the children were more at peace in the classroom; suddenly they could listen to stories, they enjoyed our painting time, and the playtime was the most productive that I had seen so far. Everyone rallied for cleanup time and I noticed, as well, that they were working together. "Here, I'll help you" and "Let's do it together" began to echo through the classroom. I also noticed that there was more respect for all of our materials; no more scrubbing with the paint brushes on painting day, no toys ever placed carelessly on the shelf, crumbs cleaned up from the floor without anyone being asked to do it; in short, I noticed that the children had real respect for their "tools," whatever they were. At home, too, parents noticed a difference. Children were, of their own accord, volunteering to help—washing dishes, cleaning floors, fixing things around the house—and there was the overall sentiment of "I can do it," as the children grew in confidence, strength and stamina.

Of course we still continued with most of our regular kindergarten activities; we did beeswax modeling, baked bread, moved and sang in our circles, had stories, puppet shows and plenty of indoor and outdoor play. Rest time, which we had after returning from the pond, became a time of deep silence and true rest and was a balm for our bodies and souls after our hard work. The more we worked and created, the more problems we solved with our raft, the more deeply the children entered into the content of our activities. Something within them—their profound intention to transform, to make changes, to contribute to the world— had been satisfied, and out of that satisfaction, they were ready to receive all that the world (in our small classroom) had to offer. Their potential was recognized, their intense desire to contribute was seen and used and they were at peace with themselves and the world around them.

I, however, was a mess. Would this thing ever float? Was this safe? Would we ever be done? I was bolstered by the children's enthusiasm and by the changes I had seen in them over the course of the year, but I still did not know what I was doing. Was this the right thing to be doing with kindergarteners? I had never seen anyone else do anything even close to this and I wondered if I had strayed too far from kindergarten pedagogy. But my children led me on and, in spite of my lack of boat-building confidence and my inner doubts, I persevered with the project, and at last everything seemed ready to set sail.

When we were finally done, the raft was just a platform of logs and we planned to use a pole, Tom Sawyer-style, to push it over the water. It was late spring, by now, and we had planned a festival around the launching of our (hopefully) pond-worthy vessel. All the parents had been invited for a picnic at the pond (the children did not know that they were coming), life jackets had been gathered for the children to wear and great excitement was in the air. A few weeks before the formal launching, Eve and I decided that we should test-sail it and, using leftover logs to roll it into the water, we gave it a push… and watched it sink! Not totally, but it was riding awfully low in the water. What now? Looking back after so many years, I do not even know how we got it out of the water again and tipped it over; I'm sure it was not easy, but turn it over we did! Then a quick trip to a lumberyard where we bought a long piece of Styrofoam, doubled it and nailed it onto the bottom of the raft. We covered the Styrofoam with paneling to both hold it in place and protect it from scrapes against rocks, and once more pushed the raft into the pond. Success! It bobbed along the surface of the pond, just waiting for the children. Then we pulled it out of the water again and left it ready for our launching.

Only a few weeks were left before the end of school and the day of our "festival" dawned bright and sunny. I was as excited as the children to set off towards the pond! With grunts and groans, the children pushed the raft into the water and a cheer went up as it floated next to the shore. Eve volunteered to pole them across the pond, two by two, while I maintained order on the shore. As the first two children stood on the raft and glided from shore, silence enveloped the children as they watched, wide-eyed, all senses alert. Another cheer went up as they reached the middle of the pond. Parents began to arrive and, seeing the children already sailing, added their voices to the enthusiastic congratulations and wonder. One child said to his mother when she arrived, "We're boat builders," and so they were.

Children need experiences that tap their enormous potential, that spark their imaginations and that give them the opportunity to transform substance.

Each child had a turn to go on the raft and many had several. And each time, the raft held strong. There was an anxious moment when a heavier child, accompanied by a smaller friend, stepped on the raft. It floated very low in the water and we all held our breath as we watched the water inch up around the ankles of the children on the raft. But it made it back to shore with no one having to test their life jackets and a sigh of relief was breathed by all. After everyone had had a turn, we spread our blankets and shared the food that each family had brought and relived the steps in making this raft. Each child pointed to different parts of the raft and explained how it was made, and every peg, every tie, every cut piece was admired by all.

The raft stayed at the pond and was much-used by the son of my colleague (who was in my class) and his friends, and I'm sure many adventures were had on it over the summer. In the fall, a hurricane smashed it to pieces against a culvert and parts of it floated downstream, perhaps to spark the imagination and will of yet another group of children. In any case, the raft is still alive in my children's memory, in their hands and in their hearts.

I am aware that not everyone is going to go out and build a raft with their older children. In sharing this story, I am encouraging you to listen to your children, to hear what they are asking for and to dare to bring them an experience that will meet their needs. There is nobility in work and the children recognize and embrace this. We have all seen that the generation coming into the world now is one that is longing to make a difference, one with strong earthly intentions and a deep desire to fulfill those intentions. They are wise beyond their years and long for recognition. They need experiences that tap their enormous potential, that spark their imaginations and that give them the opportunity to transform substance. As we know, the culture in which we now live is one that is hard for the child to adapt to; "Is there a place in the world for me?" is an unconscious question that all children carry. I believe that if we can offer them worthy experiences, we welcome them into this world, and the children can find their places, full of confidence and joy and ready to take up their particular tasks.   ✦

The Little Ones in the Classroom

Barbara Klocek

After circle time in our morning routine, as the children move into free play time, there is a rush to the bookshelf under the loft. This is where the Little Ones live, small dolls (one for each child) gathered in two baskets where they rest. The first thing in the morning, many children seek out their Little Ones. Some are tucked into shirt pockets or jumper tops and are carried away into play. As the children become gnomes, knights, and princesses, their Little Ones accompany them on their imaginative journeys. Some Little Ones are central to the play as elaborate ships and houses are built for them and all sorts of adventures are played out with them.

The idea of the Little Ones was brought to our class by my colleague, Cynthia Lambert. In her previous school, they were part of the kindergarten tradition and she was continuing the tradition, busily making many Little Ones. I have traced the original idea back to Bonnie River-Bento, who initially developed them as a therapeutic tool. What a wonderful addition they have been to our classroom because of the way they develop anticipation and patience, kindness and caring.

How do they come into the classroom? The timing of their arrival has been an important teaching tool. I find that in my teaching I am continually moving on all levels between being a strong, upright presence, such as in leading the circle, to a soft gentle holding from the periphery, as in free play. This gesture varies throughout the seasons as well. Early in the school year we take up the quality of strength in our hearts, heads and hands. From the gesture of conquering with the help of Michael by making swords, we are learning to be brave and to do what is right by being an upright, noble knight. This could be seen as helping the children experience their own strong uprightness. Then this posture is balanced by gentle nurturing with the arrival of the Little Ones.

Often early in October we find a note in the kindergarten from the Fairy Mother on the top of the bookshelf under the loft. She has noticed how nicely the children are playing and that some of the Little Ones from Fairy Land want to come and play with the children. The first year, two or three Little Ones came nearly every day, with an exception if there was a birthday celebration that day. We tried to choose the children with nurturing natures to receive their Little Ones first, in order to encourage other children to imitate this. What excitement there was! We would look to see who had arrived after circle, when one teacher would look in the basket on the top of the bookshelf. Each Little One would have a tag on its sleeve with its name and the name of the child for which it had come. The Little One's names were taken from nature, such as River, Dewdrop, Daisy or Dandelion. There were many lessons in patience as some of the children had to wait for a long time. We, and their parents, assured the children that each child would receive one and, sure enough, before the month was out, every child did.

What a wonderful addition they have been to our classroom because of the way they develop anticipation and patience, kindness and caring.

Behind the scenes, where did they come from? The teachers made them out of cotton knit, 11 inches square, made somewhat like a knot doll. We crocheted the hair, choosing the same color as the child's hair. At our parent orientation before school, we gave one to each of the parents and asked them to dress them secretly by the end of September, so that the children would not know. One of my friends, who is a quilter, gave us many pieces of fabric from which the parents could choose. We had a rough pattern and asked that the clothes be sewn onto the doll. Some made a simple shirt and pants, others were more elaborate, but we sought to keep them simple. For some parents, this task was overwhelming, so we or another parent would help them. Another teacher, who has Little Ones in her classroom, has a dollmaker make them and the parents dress them with soft velour.

One of the children asked if he could take his home, so we wrote a letter to the Fairy Mother and put it in the basket. She wrote back that "the Little Ones were too shy to leave the classroom but would go home with the children on the last day of school before they were going on into the first grade. The younger children's Little Ones would go back to Fairy Land over the summer to help with the harvest." When the children returned to school the following September, they would ask about their Little Ones and were content to wait when they heard that the Little Ones did not like dragons and would be coming later. When the time came for the Little Ones to come, we began with those belonging to the returning children. What a joyous reunion they had, and the children continued some of the elaborate play from the previous year. With growing anticipation, the younger children would watch and wait eagerly for their own little friends to appear.

What do they do with them? As with all children's play, there are endless possibilities. At first, houses are built for them out of blocks and wood or out of boxes in the room. This year, there were ocean liners with several levels for beds and kitchens and a top layer for the smoke stacks. We found we needed to bring in extra baskets as boats, strollers or cars because our older baskets began to fall apart with this enthusiastic play. Sometimes the Little Ones will be part of a puppet show or will be part of the audience watching these shows. I have been surprised by how the boys play with them like little action figures, as deep sea divers, circus men, telephone line workers, etc. The girls often have adventures as well, although they especially enjoy creating wonderful homes and castles.

The first year or two, the children created many, many airplanes in which the Little Ones could fly, but it became chaotic and too loud, so we said that the Little Ones liked to stay on the ground. In this way, there is much more calm floor play.

It is most amazing to see the transformation possible with the Little Ones. Often a child may be too rough with her Little One, stuffing it in something upside down, or having it leap from high places and land on its head. I will go over and say, "Oh, I heard a Little One crying," and give it a kiss. Sometimes we will create a hospital and put on cloth bandages if the Little One has broken its leg. If the child continues to be too rough with her Little One, I will gently take it and say that it is too frightened by this play and wants to go up by our Michael puppet to gather some courage. How wonderful it is to teach gentleness and respect in this way.

If a child is absent, often a friend will ask to babysit the Little One. One year the parents knitted twenty-four squares as wool blankets for the Little Ones. We then also dyed 11 x 11-inch silk squares for sheets, capes, and so on for the Little Ones.

The first year we had one boy who had lost his father and he did not play with his Little One at all. I just watched and wondered. The next year, his Little One was an important part of most of his play. This was an indication to me of his coming to terms with his own home situation.

The last week of class the children have rest time (just before snack) with their Little Ones. On the last day, the younger children give a kiss goodbye to their Little Ones and place them all in a basket. They know they will be returning to Fairy Land to help with the planting and harvest there and will return to them in the kindergarten after Michaelmas. The older children take theirs carefully home where some children have created a cozy spot for them there. We have been told that they remain in a special place in the children's hearts and rooms for many years. Over the years, the children have been playing less and less with the kindergarten dolls. The Little Ones have transformed this lack of interest in doll-play into a whole new imaginative level. What a wonderful way to bring doll-play back into the kindergarten. ✦

Girls and Boys— Feminine and Masculine

Louise deForest

When I was coming of age in the late sixties, one of the central ideas of the feminist movement was that boys and girls were essentially the same in nature, and that it was the cultural environment around the child that helped to create the traditional masculine and feminine roles that the child would eventually adopt as his or her own. The materialistic viewpoint of the time was that if you raised a boy as a nurturer, that was what he would become; if a girl were raised to be competitive and more aggressive, she would develop a more masculine relationship to the world. In other words, it was the old nature-or-nurture question, and it was believed that we, as parents and educators, could determine through our cultural expectations the gender characteristics we wanted to foster in the next generation, regardless of the sex of the children in question.

I tried hard to believe this and closely examined my own gender beliefs and behaviors, but there was also something that did not ring quite true about this picture. In looking back, I think my uneasiness with this viewpoint was that it was too one-dimensional. It assumed that we were all blank slates at birth, waiting to be formed and molded by the world around us, instead of recognizing that we all come to earth with certain talents and experiences and intentions. This way of thinking also did not recognize that everything in this world exists between polarities, and that the masculine and feminine poles are archetypal forces that live and are at work in everything to do with life. These archetypal polarities are central to the development and expression of the human spirit. I know that, as a girl, I experienced life differently than my brothers and that it was significant to me that I was born with a female body. I also know that growing up in a male-dominated family and being the mother of three sons encouraged me to diligently pursue my tasks of uncovering, strengthening and developing my more feminine qualities.

It is a tricky and dangerous undertaking to make generalized observations and express personal thoughts about the genders, and I do so with hesitation and a bit of reluctance. Each individual is so unique and mysterious and none of us is one-sided—purely masculine or purely feminine—but, rather, always weaving an intricate tapestry of the two together. To say "This is masculine, this is feminine," negates the individuality of each one of us, so I beg you to remember that with each generalization mentioned in this article, there is an equal number of exceptions. Ultimately, the higher inner essence of a human being has nothing to do with being a man or a woman.

The differences between male and female have been a source of interest, debate, and deep mystery since time began, or at least since humanity has been so divided. Rudolf Steiner tells us that it has not always been so in the evolution of humanity. In the epoch of Lemuria (over a million years ago), when the earth and what could then be called the human being were still in a fluid and malleable state, there was no differentiation of the sexes; each androgynous being carried both masculine and feminine forces within, and reproduced through a kind of divinely ordered self-impregnation. In the interest of human evolution, these unisexual beings slowly separated into two genders, thus taking the first steps away from an unconscious unity with the spiritual world and introducing dualism into our reality. This process also enabled us to become thinking beings and to be able to develop an individual, self-conscious relationship to the spirit:

> Thus man could use a portion of the energy which previously he employed for the production of beings like himself, in order to perfect his own nature. The force by which mankind forms a thinking brain for itself is the same by which man impregnated himself in ancient times. The price of thought is single-sexedness. By no longer impregnating themselves, but rather by impregnating each other, human beings can turn a part of their productive energy within, and so become thinking creatures. Thus the male and female body each represent an imperfect external embodiment of the soul, but thereby they become more perfect creatures inwardly.[1]

Steiner tells us that in a far-distant future time, we will once again return to a genderless form but now with the self-acquired ability to reproduce ourselves through the power of the word. He says, "And this in the future will be the birth of the new human being—that he is spoken forth by another."[2]

So what it means to live life as a man or as a woman has relevance for the individual as well as for all of humanity and is one of the profoundest mysteries of being human. Steiner does tell us that, through repeated earthly lives, we have the opportunity to experience both realities, taking on a male or a female body in an effort to most effectively meet our karma and our destiny in each life. We tend to swing between the two from life to life

1   Rudolf Steiner, *Cosmic Memory*, 90.
2   Rudolf Steiner, *The Theosophy of the Rosicrucians*, 148.

but occasionally, in the interest of developing certain experiences or capacities, we can reincarnate repeatedly in one gender. "[A] human being's experience as a man or a woman in one incarnation will determine what this person will do outwardly in the next: the female experience will produce an inclination to build a male organism and the male experience will produce an inclination to build a female organism. Incarnations in the same sex rarely succeed one another; at the most it can happen seven times."[3] He goes on to describe how women, who are more disposed to soul experiences than men, take everything they experience in life more deeply into their soul lives, while men tend to be more disposed to intellectuality and materialism, which deal mainly with the physical plane. Men enter into matter more thoroughly and embrace it more completely than do women. Women retain more of the spiritual and non-physical sphere within their disposition, keeping what is physical more a flexible part of their interest. Therefore, men tend to grasp the external in things, and experiences make less of an impression in the depths of their souls. "A deep working into and working through the organism will bring forth a male organism. A male organism appears when the forces of the soul desire to be more deeply graven into matter... man is woman's karma."[4] And woman is man's karma.

> *What is clear is that the masculine and the feminine are two sides of the same polarity and that together they form a whole.*

I tremble as I enter into a discussion of the stereotypes of the masculine and feminine, realizing as I do so that this is potentially dangerous ground. Again, I reiterate that in the realm of spiritual companionship, male and female are balanced, and that the generalizations that follow have no judgments attached. So, could we characterize the feminine impulses as: intuitive, reflective, inward, process-oriented, fluid and flexible, receptive, softer (both physically and psychologically), subjective, spiritually-oriented, emotional, imaginative and nurturing? To characterize men, could we say that they tend towards being more individualistic, denser and harder (both physically and psychologically), goal-oriented, objective, intellectual, clear and detached, rational, and more earthly and concentrated? The physical bodies of men and woman say much about their inner soul gestures. Aside from the obvious outer physical differences, men have denser bones and more muscle mass than do women, making men, by their very physicality, more removed from the spirit and more deeply embedded in the earthly realm. If one thought in terms of forms, the male would be the straight line, the female, a circle; if they were represented by the elements, one would be fire and the other water. But what is clear is that the masculine and the feminine are two sides of the same polarity and that together they form a whole. They are day (the masculine) and night (feminine). The female, through her imagination, longs for an intuitive union with the spiritual world. Through the soul life of woman and through her thoughtful understanding of nature, woman can ennoble and refine the willful nature and the vigorous strength of men. Men, on the other hand, through their deep empathy with the material world and their capacity for clear, objective thought

---

3   Rudolf Steiner, *Manifestations of Karma*, 177.
4   Ibid., 174.

and their ability to judge and evaluate, can both transform physical substance and support the evolutionary task of the development of a sense of self for all of humanity.

These attributes also have a shadow side; the clarity of masculine thought can become cold or theoretical and dry. Male strength can turn into violence or domination and the sense of individuality can turn towards lust for power and selfishness. The dangers for the feminine are equally familiar to us: the connection to cosmic realities can become a loosening of the sense of reality; the rich feeling life can become chaotic emotions; and nurturing can turn into smothering. And yet, the possibility of integrating the masculine and the feminine, of bringing these poles into balance, could be the golden kernel of our existence and the way to become truly human beings. Rudolf Steiner describes women as "soul divine" and men as "physical divine,"[5] and these two do seem to call to each other to uncover the cosmic intentions for both.

On the level of the older child in the kindergarten, those of us who work with these children are well aware of the differences between boys and girls and are often at our wit's end to carry their impulses with love and deep respect. Let's take a look at two average six-year-olds who have been in the kindergarten and know how to play; we'll call them David and Sophia.

Setting the stage, let's say that it's eight o'clock in the morning and the kindergarten is now open. I can hear someone crashing against the outer door and I know it is David. David is hypo-tactile (many boys are burdened with sensory-integration disorders, especially regarding the sense of touch) and must bang against things to get a sense of where he is in space and where he ends and where the world begins. He throws his jacket towards his cubby (not in it, mind you), and bursts into the room with a familiar look in his eye. The calm

> *Rudolf Steiner describes women as "soul divine" and men as "physical divine," and these two do seem to call to each other to uncover the cosmic intentions for both.*

orderliness of the classroom seems suddenly shattered by a wild wind. He looks around to see who is here; if he is the first one to arrive, he may run over to me to tell me the latest news, but if there are other boys already present, he does not give me so much as a glance but, with booming voice, begins to organize the play. Chairs are turned over and become trucks or snowplows; blocks are used to build space ships or piled one on top of the other to make a restaurant or an office building. Voices get louder and the play can quickly get out of hand as the boys rush to grab other materials or "rob" another house. The sounds of motors or explosions fill the air as they career from one scenario to another, barking orders and playing with an intensity and concentration that is often exhausting to watch. When it is time to go outside, David can hardly contain himself; he pushes and shoves to be the leader of our walk and, when told he must learn how to wait patiently before he can be a leader, he may kick the cubby (or punch the chosen leader as he or she passes him), and then he mopes for the whole time that we are going on our walk. When we finally arrive at our chosen play spot, again David launches

5   Margli Matthews et al., *Ariadne's Awakening*, 163. This book is highly recommended for a thorough and in-depth exploration of masculine and feminine.

himself forward, running off with his friends and in no time at all the boys are wrestling, pushing, and shouting. They run at full speed and crash into each other or tackle each other as they pass by; sticks become guns and they hide in the bushes waiting to ambush an innocent (or not) passerby. Sometimes they will build traps made of sticks over holes they have just dug, hoping to trap the girls or an animal—preferably one or several of the girls. They test their strength and agility, hanging from ropes or pulling themselves up into the trees, going across the monkey bars or digging to China in the sandbox.

For a few years I had a kindergarten on a farm and the children engaged in caring for the animals and tending the land. When it was a workday, David would engage in the work with the same enthusiasm and concentration he used when at play, and he prided himself (and competed with the others) on his work. Indeed, I often noticed that after working hard physically, David could enter into play more easily and did not seem so out of touch with himself and others. Always one to make himself scarce when it was dishwashing time, on the farm he was always the first to volunteer and the last to finish and he had a special affinity with all the animals. At circle time, he balked at the group activity and remarked that what we did was "too babyish" for him. It was only his love and respect for me and the boundaries that I provided for him that carried him through this difficult time.

Sophia, on the other hand, comes into the kindergarten more quietly, pausing on the threshold to our room, and often has difficulty separating from her parents. She, too, looks around the room and greets her friends but always comes over to lean against me or to tell me a little secret before searching out her playmates. Sophia's play tends to be quieter and more family-oriented and, just as with the boys, much time is spent assigning roles: "You can be the baby, you can be the Daddy and I'll be the babysitter." While all older children tend to talk more than actually play, Sophia and her "family" of friends spend a lot of time talking and whispering and watching the boys. Every time someone bothers them or does something they shouldn't do, especially if that person is a boy, Sophia comes running to me to recount the latest outrage and often a few tears are shed. Sophia and her "family" now put on a puppet show, draping the cloths beautifully on a playstand and gathering all the materials they will need. An argument breaks out among the girls over who should use which puppet: who had a turn last time and who should rightfully do it this time. More tears are shed and a few mean words are spoken before peace once again is restored and all the chairs are placed around the puppet show. After much persuasion (and manipulation) on the part of the girls, everyone is seated to watch the puppet show but Sophia spends most of her time reminding the boys to sit still or to be quiet rather than moving the puppets. The boys soon tire of this and wander back to their play.

Sophia and her friends are now all seated in a corner of the classroom making plans for seeing each other after school. As another girl in the class approaches to play with them, Sophia quickly tells her that she cannot play and closes off their corner with a playstand while she and her friends giggle. "We don't want to play with her," says Sophia to her friends and they all snicker in agreement. The excluded child comes to me in tears, we re-approach the group, and Sophia and her friends reluctantly make room for her in their house. When it is outside time, Sophia hurries to hold hands with her "best friend" (which changes frequently) and pushes all others away. She is quiet once she has her partner and is ready to go for a walk, watching me all the while, hoping that I will see how well-behaved she is and choose her to be the leader.

While Sophia loves to swing holding hands with her friend in the next swing, today she runs to sit under the low hanging branches of a pine tree and there she and a few other girls make fairy rings and gnome houses. They are very intent in their play and wonderful miniature worlds are created. Of course, they also like to run and are physically active—especially if there is a boy or two who wants to chase them, whereupon they run screaming to the teacher complaining that the boys are bothering them.

On the farm, Sophia was initially hesitant to take up the work, not wanting to get dirty and showing disinterest in that kind of work. After a few months, however, she became a very hard and capable worker and took special pride in pushing the full wheelbarrow over to the compost pile all by herself. She loved the baby lambs and calves but was a bit hesitant with the larger animals. In the classroom, Sophia knew all the words to the songs and all the gestures of the circle and primly took part in the circle, occasionally casting a disparaging look at any boy who was not participating as he should. She would also try to catch my eyes so that I would be sure to see the boy who was misbehaving and that she herself was not. At goodbye time she would give me and her current favorite friends a hug before skipping off with her parent.

Of course this is a one-sided and exaggerated picture. Many boys love to play with the dolls and many girls are incredibly active physically. But these examples do highlight the different ways that boys and girls tend to learn about the world and each other. Boys tend to know each other physically, bumping up against each other and wrestling; girls tend to meet on a more emotional, feeling level, and it is the social world which holds their interest.

I should also hasten to add that children in early childhood are not as fixed in their gender-tendencies as we observe people in their later years to be. In a way, children in these early years are still beyond gender, still living in the unity of the spiritual world and in the impulses that brought them to earth. Only very gradually will they solidify into male and female, through the seven-year phases of human development, until finally, as young adults, the higher self will take on these gender qualities more strongly. But all children carry the seeds of gender identity within them. What a responsibility it is for parents and teachers today to keep open to the possibility that children need to be free to establish their pre-birth intentions about the particular configuration of their masculine and feminine qualities.

And so what does this mean for the teacher working with boys and girls in a mixed-age classroom?

Several years ago, WECAN put out a questionnaire to kindergarten teachers asking what joys and challenges they were facing in their classrooms. The majority of the questions the teachers were carrying were about the older child in the kindergarten—hence this book—and how to deal with the boy-energy in their classes. Our kindergarten classrooms tend to be very feminine in nature, striving to meet the young child's sense of wholeness and to welcome them with beauty to their time here on earth. The rhythms of the day, week, and year give them security and help them to enter into earthly rhythms. These, too, can be presented in very feminine ways. So when boys enter into our classrooms in their often boisterous way, it can feel as if they are wrecking what we have worked so hard to create. We want things to remain soft, ordered, and controlled. I am by no means suggesting that we should throw up our hands and "let boys be boys." But I do think the key to working with boys is to love their energy, to be thankful for their urge to transform the physical, to enjoy how they get things done, and to celebrate how they can make a difference. We must admire and enjoy their physicality and meet their bumping, banging and yelling with good humor and understanding. We can gently or more sternly bring them back to rightful behavior, but we must carry an inner picture of the masculine forces that are expressing themselves and know that this child really cannot do otherwise, for it would be against his nature.

> *The key to working with boys is to love their energy, to be thankful for their urge to transform the physical, to enjoy how they get things done, and to celebrate how they can make a difference.*

The girls, too, need our patient understanding, but for many of us they are easier to deal with because they are willing and able to sit quietly, doing handwork or keeping us company, and they are so much more demonstrative with their affection. As women, we tend to relate to them more easily than we do to the boys. However, girls certainly have their challenges too, with their tendency to manipulate, to hold grudges and to play emotional games. How straightforward boys can seem in comparison! The tendency of girls to be "hurt to the core" also needs our guidance and courage. And here, I must express my undying appreciation for the male kindergarten teachers and the invaluable role they play in our early childhood programs. Would that there were more men for our little ones! But I daresay that, for the men working in the nursery or kindergarten, it is the girls, not the boys, that they find most confusing. It's interesting to contemplate whether, in the classroom, it might be that women find it more difficult to understand boys, while men might feel more at a loss to find a way to embrace what girls bring.

Gender roles are always shifting to meet and reflect the times and today I can see efforts being made by people all over the globe to bring together masculine and feminine, to expand what it means to be a woman or a man, and to break apart old stereotypes. We are no longer content or fulfilled living in predetermined roles. Today, many men are the primary caretakers of their children while their wives carry the financial responsibility of the family. Women are encouraged to satisfy their intellectual curiosity and their work is finally being acknowledged and compensated on a level commensurate with men. Men are reveling in exploring what it means to be a man, broadening that definition from the narrow constraints of their fathers' interpretations, through deep questions, self-reflection and open sharing with each other. But our explorations of masculine and feminine are still deeply mystifying and we have a long way to go. Recently, I heard in the kindergarten that "pink is a girl's color."

So it seems to me that one of the many challenges presented by working with boys and girls every day in our classrooms is to come to know and embrace the male and female qualities living in each one of us. I am more masculine in nature and I find it easy and enjoyable to work in the fields, to build furniture, to cut down trees, all of which I have done with my classes. It is harder for me to create a space—a beautifully-draped, well-ordered classroom with exquisite wool pictures, a full nature table, and so on—and then to sit back and allow whatever will come, to come. Quietly sewing in a corner was, in the beginning of my years of teaching, an excruciatingly difficult endeavor. And yet, through the children, I was able to learn to connect with parts of myself that longed for expression.

> *Both boys and girls are hungry to be led by our healing example.*

Both boys and girls are hungry to be led by our healing example. Children want to see that we as teachers and parents, through our own comfort with the many dimensions of who we are, can accept, love and respect the life of unknown possibilities that lie before them. This requires flexibility of soul and a sense of adventure on our part. How can we stretch our understanding so that we can truly say, whether we are male or female ourselves, "I love the way girls and boys manifest the essence of who they are!"

As I have been stumbling my way down this dimly-lit path full of minefields, I hope I have offended no one. And I have to admit that I do have another thought that may engage your interest. The more I have been writing, the more I have been thinking of the masculine-feminine polarity as being related to another polarity: that of light (male) and love (female). In talking about the human being's ability to offer healing to others and to the world, Rudolf Steiner says: "Ultimately everything that happens in the realms of soul and matter on earth depends on the way in which these elements [light and love] weave into one another in our life."[6]

I wish you well in the balancing of your own masculine and feminine tendencies as you appreciate the love and light in the children to whom you mean so much. ✦

References

Matthews, Margli, Signe Schaefer, and Betty Staley. *Ariadne's Awakening*. Gloucestershire, UK: Hawthorn Press, 1986.

Steiner, Rudolf. *Cosmic Memory: Prehistory of Earth and Man*. West Nyack, NY: Rudolf Steiner Publications, 1959.

_____ . *The Theosophy of the Rosicrucians*. London: Rudolf Steiner Press, 1966.

_____ . *Manifestations of Karma*. London: Rudolf Steiner Press, 2004.

6   Rudolf Steiner, *Manifestations of Karma*, 198.

Beer and Lollipops

Melissa Borden

In a fishing village in coastal Alaska, two six-year-old boys strut down the street side by side. They are decked out in Xtratuff boots, T-shirts, and shorts. Their mother has already disappeared into the grocery store, giving the two boys the momentary thrill of being on their own. With unabashed bravado, the taller one leans an arm on his friend's shoulder to say, "Dude! You get the beer! I'll get the lollipops!"

Boys! We know them to be a confounding mixture of sweetness and daredevilry. Our little dudes at six years old are already embarking on the path to becoming men. These boys of ours can often display a brilliant aptitude for being noisy, physically energetic, adventuresome, risk-taking, and, certainly, naughty and defiant. They can also be emotionally tender and sensitive and can have a tendency to struggle with expressing and integrating strong feelings. As parents and teachers, we embrace these delightful contradictions and hope to raise and educate our boys in an atmosphere that cultivates healthy masculinity.

However, we may question the efficacy of societal and educational norms that create environments in which boys in large numbers are failing. A newspaper editorial titled "Has Boyhood Become a Disease?" discusses classroom settings that discriminate against kinesthetic learners, where boys comprise the bulk of failing students.[1] As parents and teachers, we are concerned about classroom and social environments for children that discriminate against noisy, physically active, emotionally young children, and about an educational system that relies on the use of drugs such as Ritalin to manage these children. As kindergarten teachers, many of us have met at our gates the four-year-old boys who

---

1   Jeanne Sather, "Has Boyhood Become a Disease?" *Wall Street Journal*, 1997.

already sense themselves to be failures because of their experiences in preschool and even in their own home lives. We are concerned about a culture that does not protect childhood and where neighborhood and village communities are no longer the assumed backdrops for family life. It is sadly true that in our times, children often have little or no relationship to the work their parents, particularly their fathers, do in the community. Healthy role models for children are often lacking and those projected by movies and commercial advertising can be hollow and unwholesome. We are concerned about the shrinking number of male college graduates and the growing number of young men in the prison system. Children, particularly boys, are vulnerable to overt market manipulation by the toy, video game, and cigarette industries.[2] We are concerned about the reported phenomenon that boys in schools are falling behind girls in every subject.[3] There is plausible doubt about the suitability of many school environments where this inequality exists. There is a growing body of literature on the subject and newspapers and the Internet are full of alarming stories attesting to the challenges of raising and educating our boys. As parents and teachers, we would do well to engage in discussions that could contribute to a positive societal shift toward supporting the healthy development of our boys. We need to meet with enthusiasm the contradictions in our boys and honor the imperative that commands our boys to become healthy men.

Who, then, are these little dudes who share our homes and comprise half of our classroom population? We can bring to mind the English rhyme that asks,

> *And what are little boys made of?*
> *Snails and nails and puppy dog tails*
> *That's what little boys are made of.*

We may wonder if the picture of boyhood portrayed in this little verse has relevance to modern children, and it brings up the question of whether boys have changed or whether societal norms around them have changed. A Tom Sawyer in a modern classroom might very well be seen as a boy suffering from hyperactivity or in need of drug therapy. It has been argued by Sally Jenkinson that the rise in antisocial behavior in children is due in part to the dwindling opportunities for unstructured free play.[4] With the intention of providing children with good education, many schools have dramatically reduced the opportunity for play during school hours. Some schools have eliminated recess altogether. Mainstream kindergartens and even preschools orient themselves increasingly in the direction of academic skill building. Wendy Mogel writes, "In many schools today, the early elementary grades have become a time for mastering high-level academic tasks, and this takes a level of concentration, discipline, and fine motor skill that lots of boys haven't yet developed."[5] She

2   Ellen Seiter, *Sold Separately: Children and Parents in Consumer Culture*.
3   Steve Biddulph, *Raising Boys*, 133.
4   Sally Jenkinson, *The Genius of Play*, 13-32.
5   Wendy Mogel, *The Blessing of a Skinned Knee*, 47.

goes on to say that inappropriate expectations of our boys both in school and at home "[are] a recipe for resentment of adults, demoralizing, bitterness about homework, and shame about normal boyishness."[6]

Steve Biddulph writes that at the age of six or seven, "boys are six to twelve months less developed mentally than girls."[7] Considering carefully the proper readiness for first grade is an important factor in the success of our boys in their grade school years.

While it is acknowledged that boys and girls are each born with inherent gifts that allow them to thrive in relation to one another, it is also conceded that in the context of modern society, boys spend childhood catching up with girls in several key areas. Researchers ponder what appears to be a growing gender gap in education and attempt to understand the alarming statistics about boys in Europe and America (more about these statistics to follow). The gap encompasses the physical, cognitive and social aspects of developing children.

Physical Development of Boys

When speaking of the physical development of the boys in their lives, parents and teachers often refer to a certain recognizable "boy energy." This kinesthetic energy shows us that boys have an evident need for and an intrinsic love for physical movement. Often, with this comes an apparent drive for physical contact, as boys of all ages seem to take infinite delight in colliding with one another. Arms and legs seem to demand and rejoice in the opportunity to move freely. Research tells us that, in fact, young boys have approximately 30 percent more muscle mass than girls.[8] Their physical metabolism is slightly higher and this is probably why little boys often sweat so freely, even in their sleep. It has also been found that, for most boys, gross-motor outpaces fine-motor development in the early years.[9]

Clearly, expectations in school settings can be challenging for boys as they struggle to sit for extended periods of time.

Clearly, expectations in school settings can be challenging for boys as they struggle to sit for extended periods of time. Boys can also find the use of classroom materials to be awkward. It has been shown that young boys struggle more than girls to develop proper handwriting skills.[10] Recent research has also led to the belief that throughout childhood boys experience growth spurts that effect the development of the ear canal in such a way that boys can have intermittent hearing loss.[11] In terms of physical development, I have observed that most boys are movers, love physical contact, favor gross-motor activities over fine-motor activities, and may at times struggle to process verbal signals from parents and teachers.

6   Ibid., 48.
7   Biddulph, *Raising Boys*, 62-63.
8   Ibid., 34.
9   Ibid., 133.
10 Michael Gurian, *The Minds of Boys*, 85.
11 Lucinda Neall, *Bringing Out the Best in Boys*, 5.

Cognitive Development in Boys

Extensive research has been conducted on cognitive and neurological development in young children. The current thinking suggests that boys tend to be born with fewer neural connectors between the two hemispheres of the brain. These pathways eventually establish themselves, but at birth, girl babies have a greater capacity to integrate right-brain and left-brain activity.[12] This is of particular significance for language and communication development in young children. Steve Biddulph points out that brain integration involves the development of such skills as "reading, talking about feelings and solving problems through quiet introspection."[13] Young boys may need extra patience and support from parents and teachers in developing good communication skills. Adam Cox explores this matter in relation to auditory processing, which he points out can be an area of difficulty for many young boys.[14] This can continue throughout the early years, although in most cases the difficulty resolves itself later in childhood. However, with ear canals that may be expanding and contracting, auditory intake with young boys is not always reliable. This, of course, can be problematic in both school and social settings. Boys tend to do better when parents and teachers use simple, direct speech, and when they rely on less complex verbal communications with them. In addition, short-term memory tends to be somewhat stronger in girls than in boys.[15] This, too, is a factor in many learning environments.

Among the cognitive gifts granted to boys is a wonderful capacity for mechanical and spatial thinking. This often expresses itself in a passion for building and construction. The confluence of muscle and mental acuity makes young boys brilliant builders and sandbox engineers. Sally Jenkinson writes that "[boys] need opportunities to build every day." She also acknowledges the value of outdoor play for all children.[16]

Emotional Development in Boys

The social development of young children is clearly influenced by physical and cognitive factors. The struggle to integrate sensory information and to master language skills can put young boys at a social disadvantage. Boys can struggle to identify their own feelings and to express emotions.[17] This often results in frustration and angry behavior that may mask anxiety and emotional confusion. While defiant and even aggressive behavior in boys is often attributed to testosterone, Steve Biddulph points out that the influence of testosterone, significant in later childhood and adolescence, is minimal for boys under the age of eleven. Between infancy and eleven years old testosterone levels in boys and girls are roughly the same.[18] Do problems with aggression and violence in young boys result, in large part, from emotional issues? Do the majority of boys only gradually build up the capacity

12   Adam J. Cox, *Boys of Few Words*, 23.
13   Biddulph, *Raising Boys*, 60.
14   Cox, *Boys of Few Words*, 21.
15   Ibid., 24.
16   Jenkinson, *The Genius of Play*, 13.
17   Neall, *Bringing Out the Best in Boys*, 89
18   Ibid., 8.

to integrate, understand and manage their own feelings? We often see that they have an emotional fragility that is obscured by outward bravado and an attempt to be "tough." Boys look to and benefit from appropriate role models to guide them through this. Michael Gurian, in his book, *The Wonder of Boys*, describes the particular significance of the father-son relationship in a boy's life.[19]

One may wonder how much of what we know of boys is given to them at birth. What do they bring with them over the threshold? Have the enduring qualities of boyhood remained the same from the time that Mark Twain wrote *Tom Sawyer* to the present? At the same time, we may observe that social norms and school environments do not receive our boys with enthusiasm for their innate qualities. William Pollack dismisses what could be termed "the myths of boyhood," but ponders the question of whether the intrinsic qualities within our boys compromise the prospects of their success.[20] Today, boys are found to be struggling, and it is sadly true that the vast majority of children in the United States who are considered to be "at risk" are boys.

The following statistics may paint a grim picture. The information included here is not intended to define the problem but may be useful as a backdrop for understanding some of the challenges of raising and educating boys today.

- 80–90% of children diagnosed with ADD or ADHD are boys.[21]

- 80–90% of children on Ritalin (or similar drugs) are boys.[22]

- The vast majority of "successful" suicides occur in boys.[23]

- Boys account for 71% of school dropouts.[24]

- Boys are 4–5 times more vulnerable to neurological disorders, including learning disabilities, autism and a host of variants of these disorders.[25]

- 80% of high school dropouts are boys.[26]

- Over two-thirds of children with learning disorders and 90% of those labeled behaviorally disabled are boys.[27]

---

19 Michael Gurian, *The Wonder of Boys*, 106-127.
20 William Pollack, *Real Boys*, 52-64.
21 Michael Gurian, *Boys and Girls Learn Differently*, 25.
22 Ibid., 22.
23 Dan Kindlon and Michael Thompson, *Raising Cain*, 6.
24 Pollack, *Real Boys*, 15.
25 Cox, *Boys of Few Words*, 17.
26 Gurian, *Boys and Girls Learn Differently*, 22.
27 Ibid., 219.

- Today in America 43% of university and college freshmen are boys. This number is shrinking at an alarming rate. The number of male college graduates continues to go down.[28]

- Boys constitute 71% of school suspensions.[29]

- Two-thirds of special education classes in high schools are made up of boys.[30]

- 95% of all juvenile homicides are committed by boys.[31]

- 4 out of 5 crimes that end in juvenile court are committed by boys.[32]

- Boys account for 9 out of 10 alcohol and drug related crimes.[33]

- 1 in 75 men in America today is in jail.[34]

The pendulum of societal attitude has swung in the past thirty years. We now raise our daughters in an era where we celebrate the joyful liberation and empowerment of girls. Though the supportive attitude towards girls is still unfolding, one cannot help but feel heartened by the prospects for the future. Sadly, it seems to be another matter for boys. William Pollack writes of new research "that shows that boys are faring less well in school than they did in the past and, in comparison to girls, that many boys have remarkably fragile self-esteem, and that the rates of both depression and suicide in boys are frighteningly on the rise."[35] As parents and teachers, we must wonder how we can help the pendulum to swing into a place of balance for both boys and girls. How can we apply our imagination and our enthusiasm to this task?

From the Kindergarten

We who work with young children in a Waldorf/Steiner setting are daily reminded of the privilege that is given to us. In a sense, we stand as sentinels before the gates of a protected realm where light-filled imaginations, music, stories and play opportunities bid the young child to enter. Our task as adults is to uphold an encircling spell that protects the kingdom of childhood. We respect the imperative that beckons the young child to practice social skills and explore fantasy play and we strive to set up creative environments that support these healthy impulses. Acknowledging the importance of play as a vehicle for promoting the children's physical, social and mental well-being, we know about and cater to the need for objects in the children's environment that foster the mutable nature of their imaginations. We also work to conceive early childhood programs that can encompass the overlapping and the distinct needs of boys and girls.

28 Pollack, *Real Boys*, 235.
29 Ibid.
30 Ibid.
31 Kindlon and Thompson, *Raising Cain*, 6.
32 Ibid.
33 Ibid.
34 www.commondreams.org/cgi-bin.
35 Pollack, *Real Boys*, xxxii.

In light of the growing concerns about the welfare of boys, let's look closer at some considerations suitable for meeting the needs of young boys within the context of the kindergarten setting.

Movement

We have learned that the opportunity for free, unstructured outdoor play promotes social, physical and cognitive development in young children. There is no denying that boys need plenty of opportunity to move. The outdoor classroom is particularly suitable for young boys who revel in gross-motor activity, love to make as much racket as possible, and look for opportunities to meet each other through physical contact. Boys tend to be kinesthetic learners.[36] They are gifted sandbox engineers and are given some social advantages in environments that do not heavily favor verbal precociousness and fine-motor skills. The great outdoors and the wonder of the natural world encourage little scientists to explore and young artists to feel delight. Children, and most notably boys, need space and permission to run, tumble, wrestle, and roughhouse. Daily walks to local parks and green spaces can promote a sense of freedom and exploration of physical movement. The rhythmic nature of walking seems to have harmonizing effects on children, socially as well as physically. Healthy young boys can be seen to enter into movement in its most carefree form, fuelled by the wealth of etheric forces in the surroundings. Indeed, opportunities for movement in outdoor play bring a sense of well-being to young children and can be especially liberating for boys. Some teachers have found that a day that begins with one or two hours of outdoor time and includes a walk is especially suitable for young boys.

Boys need to feel safe and to be certain that they will be successfully guided through difficult moments by trusted adults.

Managing Conflict

In the kindergarten we can see that boys need to know who is the "boss." They easily establish a social pecking order with one strong "captain" at the top. This behavior is even more evident during the six-year-old change. It is important that an adult take on this role of "captain of the ship." There are far fewer problems with bullying and social dominance if it is very clear to the boys that the adult is the boss. Boys need clear, strong boundaries and limits firmly established. They do better when the rules of conduct are simple and do not require elaborate explanations. In fact, for young boys, the fewer words used, the better. Discipline approaches should, in general, be matter-of-fact and rely minimally on complex verbal input. It has been noted that many young boys struggle to express things of a feeling nature and that they can be inwardly tender.[37]

Lucinda Neall affirms William Pollack's viewpoint as she expresses her thoughts about emotional literacy, communication and self discipline, "which are skills to prepare [boys] for

36 Cox, *Boys of Few Words*, 21.
37 Jenkinson, *The Genius of Play*, 13.

adolescence and manhood."[38] This, she points out, is an area where parents and teachers can be supportive by keeping things simple and clear and respectful.[39] Boys need to feel safe and to be certain that they will be successfully guided through difficult moments by trusted adults who will live up to the responsibility of being in charge.

Humor

The countless hilarious moments in the world of young children can offer parents and teachers a deep well of good humor. The joy of childhood is infectious. Though times may arise when a sober response is called for, humor will always carry the day with the children. Humor facilitates the management of conflict too. Teachers and parents find it a wonder to observe little boys who just have been involved in a tussle parading arm-in-arm as if they are now best friends. Sometimes, the impulse for conflict arises from a simple urge in boys to have physical contact with one another. It is important for parents and teachers to realize that boys place a high value on peer respect and tend to be quite concerned about their own status in relation to the other boys. In the kindergarten, this tendency is particularly notable among the six-year-olds. Thus, allowing boys to "save face" is an important component of managing conflict. Again, humor can save the day!

Speech

Research and experience show that, in general, boys—even those who are gifted with verbal precocity—do better when communications from adults are direct and simple. I work with the "Rule of One" as a starting point when communicating with groups of boys: one noun, one verb! This is often all that is required. Too many words can be overwhelming for many children and young boys in particular. We hope to help our boys experience success in communication, even though experience tells us that some boys are not good listeners. It may take them extra time to develop strong language and communication skills. We need to make it easy for them to understand us and then lead them carefully into the next steps in their development. Ideally, boys and girls who are ready for first grade are able to follow through with simple directions that include two or more tasks. Teachers and parents can cultivate this skill in their boys by using careful, clear speech and patient guidance.

Role Models

Home life, childcare, preschool and school environments have a preponderance of women teachers and caregivers. William Pollack discusses the challenges of educational environments that are staffed by "all or almost all" women. While traditionally women were the caregivers for young children, still, at one time men had a greater presence in children's daily lives. Today children often have no relationship to the work their fathers do. Boys are

---

38 Pollack, *Real Boys*, 268.
39 Neall, *Bringing Out the Best in Boys*, 240.

in desperate need of healthy role models to help guide them along the path to adulthood.[40] In particular, men can help boys learn physical limits and how to manage strong feelings. They can also model respect for others, especially women. What a difference it would make for the boys if schools could make strong efforts to include gifted male teachers in their programs. Male teachers can help bring gender balance to the school environment and can help women teachers understand the ways of boys. The presence of male teachers who can model healthy, respectful behavior is beneficial for girls as well as boys. Early childhood settings that do not have the benefit of male teachers or staff can look for opportunities to incorporate fathers and other men into the classroom. The sound of men's voices and their physical presence in our preschools and kindergartens can bring a soothing sense of balance to the atmosphere of the classroom. Older kindergarten boys can experience an affinity with elders of their own gender that can make them especially eager for impressions of masculinity.[41] As teachers, we can support the development of our boys by integrating more men into our early childhood work. We can offer healthy role models if we draw thoughtfully from the resources in our communities.

Emotional Well-being

Parents and teachers can observe the emotional tenderness and sensitivity of the boys in their care. Lucinda Neall writes that girls' verbal development "is generally faster than [that of] boys." She adds that this puts girls at an advantage when processing and expressing emotions.[42] Boys need protection and respect for their emotional lives. It is unreasonable to expect young children to analyze their feelings to any significant extent. This is a skill that can be modeled by adults and will take time to develop. When managing conflict or difficult moments with boys, it is advisable to separate behavior from feelings. A boy's feelings need to be acknowledged and respected. Behavior and the consequences of behavior can be guided simply and corrected with as little fuss as possible. At the time of the six-year-old change, children begin to understand causality and can see a relationship between their actions and the consequences. Because boys struggle to identify and understand their own feelings, they can project a tough exterior to protect a tender inner dimension. It is important for teachers and parents to recognize this when interacting with boys.

Affection

Soul warmth from parents and teachers is the food that feeds a sense of well-being in children. Both boys and girls thrive, even in adversity, if they dwell in an atmosphere of love and joy. Our sensitive little boys, who can be such noisy, boisterous handfuls, ask us to

---

40 Pollack, *Real Boys*, 268.
41 Biddulph, *Raising Boys*, 31.
42 Neall, *Bringing Out the Best in Boys*, 83.

embrace the wholeness of who they are. Expressions of love and ample physical contact foster healthy children. For boys, unsolicited affection, in particular, tells them that we love them unconditionally. Our boys ask us to admire their intrinsic qualities, to accept and support them as they grow, and to impart to them our enthusiasm for their developing masculinity.

Understanding the Six-year-old Boy

Sometime around the sixth year, we begin to see the emergence of a new boy. He is identifiable by his stretching limbs, his new teeth and a jawline that emerges from his round cheeks. Sometimes, indoor spaces seem to be too confining for him. Outside, he is eager to challenge himself physically and loves to show off new skills to his teachers and parents as he calls out, "Look at ME!" He often defies his mother and would like to try the same with his teachers. He is looking for a new "boss" who can embrace the boy he is becoming. To the love he has for the adults around him, he now adds the wish to challenge them so that they set boundaries he can respect. The wellspring of imagination that has so bountifully nurtured his play seems temporarily to have run dry. He has become impatient with the play of his younger four- and five-year-old friends and shows a new inclination to be "naughty and disruptive" to the social order. This is a crisis in his young life. The lives of his six-year-old sisters foretell a slightly different transformation—a significant and important internal developmental shift. Children of this age look now to the wide world around them for new impulses to feed their imaginations and teach them valuable skills. They are beginning to develop a new capacity for holding concepts or pictures in their minds. The etheric forces that have been busy in the task of shaping their physical body are now becoming freed for other tasks as the children enter a new epoch of childhood.

One day we see our six-year-old boys blithely engaged in play with the younger children; the next, they are looking for trouble and scheming about how to climb over the fence into the neighbor's garden. They can be restless creatures at six years old, with one foot in early childhood and the other poised to step into the future. Two little six-year-old dudes walk down the street side by side. They eagerly imagine a world full of "beer and lollipops." They are bold. They are impossibly sweet. They are the boys who need our admiration and love. ✦

References

Biddulph, Steve. *Raising Boys*. London: Thorsons, 2003.

Cox, Adam J. *Boys of Few Words*. New York and London: The Guilford Press, 2006.

Gurian, Michael. *Boys and Girls Learn Differently*. San Francisco: Jossey-Bass, 2003.

_____ . *The Minds of Boys*. San Francisco: Jossey-Bass, 2005.

_____ . *The Wonder of Boys*. New York: Tarcher/Putnam, 1997.

Kindlon, Dan, and Michael Thompson. *Raising Cain*. Toronto: Random House, 2000.

Jenkinson, Sally. *The Genius of Play*. Stroud, UK: Hawthorn Press, 2001.

Mogel, Wendy. *The Blessing of a Skinned Knee*. New York: Penguin, 2001.

Neall, Lucinda. *Bringing Out the Best in Boys*. Stroud, UK: Hawthorn Press, 2002.

Pollack, William. *Real Boys*. New York: Owl Books, 1998.

Sather, Jeanne. "Has Boyhood Become a Disease?" *Wall Street Journal*, May 2, 1997.

Seiter, Ellen. *Sold Separately: Children and Parents in Consumer Culture*. Piscataway, NJ: Rutgers University Press, 1995.

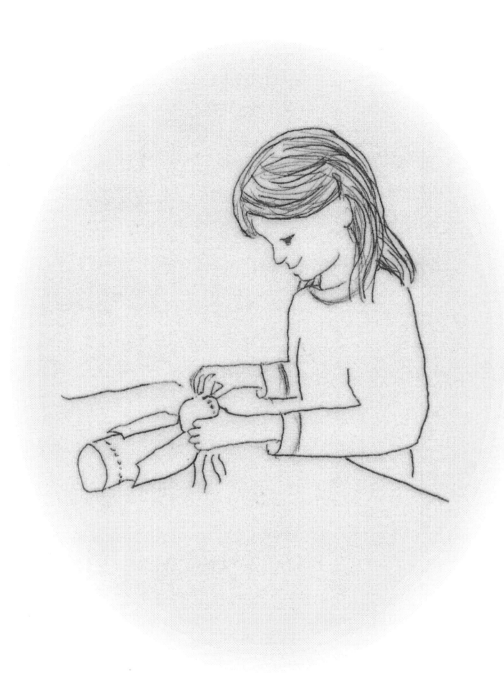

Meeting the Child's Needs—
Suggestions for Working in the Classroom

An intense impression of the child as a whole being must arise within the whole human nature of the teacher, and what is perceived in the child must awaken joy and vitality. This same joyful and enlivening spirit in the teacher must be able to grow and develop until it becomes direct inspiration in answer to the question: What must I do with this child?

Rudolf Steiner
The Essentials of Education

A Working
Kindergarten

Louise deForest

This article, written in 2005, originally appeared in a different form in *LILIPOH* in 2006. Louise deForest's success with the kindergarten program at Green Meadow Waldorf School enabled others to carry on in her footsteps. Now Louise is working for part of the week in downtown Manhattan. In light of her words in the last paragraph of this article, we can imagine the valuable service she is imparting to the children and parents in her parent-child group there, as she connects the families to purposeful work activities. —*Ruth Ker*

Three years ago a unique collaboration between Green Meadow Waldorf School and the neighboring Rudolf Steiner Fellowship Community began, with the incorporation of a Waldorf kindergarten into a community focused on the care of the elderly.

At the intergenerational Fellowship Community, founded in 1957 and based on the insights of Rudolf Steiner, co-workers and their families both live and work in the community, and the elderly participate in all aspects of life. For those in need of nursing care, there is Hilltop House, the heart of the community. This is where all meals are served, where lectures, conferences and performances are held, and where even the laundry room is located, so that those who are limited to wheelchairs or are bedridden can still take part in the extended family life around them. For the more independent retirees, there are three separate buildings around Hilltop House with a playground between them where the children of the co-workers often play. Around all this are many fields and flower gardens where biodynamic food is grown and animals are cared for, including sheep, dairy cows, horses, and chickens. It is a community brimming with life and purposeful activity, where each individual, no matter what his or her age, is able to contribute in a meaningful way to the benefit of the whole.

Just down the road, Green Meadow, founded in 1950 and serving children from nursery to twelfth grade, is one of the oldest and most respected Waldorf schools in the country. Three years ago the lower school, wanting to have more children from Green Meadow's kindergartens entering first grade, requested to add a few more children to each of the three kindergartens. For the past dozen years or so, the kindergarten faculty has felt that children today do not have the stamina or etheric forces to thrive in large classes, so the class size was limited to fourteen; to make this compatible with the budget, the teachers decided to work without assistants, which worked very well for years. When we were asked to enlarge our classes, though, an alternative had to be sought. And so the Green Meadow Child's Garden was born, housed in one of the independent living houses in the Fellowship Community.

As lead teacher in the new program, I designed the Child's Garden class to weave the Waldorf early childhood curriculum into the context of a work-based community in order to benefit everyone. Much thought has been given to providing the children in this class with as many opportunities as possible to participate in the varied activities of our adopted community, as well as to continue with the artistic activities and rhythms so important in a Waldorf kindergarten. We started the year this fall harvesting beets and leeks from the outer fields. We did this job for six weeks before moving on to the chicken house for another six weeks; then to the barn to clean out the horses' stalls, to Hilltop House to help prepare dessert for 150 people, to the greenhouse to prepare trays for planting, and so on. We do these jobs, rotating every six weeks, twice a week, Mondays and Fridays, first thing in the morning. After our tasks are completed we return to our class for rest, verse, artistic activity, snack and free play. Parents can also sign up to accompany us in our chosen work, getting to know the class in the process and seeing firsthand how very capable their children—and all the children—are.

While all children in kindergarten "work," what is unique about this group is that the whole community depends upon their effort.

While all children in kindergarten "work," what is unique about this group is that the whole community depends upon their effort. No one else will clean out the chicken house, or sweep the barn, when it is the children's turn to do so, and it deepens their experience to know that they are serving both the animals and the people around them and that they are entrusted with a significant task. Another unique aspect of this work is that nothing is done just for the class's own benefit. The vegetables harvested from the fields are sold in the Fellowship store, the eggs go directly to the kitchen for the members and co-workers, and the delicious cobblers we make are eaten at Hilltop House or sold in the store. We do the work we do because it needs to be done; our reward for work is the work itself and the joy of stepping back and looking, for example, at a clean, aired barn waiting for the animals to return in the evening. As John Donne said, "All in order, sweet and lovely."

It has been more challenging to find ways to connect and form relationships with the elderly and still keep to rather tight time constraints. Of course, we have an open-door policy and members of the Fellowship, as well as co-workers, have a standing invitation to drop in any time. One fairly independent eighty-something-year-old woman comes every Tuesday to help make bread. She stays until after snack, often reading a story to the children after their rest time; she always forgets everyone's name, but the children accept this as part of who she is, and upon seeing her coming into the room, they rush over to remind her of their names.

Those who are more confined are not able to make such spontaneous visits. So once a week the class spends the last forty minutes of the day in Hilltop House, right in the large main gathering room, the Goethe Room, and there we play traditional games such as The Farmer in the Dell or Ring-a-round the Rosie. The younger children of the co-workers and the volunteers join in our games and the elderly in wheelchairs sit around us, some watching, some sleeping and some singing right along with us. It is significant to me that this is the children's favorite day, supporting my conviction that there is a unique bond between those souls just beginning their life on earth and those who are reaching the end of their present destinies.

At least once a year, the kindergarten faculty gives the gift of a puppet show to the residents of the Fellowship. The weekly, smaller puppet shows of the Child's Garden are often held in the independent houses around Hilltop House, and all the members and co-workers who live there are invited to sit with the children and watch the puppet show. While it is often a challenge for the teacher to clear the space in the lobby, set up and take apart the puppet show afterwards, the reward happens upon looking out at our audience. We see small children, recently descended from the spiritual world, still enveloped in the intentions that brought them to earth, who are nestled up to the old men and women who are also close to the spiritual world, with their rich biographies and near-completion of their destinies. All are transported to the dreamy, honest world of the fairy tale.

All over the country and the world, teachers are noticing a difference in the children who are now incarnating. These children are incredibly smart—brilliant, even—yet socially appear at first glance rather cold, lonely, and inept. It is increasingly difficult for these children to incarnate, and we are seeing an increase in learning difficulties and sensory-integration challenges; yet they also have the ability to read us like open books. They can have wonderful, rather dry senses of humor, and a keen eye for the truth. What all of them seem to share is a certain impatience with childhood, as if they have done this already, and a strong desire to start making a difference in this world. While all of this can be a gift to any teacher, it is also increasingly difficult to carry these determined individuals in the kindergarten.

Many of us who work with these children have adapted our programs to try to meet the challenge they bring us. Some of us have incorporated more movement into our days; others have rearranged their daily schedules to allow for more time outside. Some are introducing more complicated craft projects or telling stronger fairy tales, and all of us are working more closely with doctors, therapists and eurythmists, as well as parents, to help these dear ones overcome the hindrances that stand in the way of their full potential.

While it may be too early in the life of this program to make definitive judgments, I do see a difference in the children who have participated in the Child's Garden. After their initial surprise wears off, they love to work, be it washing dishes, collecting eggs, or carrying manure in their wheelbarrows to the manure pile. More and more they come to see work as a privilege, and I have actually found that they are so satisfied by it that I have fewer discipline problems in the class. They take great pride in the fact that they know how to do whatever needs to be done and many is the time that they beg me to please not help them so they can do it themselves… and they can. Not only are their bodies strengthened and their wills engaged, but their confidence increases each day. Parents tell me that one of the biggest changes they notice in their children at home is that suddenly they want to take part in all the tasks and chores around the house. The very feminine girls who would initially prefer to sit talking in a corner soon take pride in the strength of their arms and often beg to do the most difficult task. The boys who tend to be unruly are held by the form and direction of the work itself, which carries through the whole morning. Boys and girls work together in small groups, thereby overcoming gender barriers and creating a ground on which they can later meet in play. After our work, all the children enter into their free play time with a focus and concentration that I do not see so clearly on other days, as if the movement of their limbs has now freed them to enter into imaginative and creative play. For the older children who are making the often turbulent and difficult transition between the phase of imitation and that of learning through authority, seeing me working along with them, directing them in their activities, establishes me as a true authority: one who knows how to do.

In an age when there are so many untruths for young children to sort through, work provides them with a connection to the world around them based on truth and service. Their impulse to incarnate is satisfied to some degree by the true and direct connections they make with the world around them and their spiritual intentions to contribute and make a difference in the world begin to find expression.

Many people have said to me that they wished they had a farm to which they could bring their children. While being on a farm is wonderful, the opportunities to work in the world are unlimited. Even in the innermost city, one can find meaningful ways to engage the children in work and make connections with the adults around them. Perhaps the onion bins in the corner grocery store need to be cleaned out regularly; perhaps you can pick up fallen branches in the nearby park or trim bushes. Sidewalks and stairs could use a good sweeping, trash can be picked up, doors painted, handrails sanded and oiled… the list is infinite for those with eyes to see. There may even be someone in a neighboring building who is ill and would love visits and some good kindergarten bread. As Kahlil Gibran wrote, "to love life through labor is to be intimate with life's inmost secret… and when you work with love you bind yourself to yourself and to one another." ✦

Creating a Flow in Time: Breathing through the Day with a Mixed-age Kindergarten

Barbara Klocek

There are many possibilities in shaping our time with the children in a mixed-age kindergarten. We all know that Waldorf education stresses the fundamental value of rhythm in organizing our time with the children. A health-giving foundation is laid as we breathe in and out of our activities during the day. It has been wonderful to be a part of the working group on the older child in the kindergarten and to experience the various ways that each of us have met this challenge. We thought it would be helpful to share these various ways with you to encourage you to find one that fits you, your children and your situation. Over the years I have experimented with different rhythms and have found this to be the one that is working best for me at this time.

8:00–8:20	Outdoor arrival, play, visiting with parents and children
8:20–8:40	Change shoes and circle time
8:40–9:30	Free play inside and snack preparation
9:30–10:00	Cleanup and rest time
10:00–10:30	Snack
10:30–11:30	Outdoor play
11:30–12:00	Story three days a week; walk and painting on the other days
12:00–12:30	Lunch
12:30	End of morning

Our day with the children begins at 8:00 as they and their parents begin to arrive. For the next twenty minutes the yard fills and there is the hum of voices as the children greet each other and the parents visit. We have designated this time as a "walking time," instead of running, out of respect for the many toddling brothers and sisters. At 8:20 the bell is rung and the children enter slowly into our entrance space with cubbies and change into their slippers. Then we gather on the red rug and play finger games and quiet games until all of the children have finished getting on their slippers. We sing our opening songs and verses (see below) and then joyfully dance together through circle. There is a mood of satisfaction as we finish this breathing together. We then breathe out into free play. The children eagerly flow into play, often taking up images from the circle. An activity such as bread- or soup-making, sewing, felting, fingerknitting or woodworking is begun by the teachers. Often children are invited to join these activities, especially if they were restless during circle. On Monday the older children are asked to help fold napkins, small towels, or painting cloths. This allows the younger children to find their way into the space and begin their play while the older children are helping. Often the older children can dominate the play and it is good to give the younger children an opportunity to initiate their own play first sometimes. What a nice mood it creates at the beginning of the week.

During this wonderful out-breathing of free play, the room is transformed into boats, houses, bridges, etc. A happy hum fills the room. Sometimes I hum or sing softly some of the songs from circle if the noise level is getting too loud. As we are nearing the end of free play, we ask some of the older children to help set the table for snack by carrying pitchers of water, bowls and cups. When all that preparation is finished, the teachers sit on two little chairs on the red rug (our open space) and then sing,

> With a voice so tiny, and with eyes so shiny,
> Our house elf says, let's clean our room. Can I help?

All the children gather, and our two little house elves—small dolls about four inches tall with gnome-like hats—often comment on what has been happening or make up a little movement game with the children. Then the children hear their task for the day. We keep the same task for three weeks, the same rhythm as our story. We use this time to have two or three children work together who might benefit from being together, to develop a friendship or to help learn how to do the task, often having the younger and older children work together. This conscious transition from free play to bringing order to the room has made cleanup time so much more pleasant. It creates an opportunity to let go of the imaginations from free play, and, with a fresh breath, we can then move into another activity and imagination. I find there is much less chaos. When their task is done we ask the children to come to us to see what needs to be done next so they can help with another task or wash their hands. It is wonderful to see how the tasks become easier over the three weeks and what joy the children have in completing them with a friend.

We then have a short in-breath. After the children wash their hands, they lie down on the red rug. This brings the children into stillness as I am sitting on a chair on the rug singing,

> I'm looking to see who is quiet as can be.

When I see a child is quiet I call them to me and each day a few children can sit on my lap and play the kinderharp. The older children often still want to be active and are given the opportunity to tidy the corners and to wash some of the surfaces and floors. They love this because it's almost as if they get to stay up later while the little children have gone to rest. After all are resting, there is a short lullaby sung and a few minutes of quiet. We all relax into this silence after play and clean up.

We then go on to our snack time. After snack, some children wash the tables, others set out chairs, and two older children wash the dishes with the teacher. Again, these tasks provide time for certain children to be working together and have the added advantage of promoting smoother social interactions. One year we had an older girl who frequently excluded the same other girl. We gave them the task of washing the dishes together for three weeks, and sure enough, they became friends. If we are setting up a puppet show or play many of the older children will ask to stay in and help. Usually two or three are chosen and they eagerly help, and nearly set it all up if it is the second or third time for the puppet show or play. As the year progresses sometimes the younger children also ask to help and enjoy participating "backstage."

As we go outside, often the older children will help the younger children with tying shoes or putting on rain pants. We have a large yard with a digging hole or hill (depending on the time of year), garden, sandbox, climbing structure and wagons. We have horse reins, which are a favorite activity, as well as ropes for jumping, tying, and all sorts of creative uses. All the older children learn to jump rope as the teacher turns it. Sometimes the younger ones surprise us with their ability to jump as well.

After an hourlong outside play time we come in for story on Monday, Tuesday and Friday. On Wednesday we go for a long walk and on Thursday we paint. Our story rhythm usually runs in a three-week cycle. The first week is for telling, followed on one occasion by beeswax modeling. The second week is for puppet shows, first done by the teacher, then by a few older children and then often done as a puppet show in the round where everyone participates as we pass the puppets on their journey around the red rug. The third week the story is done three times as a play. These plays are usually done in the round with simple capes and caps or crowns. Mostly everyone participates, with some children being trees in the forest, or a well or a basket—whatever images are part of the story. The parts are planned in advance and I try to choose the children for the first play who can carry it the most deeply. Often, in the following plays for pedagogical reasons children are chosen who could benefit from the role. The plays offer a wonderful opportunity for the older children to learn to carry larger parts. Children who are self-conscious or silly early in the year learn to live into the imaginations deeply and, with practice, develop poise. These plays continue the dream-like consciousness of the kindergarten, with the teacher walking beside the different children and speaking the parts,

Children who are self-conscious or silly early in the year learn to live into the imaginations deeply and, with practice, develop poise.

guiding the children throughout. So the children are not usually speaking or even acting out but rather dreaming through the story.

We have a short goodbye song (from *Let Us Form a Ring*):

> *Oh lovely sun, oh lovely earth, good friends all gathered here.*
> *Let's all join hands so there may flow, a stream of warmth and golden glow.*
> *Goodbye.*

We then all sit and have lunch, which has been brought from home, together. We used to end the day at 12:00, but found that many children were very hungry and were having meltdowns or eating in the car on the way home. When we first started having lunch at school, the children would love to sit and talk rather than eat. But when it was time to pack up they complained they had not yet eaten. We now light a quiet candle for the first fifteen minutes of lunch with the song,

> *See the little candle, shining, shining bright.*
> *Quietly we eat as we watch your light.*

After we see that many of the children have eaten most of their lunch we sing, "Thank you little candle for your golden light." When it is blown out, it is a sign that we can now talk quietly. This has led to a very peaceful lunchtime. There are always children who take more time to eat, so we often have the ones that have finished come and sit on our laps as we sing a song to them. It is a nice way to have music surrounding the children in an informal way.

Our day ends at 12:30 as the children put on their shoes to go outside and meet their parents. In our kindergarten yard there are two kindergarten classes present at the end of the day going-home time. We struggled with having so many people on the yard for several years because the children wanted to play with their friends and the parents wanted to visit; it was chaotic with so many people, large and small. Now after five to ten minutes we ring a large cowbell and everyone knows it is time to leave. Then the children staying on for nap have a peaceful yard in which to play. What a "wonder-full" day it has been.

Here are some of the songs and verses that surround our morning circle:

Circle beginning

Gentle fairies, wise elf men, come join us please do.
We bring golden light from our garden to you.
Our angels they guard us by day and by night,
From the sun and the moon and the stars shining bright,
Light fairies come to us, bring to us your golden light.

When everything is so quiet … the light fairies come, bringing light from stars and sun.
(to light the morning circle candle)

Down is the earth, up is the sky, there are my friends and here am I.

Good morning dear Earth, good morning dear Sun,
Good morning dear stones and the flowers every one.
Good morning dear creatures and the birds in the trees.
Good morning to you and good morning to me.
 (sung once in standing and again holding hands and moving around circle)

For we are guarded from harm, cared for by angels,
Here we stand, loving and strong, truthful and good.

Circle ending

I dance with the flowers, I sing with the sun. My warmth I give to everyone.

Here is a spark of Father Sun's light, to keep in our hearts so warm and bright.
(to put out morning circle candle)

References

Foster, Nancy, ed. *Let Us Form a Ring: An Acorn Hill Anthology.* Silver Spring, MD: Acorn Hill Waldorf Kindergarten and Nursery, 1989.

Sailing Our Ship
in Fair
or Stormy
Weather

Tim Bennett

As the teacher of the Rosemary Kindergarten in Seattle, I am the captain of my ship, as well as the navigator of its daily journeys into charted and uncharted waters. Inwardly the captain's heart holds two questions: Who are these children? What are their needs? Because of my responsibility for these children from the moment they pass through the gate until the moment when they return into their parents' arms, there are a few important rules I follow when on board this ship: *keep things simple, slow down, be present* for each family and child, and don't forget to *have fun and smile*.

The parents are asked to drop off their children between 8:30 and 9:00 a.m. I use this time of arrival to tidy up outside, do garden tasks, talk to parents and so on. It is the transition time from home to school and an opportunity to play outside in our schoolyard. We have swings, a slide, balance boards, stilts (for the six-year-olds), and shovels in our sandbox ready to dig for pleasure or for treasure. I also have parents turning a jump rope. And of course there are the chickens: Honey, Ruby and Blackie. We check for eggs and say good morning to our beloved chickens. Sometimes our chickens also have unusual adventures—like the day when one of the older children took Ruby from the chicken house and held her while skipping rope.

Ahoy mateys! At 9:00 a.m., I gather the families together and we begin to form a circle. As a community of people, we greet each other and greet the day. I always have a little song or verse for the season. If it's raining, as is sometimes the case in our fair city, I sing:

John has a great big pair of waterproof boots on.
Splish splash, splish splash, splish splash splish!
And John has a great big waterproof mackintosh
and John has a great big waterproof hat!
And that, says John, is that, and that, says John, is that!

Then we become a bit more reverent for a moment and we say our morning verse:

Our hearts open wide, light streams deep inside.
Stars, moon and sun shine down on everyone.
On earth now we stand, giving all our hands.
Good morning, dear friends.

Then I sing what will happen today: "Ring a ring a Rosemary day, welcome, welcome, nature walk day and painting day." After this opening to the day, I begin to feel that we are a group and that we have built up some substance through our interest in each other and our movement together as we have our daily greeting.

It is time for our ship to set sail! We head for the school gate, where we find walking partners and say goodbye to the parents and little brothers and sisters. The captain is at the helm, the crew is ready and we set out to seek an adventure in the great wide world, waving to the parents as we go. As the captain, I carry a sturdy backpack, filled with a long rope, snacks, water, a first aid kit and a cell phone. My faithful first mate (also known as the kindergarten assistant) has a red flag that we take with us to help us get across the five-way intersection on our way to the park. My rule for crossing the street is that the red flag must be in the middle of the street before any child takes a step off the curb. My intrepid assistant goes out onto the road, makes sure the coast is clear, and then we can all safely cross the street. Upon reaching the other side, the children know that they are free to run, skip, and cavort. Our nature walk has truly begun.

We have set sail and are now out on the open seas, surveying the landscape far and wide! Nature adventures are rich and nourishing for the children in so many ways. The most obvious healing aspect is simply being in nature, in the outdoors in all kinds of weather during the four seasons of the year. In the Pacific Northwest, this is possible because of the mild temperatures in both winter and summer. The children really have a daily dose of what it means to be on the earth, surrounded by nature and the ever-changing weather. We always "dress" for the weather. For most of the fall and winter, we wear raingear and a warm hat. Being in nature also brings the possibility for a strong connection with the fairy world and the materials of the earth: sticks, stones, leaves, moss and so on. The senses are enlivened when out in nature and the children more easily fall into play in a lively and healthy manner. Dirt, mud, dust, rivulets of water, autumn leaves, bugs, squirrels, spring blossoms, still air, and whipping winds all build their feeling for beauty, goodness and truth. These experiences provide a foundation in the child's will and feeling life to support the science lessons that will have deeper impact in future years. Experiencing the gifts of the earth in these early years will plant the seed for caring about the future of our planet in later years.

Experiencing the gifts of the earth in these early years will plant the seed for caring about the future of our planet in later years.

I started the daily nature walks because more children were coming to me who were weak in their physical and etheric bodies. There were also other children who were overly physical in their limbs and could not find any rest or peace. Both of these kinds of children found a healing in the movement possibilities of the nature walks. The weaker children found strength and eventually a great joy in movement. The overly physical ones could freely move and gradually come into a rhythm through the regularity of our walks. Being among the trees and under the great sky gives the children a picture and a feeling that they are a part of the kingdoms of nature. In sharing the space with the elements of the earth and the kingdoms of nature, they can find their place in the world. Of course, this happens for them in an unconscious and powerful way.

As the navigator of the journey, I chose to go to different parks during the week; we have three parks within walking distance. We go to a large woodsy park twice a week. This place is full of maple, fir and cedar trees. There are lots of hills and valleys to explore. Here the children can really get a taste for adventure, sliding down muddy hills, climbing up a fallen tree, jumping off small rocks and cliffs, and building fairy houses or shelters in the woods for those cold winter days. Sometimes I throw a rope over a tree branch and make a rope swing for the children. The older children love this. Usually we walk for a while and then stop to play in whatever secret garden we have found. This is when some of their deepest play happens. They build houses out of sticks and branches, play knights in the forest, build fairy houses or gather treasures: a bottle cap, a special key, a magic stick or stone. The children often name these beloved spots on our walk. We play at the "Rolling Hills," where there are many dirt bike hills just perfect for running up and down. Then there is "Bunny Hill," a place where a huge pile of rocks provides a home to ongoing generations of wild rabbits and former "pet" bunnies. Naming a spot makes it our own and places it on the children's growing map of their expanding world.

At this point, the crew often becomes a bit tired and hungry, so we take a short rest and serve up some grub: salt fish, biscuits and rum. Well, we've run out of fish, biscuits and rum, so it will have to be trail mix, rice crackers and water for the captain and crew today. After snack, we start back to school. On our way back, I usually play a short game to re-enliven and focus the children, helping them come along home together as a group. I like to play "Sheep and Wolves." Half the children are sheep or shepherds (the shy ones who only want to watch the game) and the other half are the wolves. I say, "Run, sheep run!" and the sheep run out from their house (a tree where they have previously gathered). Then I say, "Run wolves run!" and the wolves run and try to catch the sheep before they can get back "home." If a sheep is caught, it can become a wolf if the child wants to. I keep the game fun with a lot of running about and I always play with them. I am usually a sheep and the children love to catch me. Other games we play are seasonal games that work well outside: "What Time Is It, Mr. Fox?" or a simple version of "Red Light, Green Light." I play any simple game that has to do with running, chasing, and stopping.

I also take a jump rope along with us. We can tie one end to a tree and do all sorts of jump rope games. The games can help to build up different rhythmic movements, as well as build self-confidence in one's growing physical abilities. After games, we continue on our way back to school, stopping at different points along the way to wait for the slower ones and slow down the faster ones.

During the entire walk, I watch the children form their social connections for the day. There is something about the nature walks that helps the children breathe out into the world of the "other," not just into the world of nature. I always get the sense that the children come from all over the city and need to shed the morning car ride and whatever dramas might have been going on at home. Our adventures help the children to come into social harmony. The walks allow them to shed the past, live in the present, and move, literally, into their future. This is the magic of the act of walking into nature. The children are drawn to the world around them and then are drawn to the friends who share this world. Again and again I see the forest being the mediator in helping these friendships to blossom. For example, children who like to go "hunting" for imaginary raccoons or coyotes join together in close camaraderie. Other children who like to collect treasures gather together in search of special leaves, sticks or rocks.

There is something about the nature walks that helps the children breathe out into the world of the "other," not just into the world of nature.

Our ship glides into port at the schoolyard gate between 10:30 and 11:00 a.m. We all disembark for circle or story time. We have circle on Monday and Tuesday. We have story time on Wednesday and Thursday. On Friday, we have circle games. I also like to incorporate folk songs, simple folk dances, and some basic circus skills. All the children love to stand on my shoulders and become a giant! At story time, I usually tell the story. After the class knows the story, we can act it out. The six-year-olds always lead the acting out, showing the little ones what they know. I also do puppet shows in a similar fashion, first doing it myself and later having the six-year-olds move the puppets that have a minor role in the show. This is a place where the six-year-olds can really let their new capacities shine out for the whole class to see.

Next, we move on to our snack time, seated at three small tables. I strive to make this a time to be nourished by the food while we are in the presence of each other. I use snack time as a breathing in during the flow of the day. So we have a quiet snack with "no talking." I find that if I say, "No talking," this is clear for the six-year-olds, and the little ones will follow along. The children take this time to rest and enjoy the quiet and peace around us. Also, at snack time, I always choose two six-year-olds to be the "waiters," pouring tea and water for the others. The younger children love to be served by their older friends.

Next is our free play time. In fall and winter, we play indoors, but in spring we play outside when the weather allows. Besides the free play, in the winter we have opportunities for the six-year-olds to be involved with some projects. They make felted hats and mittens that can keep both their heads and hands cozy. I have also found that the six-year-olds like to build elaborate structures, so I make sure that there are a lot of ropes, pulleys, large pieces of driftwood and sawn wood, metal clips, and wooden clips. These materials encourage the older ones to use their growing physical strength and newly acquired ability to carry out plans to their hearts' content. It is during this free play time that we also do our artistic activities: painting, coloring, beeswax modeling, baking and cleaning.

At 12:20 p.m. we have cleanup time. First everyone leaves the room to wash their hands and get their lunches from their cubbies. When they come back into the room, they put their lunches at their places at the table and then begin to tidy away. There always seems to be a bit of magic at tidy-away time, as we set our house in order and anticipate eating our good food.

At 12:40 p.m. we have lunch. Again we begin lunch with our quiet voices, and, once everybody is settled down and eating, I tell a story from my life or stories that have been passed down to me by some colorful characters. The children love these stories and sometimes share them at their dinner tables at home! They then get ready to leave school. I often put up a balance beam on two chairs and have the children "walk over the bridge" to say goodbye to me after they have packed up their lunches. Having sailed over waters both calm and stormy, the children then find their parents, who are waiting outside on the porch to sweep them up and take them home. The old captain and his faithful first mate swab the decks, secure the rigging and make everything ship-shape for the next day's journey.   ✦

The Daily Blessing
of the Older Child
in the
Kindergarten

Ruth Ker

I cannot speak about my daily routine without acknowledging the importance of the mixed-age kindergarten configuration within which many of us work. In my opinion, the value of the mixed-age grouping for both the younger children and the older far outweighs its challenges. Repeatedly, the younger children are invaluable for keeping the older children interested in the lively play scenarios, reminding them about the wonder of new discoveries, and helping the older children to modify their robust approach to life. Of course, all of this happens spontaneously and unconsciously as they eagerly embark on the discoveries that each new day brings. During our day together, we are constantly reminded of just how important it is to the younger children that the older ones are met with limits and expectations that make the kindergarten a safe and respectful place for everyone. There is a sigh of relief and a visible change to the countenance of the older and younger children when the boundaries are maintained and disruptive behaviors are met with matter-of-fact justice. Consequently, a mood of well-being and security in the trust that the right will prevail can enter our time together.

Our day, which goes from 8:30 a.m. to noon, begins outdoors and ends with games time indoors. I find the traditional games to be a wonderful harmonizer for the social fabric of the class, so I have found a way to incorporate them into our daily routine. In the latter part of the year, in addition to ending the day with games time, we also play some of these games on our morning walks. Because we have two mixed-age kindergartens in our community, we sometimes even invite the other class of kindergarten children to join us for traditional games as the year progresses. In this way, the future first graders begin to meet each other and are already building social skills together. As the year progresses, I usually wait for the older children to request these games to be played at outdoor time as well. They often remember them from the year before when they were younger children in the kindergarten. Their awakening capacity to retrieve this memory of the favorite game for which they yearn is also a signal for me that the new consciousness of the six/seven-year change is arriving.

Below is a schedule of my daily routine followed by further explanation:

8:30-9:00	Work and play outdoors in the playground
9:00-9:30	Morning walk and play at the Big Garden
	Seasonal garden work
9:30-9:50	Lavender hand wash
	Circle time
9:50-10:00	Rest time
	Bathroom routine
10:00-10:20	Snack time
	Helpers for kitchen cleanup
10:20-11:20	Free play
	Life/artistic or handwork activity
	Coloring and handwork baskets always available
11:20-11:30	Tidy-up time
11:30-11:40	Story
11:40-12:00	Games time
	Going home or to after-school care

Day	Daily Activity	Work Activity
Monday	Painting	Spray, wrap, and iron
Tuesday	Drawing	Sewing, mending, and children's handwork
Wednesday	Bread making	Sometimes handwork
Thursday	Soup making	Watering plants
Friday	Laundry day	Washing napkins, doll clothes, etc.
	Finishing handwork	

Outdoor Play

In the morning on the play yard, time is given for a brief greeting to the children and the parents as they arrive. Some children come earlier with their parents so, when the teachers arrive on the play yard, the children are already playing together with their parents watching over them. Each year I see the need of the parents to be met in some way at this drop-off transition. A warm smile and a greeting can go a long way. I encourage the parents to visit amongst one another outside the play yard *after* they drop their children off. It can be intimidating for the young children, particularly at the beginning of the school year, to come upon a whole group of conversing adults as they (the children) try to get through the gate and into the playground. It is at this drop-off time that I can quietly say to the parents that I am seeing their child showing some of the six-year-change phenomena. They know what I mean because we have already introduced the topic of the six-year change at our beginning-of-the-year orientation meeting. We then agree to speak about this privately at a later time.

As soon as possible after entering the play yard, the teacher takes up meaningful work. The children often come to help, but many are immersed in their play and look up once in a while to see the teacher at work raking, building paths, weeding, filling birdfeeders, digging trenches, planting, pruning, edging, shovelling, digging over the compost, chopping wood, or building fires in the cob oven. Swings, a sandbox, a cob oven, a playhouse, a rolling hill, gardens, flowerbeds, compost bins, birdbaths, wheelbarrows, wagons, a water pump, grass, trees, mud, and stones provide ample opportunities for earth, air, fire, and water experiences.

As the year goes on, we begin to see the behavior manifestations of the six-year transformational change at our outdoor time. Children who, previously, were happily engaged in methodical, engrossing play begin to run around with frenzied gestures, climb as high as they can on the structures available, chant "Na, na, na, na, na" (mood of the fifth) rhymes, whisper things and giggle at the top of their lungs, and so on. Meeting these behaviors in a firm, loving way with imaginative pictures helps: "The horse next door gets frightened when he hears those loud sounds." "We need to hear Brother Robin's song instead of the squawking parrot today. That parrot is scaring away the other birds." Enlisting the children's help in a focused activity also helps.

It's important for the teacher to remember that the older child's etheric body is seeking out movements to assist it as it is actively working in the child's body to complete its task before becoming more liberated for future tasks. It is at this time that we witness many chaotic and frenzied movements on the part of the children, and often a state of disequilibrium and puzzling polarities. Please refer back to Section One to deepen your understanding of the outward signs of this time of transformation.

In order to assist the etheric body in its work, we will sometimes arrange movement journeys or obstacle courses outside on our morning walks. On our way to the Big Garden we will play "Follow the Leader" while we balance on logs, crawl through tire tunnels, roll down hills, hop on hopscotch stones, or skip across the field. Helping the children to find appropriate channels for the burst of energy they are experiencing (until they are able to self-regulate) is part of our work with the older children. It is also reassuring to see that the children themselves will unconsciously seek out different movements. This year, several times the children dropped to their knees and crawled across the one-acre meadow on our morning walk.

The children can be just as impulsive with their social blunders as they are with their body movements. Sometimes repeating what they say to one another and then giving an alternative way of saying it can be a helpful tool for the teacher. One could say to the child, for instance, "Is it better to say, 'GIVE THAT TO ME RIGHT NOW!' or, 'Can I have that when you're finished?' " The children generally hear the proper way to say things, especially if the teacher repeats accurately the voice intonations of the child.

At the end of our outdoor play time a bell is rung in the playground. (I searched for a long time to find a soft-sounding bell that has a sound close to the musical note of A). We learn at the beginning of the year that when the bell rings, we put away our things outside and come to the teacher right away. In order to accomplish this smooth transition, I spend time at the beginning of the year playing the "bell game": I hide, ring the bell, and then the children come and find me. Then, at some point I say to my colleague, "From now on every day, we'll play the bell game, and when we can remember every day to come right away after tidying, then we'll be able to go on adventures."

Talking to my colleague so that the children can overhear what I say is a tool that I have found to be very effective. The children are more likely to listen to my comments to her than if I address them directly. After we learn about the bell game, we can then go on our morning walks, and later on even to the farm and on other end-of-the-year field trips.

This is how our morning walks proceed: The bell signals that it's time to leave where we are and go on our morning walk. As we wait by the gate for everyone to put away their toys and to arrive, I choose two children who will be the kings to lead us to the Big Garden. The children are eager to be chosen to be the kings and lead the parade, so they put away their toys quickly. This satisfies a much-needed desire on the part of the older children to be the leaders or the bosses. If the kings forget to wait for everyone and consequently run on ahead, then I call them back with the bell and they wait until another day to be the kings. "A helpful king waits for all the other people when she leads the parade." Often, the younger children do not want a turn until the year is well underway, and the older children can be even more helpful by taking the hand of a younger one and assisting them to be a king for their very first time.

Our morning walk reveals many different spectacles throughout the seasons—the waxing and waning of the flowers and vegetables in our garden, how the sunflowers look up at Father Sun at the end of the summer and then hang their heads down as Autumn arrives, the colorful leaves that Lady Autumn and Fire Flick have been painting, King Winter and his Snow Fairies going up and down the mountain, Jack Frost's amazing paintings of the ice and frost crystals, mushroom fairy rings, caterpillar journeys across our vegetable garden and then the inevitable discovery that the caterpillars are gone, and now we see so many butterflies, and so on. But, most importantly, there is also work to be done at the Big Garden. This work is something the older children relish, especially if they can be "in charge" of something. Many hours are spent harvesting worms, building homes for these squirmy creatures, and seeing who can collect the biggest "family" of worms—all of this under the guise of making a trench or making a planting row for the seed children. Another valuable task is the watering of the garden—many hours have been whiled away doing water play on a sunny day. Needless to say, quick results are not the expectation!

The older children also love to make suggestions about what they think is needed (for example, a ladder to pick the beans off the bean pole) and then remind the teacher many times about its importance: "Teacher, remember about that ladder? When can we do that?" If the teacher can connect to their suggestions, the children will take up this task with great satisfaction and authority. A bond can grow between the children and the teacher that is reminiscent of the feeling "we are in this together." Because this transition into the six/seven-year change is often called "first puberty or adolescence," it is good to cultivate this feeling of togetherness, and to give the unconscious message that the teacher understands their need to have more authority and will meet it in ways that are good for the whole kindergarten family. This is one way we make a bridge from working as a model for imitation to the next developmental phase that the six- and seven-year-olds are expanding into—the stage of responding to a beloved authority.

At the Big Garden, there is also a little forest. It is here that the children believe the Fairy Mother lives. I see how important it is for the older children to deepen their imaginations about what her house looks like inside the hollow tree, where her front and back doors are, who her helpers are, and so on. They build paths for her, make stair steps out of stones, and leave little offerings by her door. Sometimes she leaves things for them, too. I am reminded that the changes the older children are experiencing do not signify that the children now need intellectual understandings. Rather, the six/seven-year transition time asks for the teacher's assistance to create opportunities that allow the older children to cultivate expansive inner landscapes into which their newfound, rich picturing capacities can pour.

If the teacher can connect to their suggestions, the children will take up this task with great satisfaction and authority.

When it is the end of our play/work time at the Big Garden, the bell rings again, our toys and tools are put away, and kings are chosen to lead us back to the school. At the beginning of the school year, we learn that the big children of the grade school are inside their rooms and do not want to be disturbed while they are writing in their books, so we walk quietly by their windows. This prepares us to arrive at the school door and enter inside with a semblance of calm and order. Of course Dusty Gnome awaits us inside, and our arrival will probably wake him and Redbird up. The children often bring back sticks, moss, berries, or rocks, and give them to Dusty in his home under our nature table. Sometimes we have to help him houseclean as the year goes on because the offerings to his underground home have become so plentiful. I also try to listen to the children's conversations and hear what was important to them during our morning outdoor time. Then I can bring some of these things to our nature table later. The older children often have wise, sometimes humorous, and vivid imaginations about the mysteries we experience. Oftentimes I get my cues from them as to how to arrange the nature table. Each time we arrive back into our classroom, there is always some child who draws our attention to what is new on the nature table. In this way, what we have enjoyed outdoors has its place inside as well.

Transition to Indoor Time

Our arrival in the classroom finds some of us changing wet socks and pants. We take off our outdoor clothes, hang them up properly, put our dirty laundry in the basket by the door, and make our way to the circle rug to put on our shoes. I find it makes a great difference if I can model a slow pace and a calm presence before we open the door from outside and after we enter the cloakroom. I even slow down my speaking and gestures as if we have all the time in the world to accomplish our next tasks.

The children's places at the rug are marked by their indoor shoes and a picture card. The card is the same symbol that also marks the child's cubby. They don their shoes, leave the cards behind, make their way to the line-up for the lavender hand-wash, wash their hands accompanied by a loving towel-dry from teacher, and then make their way back to their place still marked by their cards. They sit down and wait until the teacher asks a friend to pick up all of the cards.

Circle Time

Then circle time can begin. We begin circle with the same verses each day and end with a lullaby that beckons us into rest time. The beginning verses, along with the lavender hand-wash, are designed to help pull the children into themselves and to help ground them after our long outdoor playtime.

I value the importance of a program with a balance of outdoor and indoor opportunities. In our world where the children see the adults in their lives busily occupied with many outward activities, I think it's important that young children experience how to regulate themselves in an indoor environment. Children cannot always do this for themselves, so a well-planned circle with large and small movements can "massage" them into a receptive and calmer state.

The physical changes of the six/seven-year transition are often accompanied by what appears to be great restlessness in the children's bodies, and it's important to help the children find ways to bring control over their impulsive gestures. Otherwise, the change becomes even more distressing for them and others around them. Impulse control is something that children can learn through strong rhythms and imitation of the gestures of beloved others. Circle time provides opportunities to expand gestures and then bring them back into form, and this subtle massaging activity can have wondrous effects on the older child.

At circle time, I work with some mood-of-the-fifth circles (effective tools for pulling the older child back into a more dream-like state), developmental journeys (ample variety of movements to assist the etheric in penetrating the whole body and to help children who may have retained reflexes), fairy tale circles (to assist burgeoning picture imaginations), and seasonal or festival themes.

Sometimes the older children will have ideas about how to augment these circles. They are moving into a phase where being met as an individual becomes important. It can be therapeutic for the classroom setting to listen and respond to the older child so that he or she feels heard. The younger children are often still operating as a group ("a bunch of grapes") while the older ones are beginning to individuate. I remember a Christmas festival circle that we did with the parents present. Beforehand, one six-year-old boy said, "I think just one child should sing that part." This child's mother is Werbeck-trained and I knew he had witnessed many of her performances, so I took his response to mean that he would like to sing that part of the festival play alone. He was overjoyed when I asked him if he could sing that part of the play for us.

I do not allow the children to interrupt the circle or verse, but sometimes their impulses can be taken up into the circle and this can be satisfying for all. Another time an older child came to me at free play time and said, "Why don't the bunnies crawl into their holes?" I knew he was referring to the bunny circle that we had done together that morning, so the next day at circle time the bunnies found holes within the classroom into which they could crawl. This was great fun, we practiced crawling (which the child who had requested this activity had not practiced much of in her first year of life) and bunny games prevailed at free play time for a few weeks after that.

Sometimes the children will also give suggestions about gestures while we're in the middle of circle. "Let's do hopping steps now." This is a little trickier, but to connect to the older children's suggestions and incorporate them without reinforcing interruptions at circle time can be a valuable skill for a teacher to cultivate. However, care must be taken to ensure that it doesn't become a game to see how many times circle can be interrupted. At times when I suspect the child is wanting to deflect the attention to him- or herself in an unbeneficial way, I just insert matter-of-factly while midstream in the verse or song, "It's teacher's turn," while carrying on with my gesture and the content of the circle. One can determine when a suggestion emerges from an older child's deep-seated need, if the suggestion is something that could be important for the whole group, or if it's an attempt to interrupt the circle. In any case, it's imperative that the stream of verse, song, and gesture keep flowing.

The older children, of course, manifest responses to circle that are representative of their development. Often when they begin to experience cause and effect and the sense of time in their consciousness, they will speed up the words in a circle or they will slow it down. Or they will do gestures differently than the teachers, or they will refuse to do this "boring stuff" or repeatedly interrupt and have a "better idea." Being the center of attention and being the "boss" of things becomes important to them. Incorporating opportunities for the older children to enter the middle of the circle one at a time can change the focus so that they are awaiting their turn to do this. Circle games and some fairy tale circles can provide these opportunities.

Of course, each situation must be met with loving firmness. It is also appropriate to respond more directly to the older child. "You weren't interrupting us, were you?" or "You probably just forgot how to do this. You can watch us from the watching chair and then you'll see how we do it." Sometimes just a gentle touch or a teacher standing close by reminds an older child to join in. Also, the placement of the children at circle makes a big difference when there are those who could be disruptive while going through the stage of whispering and giggling. That is why I have the same picture cards for the child's cubby and for snack and circle placement. This way, each day I get to choose where the cards will be placed and consequently where the child will be sitting or standing.

> *I value the importance of a program with a balance of outdoor and indoor opportunities.*

During circle time, I find it is a valuable tool to just carry the assumption within myself that everyone will participate. Somehow the children pick up on this and then a gentle reminder, "Joseph, you'll be helping us," without stopping the flow of verse and gesture can serve to bring the children all along together. I also frequently imagine that I have angel wings and that I am wrapping my wings around particular children and bringing them along with me.

The eurythmist Estelle Bryer says, "When the children are school-ready, the teacher can become more authoritative and expect the children to be more correct and qualitative in their movements. Here, nods of recognition can do wonders."[1] Sometimes I have to work hard to make an individual connection with a child going through this six/seven-year transformation. If the child cares for me and we have built soul-spiritual substance between us, then it's more effective when I glance at the child across the circle with raised eyebrows.

In order to cultivate this bond of mutual interest, a home visit pays off mightily. Because of the link we have created together during our communing time in the child's home, a glance in the child's direction at circle time is all that is needed.

When I do a home visit, I tell the parents that I am coming to connect with their child, not to check out their home environment. This comment is often met with relief. Sometimes I will have a cup of tea with the parents, but mostly I am there to be with their child. In this way, the child feels my deep interest—I read his favorite story to him, watch her ride her bike, look at his very own garden space or meet her dollies. Then miracles happen overnight, and the next day in the classroom the feeling of warmth and cooperation between us is palpable.

Then comes the time in the course of the year when we can have some circle activities where the children are able to practice taking turns. This usually happens when a few of the children have completed the six/seven-year change. Then, the group dynamic can allow for waiting while watching others have turns doing something. An example of this is sitting at

Estelle Bryer, *Eurythmy for the Young Child*, 9.

circle while watching friends use the scooter boards, three at a time, or waiting while we all take turns getting wrapped in a cocoon (blanket) and then unfurled.

Another circle activity that addresses the older child's changing consciousness is, after many repetitions of a particular verse, to then begin to whisper or silently move it. During these times the whole group is very attentive, and one can see the older children looking out and away as they form the words and picture images in their mind's eye without saying them out loud. The younger children are often carried along in this circle activity just by the sheer force of their older peers' concentration.

Just as children learn through play in all other areas of life, I see that the older children in the kindergarten delight in playing with their newfound capacities. They achieve greater soul mobility by playing with their change in consciousness and the giggling, speeding-up/slowing-down, whispering, saying words internally without speaking them, and so on. If we can take up the adventure of joining them in this exploration, it can be a joy for teacher and child alike.

Rest Time

As I mentioned, the end of circle is signaled by a lullaby. The children, one by one, pick up a pillow and blanket and find a place to lie on the rug. This is a relatively new aspect of my program, something that I never attempted or felt was necessary in my earlier years as an early childhood teacher. The trigger for change for me was observing James Hillier's class at the Lake Champlain Waldorf School. The quality of peace as the children eagerly took their rest was palpable. That day, as I also used those moments to recharge myself, I realized what it could mean to a child to have regular opportunities to build the habit of "taking time." Could this be a wellspring for the child's later meditative life? I decided to incorporate a rest time into my program. And, what better time to place it than after an expansive, hour-long outdoor playtime and a vigorous circle!

At the beginning of the year, rest time is not something that some of the new children understand or have experienced as part of their routines. Fortunately, the older children have established the habit from their kindergarten experience the year before. This activity is also accompanied by an imagination: the children are the birds in the nest and Mamma Bird (the teacher) can tap the birds on their back only after she sees that they have had their rest. It generally takes about two weeks before the children are visibly drawing sustenance from these moments. Those who aren't able to settle often benefit from a little cozy nest by themselves or by being close beside the teacher. Sometimes this can be the opportunity for a foot massage or back massage—another opportunity for the teacher to bond in a loving way with the individual child and for the child to receive loving touch. It's also a valuable observation to ascertain which children respond to firm touch and which find soft touch more acceptable. It seems to me that children nowadays have very busy lives, and touch experiences are often one of the things that are sacrificed.

When Mamma Bird taps the baby birds on the back, they put away their pillows and folded blankets, go to the bathroom, wash their hands, and make their way to the snack table.

Snack Time

Our snacks vary according to the grain of the day. Keeping in mind that the children often have quick breakfasts and that they have burned off a lot of calories so far during their vigorous morning activities, we serve healthy, abundant portions. We also augment the grain with a seed or nut that then makes the food a complete protein. Children who do not have protein before coming to school can show signs of irritability, light-headedness, and lethargy. We all know how these symptoms can complicate a child's kindergarten experience! So, fresh ground almonds, ground flax seeds or ground sunflower or sesame seeds are added to the grains and a fruit or vegetable is served on the side. Drinks are made from a mixture of apple juice and herbal tea or just simply mother earth juice (water).

During snack time, we practice passing food to our neighbors. Even warm soup bowls are skillfully passed down our big, long table. We practice our social graces by asking for things with "please" and "thank you," putting our napkins on our laps, and *trying* to remain sitting with our bottoms on the benches. The act of calmly sitting, of course, becomes more difficult as the six-year-olds begin to go through the change and become like little bubbling pots.

The table has been set with placemats, cloth napkins, cups, and utensils, and our places are marked with our picture cards. The candle is lit, the blessing is sung, and then the serving and conversation begins. Some years we have quiet mealtimes because the children are unable to visit without using their loud booming voices. This also is a good opportunity for impulse control and, of course, is accompanied by an imagination so that it doesn't seem like a cruel imposition. However, most times we are able to visit, joke, and tell stories within an acceptable decibel range. Redbird inevitably lets us know if we're too loud. He hangs from a branch near our snack table and it truly is magical to see that if it gets too loud the children will report that "Redbird is turning around! It's too loud."

Redbird is a red wool bird who hangs by a string on a stick. At the beginning of the year Redbird, well known by the past year's children (who are now the older children in the kindergarten), takes up his task of accompanying my assistant around the table after snack time is over. Redbird softly "kisses" the cheek of the child whose turn it is to snuff out the candle. The children usually watch quietly as he passes to see whose turn it will be. Every year the children have their imaginations about what Redbird does when we are not at school. Often some of the things that appear in our classroom are magically attributed to Redbird. The children often leave him crumbs from festival snacks or our good bread that we bake every week. I leave it up to the returning older children to carry the imagination on to the new group of children each year.

Snack time is an opportunity to have community meals, and here I learn a lot of things: what infinity is, who God really is, that there are angels on the ceiling of the kindergarten, what video a child has watched, whose parents are arguing and about what, who is losing another tooth, who doesn't believe in Santa Claus, what misconceptions the children have, and who is starting to say and do things that signal the six/seven-year change for them. While overhearing the children as they speak to one another, I appreciate where they are in child-consciousness (which is often not where we adults perceive them to be).

At the end of snack time, Redbird kisses a child to put out the candle and we say "thank you" for the meal. We also mention the day's activity by saying "Blessings on our painting (or drawing, bakeshop, or soup-making) day." Two children are chosen to clear the table, do the dishes, and sweep the floor under the table. They don their aprons and proceed, while the other children are called to come and place their cups on the tray by the sink and then, one by one, they enter the play.

Free Play Time

Let the enthusiastic delight begin! It's a wonder how the children's eagerness and spontaneity is there day after day! The children seriously choose their props and find their way into some friend's imagination, and then the alchemy begins. I have some everyday toys that the older children tend to appreciate. Heavy wooden boxes become boats, sleighs, or nests; leftover wooden rounded pickets from our picket fence are used for skis, crutches, skateboards, and roof panels; a thickly laminated, heavy wooden slab becomes a computer, TV screen, or performance stage. All of these heavy things are lifted high into the two climbing platforms. Because these platforms are across from each other, the children often attach fingerknit wires between them and arrange pulleys for transporting baskets of things across the room or for giving babies rides. Some dress-ups also facilitate the older children's imaginations. The white skirts and tops stimulate weddings, and a variety of hats stimulate the pictures the children have of the worker archetypes of the world. Of course this leads to who is the boss of this game. There are endless conversations amongst the six-year-olds working out who gets to be the boss.

This brings to mind a day in our free play when three kings were arguing about who would be "first boss." Finally the resolve came: "You be third boss, you be second boss, and I'll be first boss. And I get to say what we do." The three kings nodded sagely and then began to argue about who got to sit on the throne. As the discussion progressed, the third boss came up with the idea that they could move the snack table into their castle and make three thrones on it. After asking the teacher if they could use the table, they then enlisted the help of eight others to move it across the room. What a moment of pride and accomplishment for the whole class! Then the kings happily played side by side for the rest of the session decorating the chairs that they had placed on top of the table for their thrones.

For the older children, there comes a time in the year when these well-loved props fall short of their developing consciousness, and then the children can be seen at free play time sitting for long periods of time talking about what they are going to do and sometimes never quite getting down to the task. They spend so much time discussing and planning that at tidy-up time they will loudly complain that they "did not get to play." Sometimes they will sit around with their fingerknitting baskets and converse or philosophize like a group of old men or women.

When the capacity to see ideas and plan ahead arrives for the older children, they can go through a time of frustration. They haven't yet developed the skills to implement their ideas, and when they do have some success in orchestrating the specific play scenarios that they are imagining, they can also become trapped in them. They can't seem to get any further than playing the same thing over and over again, and they are reluctant to let any other peer move the imagination along. The older children can benefit from the teacher being available during playtime to help them to overcome this mire of being stuck and to give a little prop or suggestion that can help the play to move on to new horizons. The younger children are also helpful at this time. The fluidity of the younger child's play, where the child responds lightly to the props involved and then freely moves on to new scenarios, is loosening and provides a helpful remedy to the older child's newfound consciousness. The interplay of the older and younger children can help massage the older child into his new reality with more grace and comfort.

It can also be helpful for the older child to be brought into the teacher's work activity. From the perspective of working with the teacher and looking out into the classroom, the child can watch the other children's play and then can be inspired to go back into the play in a freer way.

It also helps to have some general "rules of the land" during free play time. One of our necessary rules is that "we are all together in this land." This alleviates a lot of the exclusiveness that the girls, especially, will play at when they go through the six/seven-year transformation. There are still many opportunities in the kindergarten for them to have private times with their special friends. There are also many ways that we can be all together that do not crowd others. If I see that there is a particular child that disrupts the play, I have to work harder trying to find a way that he or she can be occupied serving the play, developing new skills, or perhaps that child can be distracted into another activity until the intensity of the mood shifts.

The healing basket is one of our important tools as well. If a child's gestures have gotten away from him, then this child can administer the healing salve to the offended party. The restlessness of limbs can often translate into impulsive movements that appear to be lashing out at others. It's amazing how many of these children are not aware that their limbs actually did bump into someone else. Perhaps also, the healing silk cloth that is in the basket needs to be wrapped around the child's hands or feet while the child waits quietly for her helpful ways to return. We keep this basket in a special place in the classroom, and every year we dig up some of the root of our comfrey plant and make some more healing salve for our basket. The children experience that we use the lanolin from the sheep, the wax from the bees, and the oil from the almond tree to help the comfrey do its healing work. When we as teachers see manifestations of roughness in the child's gestures, and we sense that the child is more out of control and others are being hurt, then a time to sit with the healing cloth on the offender's hands can be just the right remedy. This needn't be a presented as a punishment. It can be administered kindly and matter-of-factly, and can give the child just the right few moments to settle back into himself.

When the capacity to see ideas and plan ahead arrives for the older children, they can go through a time of frustration.

Above all, at this time in their development, I find that the older children need adults around them who are not alarmed by them but can, instead, carry the inner stance of "I know these changes are hard for you. I understand and I will help you." The older children tend to be appreciative when they can meet a firm and loving boundary. Although initially the children will push against a boundary or a teacher, when the limit is held lovingly and firmly, the eventual response is usually a fond embrace or a desire to come closer. So much is changing in their world and they need to have the assurance that they will continue to be held surely and safely in the arms of the kindergarten.

Some of the common games that I see the older children play at free play time are master/servant (mothers tending babies, owners taking dogs for walks); tying fingerknit ropes into knotted masses; building houses, preferably without windows, and then going inside them and talking; wrapping presents and delivering them; making money; building up puppet play scenes and talking the puppets through little stories on the landscapes they've created; and finding ways to elevate themselves in their play (explained later). Each year many of these same themes repeat themselves.

Another prop that I find very useful is a variety of softly stuffed cushions. The children drag them around, use them in their houses, and derive much pleasure from the kind of sensory play where they can climb underneath and be squashed, pile them up and jump into them, and so on. Although this may seem rambunctious, it actually turns out more often to be an orderly game that enables the older children to direct the taking of turns and make sure others are out of the way. This activity can take long periods of time to organize and set up. Sometimes the children will ask the teachers if they can make a sandwich with the cushions. This starts a time of the children asking for turns to be pressed in the middle of two big fluffy pillows while the mustard and mayonnaise and lettuce are pressed onto the sandwich. This is a very important experience for the children who have sensory issues and need to be informed about the boundaries of their own skin.

During free play time, the teacher takes up a work activity like folding laundry, fixing toys and props, carving, ironing, baking, chopping vegetables for soup, or making new toys. Also, at certain times of the year, life activities like threshing and grinding grain or processing wool resonate with what's happening in nature. The older children tend to become more interested in participating in these focused activities as the year progresses.

Sometimes the older children will suggest that they can do major activities by themselves. One year a group of older children told me that they didn't need my help to make the soup anymore. It was remarkable to watch how they methodically went through the same setup and procedure in the same order that we had done all year long. The beaming sense of accomplishment that showed itself the next day as we ate the soup brought strength to the whole class. Another year a child said, "When are you going to let me clean this whole kindergarten by myself?" (Needless to say, he didn't repeat that request too many times.) When the teacher consented, he set to work with great relish. The other children watched and then started to ask him if they could help. "I guess so," he said and, one by one, the children joined in "to clean the whole kindergarten by themselves." It was heartwarming to see the joy they found in their work and to hear, "Don't help us, teacher."

I find that the older children need adults around them who are not alarmed by them but can, instead, carry the inner stance of "I know these changes are hard for you. I understand and I will help you."

In our kindergarten, all of the equipment is designed to be used in play except for our two work tables. Our cupboards have been unloaded, flipped on their side and used for four-seater boats, tables have been draped for enclosures, a play-stove turned on its side with the door opened for a fish hold, and benches overturned and ridden across the floor for bus rides. This year, I looked up from my wool carding to see that the children had emptied out the baskets that contained our drapes, silks, pillows, and blankets and were balancing these same baskets on top of the playstands. Then they climbed into them while carefully balancing their steps and, from their perches on top of the playstands, surveyed the whole room. Next they began to rent out their "apartments and beds" for the money that others were making in another part of the room. The imaginations are endless when even the physical equipment can be transformed.

At the time when the children themselves are stretching taller and spreading up through their ribcage and out through their limbs, it is not uncommon to see the older children work very hard at moving pieces of furniture and hoisting them on top of other pieces until they have built structures that tower up toward the ceiling. I like to be close to make sure that these three-dimensional works of art are safe. The next inevitable step is that the creator climbs to the top of the creation and perches there contentedly while surveying others in play. The closer the children can get to the ceiling, the better! Often at this time we also see ladders and stair steps appearing in the children's drawings, and children can complain of "growing pains" in their legs, tummies, and sometimes arms.

It is during free play time that we also have our painting, drawing, baking, and handwork/craft times. Everyone comes to our table to paint and draw, but baking and handwork are not compulsory.

The older children can be very helpful to the younger children at handwork time. Threading needles, tying knots, and many other tasks can be joyfully accomplished by those who want to be in charge. However, it is my experience that children, old and young, prefer their play. And handwork projects that are begun can be soon abandoned in favor of interesting play happening somewhere else in the room. This is why I have handwork baskets for each individual child. Unfinished handwork projects go into the baskets.

The handwork program is something that I carefully monitor. While I have no expectation of the younger children to settle at the handwork table, I carefully watch the gesture of the older children towards handwork. It can be a sign of school readiness when the older child is able to hold interest for a handwork activity for a prolonged period of time and have the desire to work to completion on it. I have encountered numerous children who already have belief systems that tell them that they can't do something, so sometimes I sit with an older child until he or she is able to have a few empowering experiences. It is a healing moment for the children when the realization arrives that they can do things with their hands.

The younger children may begin a project that they complete much later or not at all. If I feel it is therapeutic for a child to complete his creation, then I will bring him over to it later, but mostly I honor his need to be in the play instead. This reminds me of Michael. Michael was born prematurely at twenty-six weeks, and has been with us in the kindergarten for three years. Each year he enthusiastically comes over to the handwork table and begs for a turn to make a heart pincushion for Valentine's Day. This year, his third year, is the first year that he has stayed with the task without being distracted into the play. For three years, he's been working on the same pincushion. This year, he has asked if he can make another one for his own sewing basket. (The kindergarten children who will be going into first grade make a sewing needle book and prepare a sewing basket as their project.) Readiness for working to completion on focused projects has finally arrived for Michael, and so have a lot of other characteristics of first-grade readiness.

Painting and drawing time are signaled by a song. Some of the older children generally voluntarily come to help me set up and tidy up afterwards. When everyone has arrived at the table, I open the window a crack to invite the color fairies to come in and dance on our paper. Of course the color fairies come in only when it's quiet. This can be quite a challenge for the older children, whose desire to socialize is so strong. However, painting and drawing provide more opportunities for the children to practice impulse control and self-regulation, and I am firm that painting and drawing times are quiet times.

When a few of the children have finished their paintings or drawings and have put their boards or books away, then the cleanup gets underway. Children volunteer or are asked to clean the paint pots or put away the drawing mats and crayons. Those who have finished and are not cleaning up the painting and drawing tables then move into the play to help tidy up the play props. My colleague is busy modeling the joy of tidying our little home, but many of the children need to be guided into which cleanup task they will complete.

Tidy-up Time

My approach to cleaning up the kindergarten with the children has changed over the past five years. When I began teaching over thirty years ago, I would sing a cleanup song and the children would willingly join in, imitating my activity. Through time I have seen many changes to children's reactions to this transition, and it has been hard for me to relinquish the ideal that the children should just calmly imitate my activity. More and more children cannot deal easily with this transition. Behaviors such as going limp, racing around the room wildly, hiding, sitting, wandering around holding the same prop for the duration of tidy-up, and going to the bathroom until cleanup is done are all common reactions. The following is what I have found works for me now.

When we have painting and drawing days, the children finish and leave the artistic activity a few at a time, and the first thing they see is one teacher already busy putting away the play props. This teacher leads the children into helping with the tidy-up tasks if they do not join in naturally (as explained above). Sometimes they have to be reminded about their task if working alongside them with enthusiastic example does not work. I have found it helpful to give some of the "nerve-sense" children their own quieter space so that they are able to focus. This can be done by having them wind ropes or fold cloths or sort crayons, for instance, away from the main tidy area where the other more thick-skinned children are moving around. For extremely sensitive children, I have given them the opportunity to do these activities inside some draped playstands so that they have a shelter from what they perceive as the chaos that erupts in the room.

On the other days, when play precedes tidying up, the teacher sings "Let us form a ring" to call the children together, sits on the floor with arms crossed, sings a song while lighting a candle, and then assigns tasks. These are the words of the song:

I'll light a little candle now,
And help it shine so bright.
It will help me tidy up,
I'll clean with all my might.

Some years, the children are able to move into the tidy-up, see what is needed, and work alongside the teachers doing the tasks. I have also found that, with some groups of children, giving specific tasks to get them started is helpful. After the tasks are assigned the teacher covers her eyes ("I'm closing up the curtains") and then counts to ten, "opens the curtains," and sees that the children are well underway with their jobs. The children love to scurry away and be busy with their task so that when the teacher "opens the curtains," she can see that they are already at work. Covering up my eyes and then opening them again adds an element of playfulness to our work. I also find it much easier for the children to transition into tidy-up time if they have an opportunity to collect themselves first. Crossing the arms and singing our tidy-up song accomplishes this. Assigning tasks gives them forward momentum, and then they are able to imitate again instead of getting caught up in the nervous agitation of the transition. As mentioned above, there are still many sensitive children who need to be removed from the change in activity as their friends scurry around the room. Scrubbing a pot, sweeping a floor away from the main area of activity, wiping down a table, sitting on a chair and coiling up fingerknit ropes can all be more solitary tasks which are calming for these sensitive children.

When all our toys are put away, the story candle is ready, and our benches are circled around the rocking chair, then story time may begin.

Story Time

Each year, the stories I tell depend on the group of children in the kindergarten. When their recall memory capacity develops, the older children will begin to request stories that they remember from the year before. I try to honor these requests, especially if they are beneficial for the younger children as well. These stories are like old friends to the older children.

A story is told at least five times, sometimes more. Then it is often pretended together as we do a play, or it is presented as a puppet play as well as a play. I usually work with a story in this way for two weeks at least, and therefore the story sinks deeper and deeper into the children's consciousness.

Each year we have a continuous nature story theme (like the adventures of a little mouse through the seasons), and during the two weeks of the main story, the nature story may be inserted. Often the nature stories can be developed to bring in a curative story element to the children. Perhaps the little mouse had some repercussions from stealing the cheese! (Stealing can be one of the habits that an older child will try out while passing through the awakening that happens at the six/seven-year transformation).

As the year progresses and after we've heard the story many times, the older children relish the opportunity to do plays of the stories. This is a way we can take the story into us on a deeper level, and pretending a play can be a beginning bridge to the drama that they will later experience in the grade school. When we line up the benches in a row at story time it's a signal that we are going to do a play. Right away the children are saying, "Can I be the princess?" or "I want to be Rumpelstiltskin." I begin by saying "The teacher will know whose turn it is," and then I place large cloths on the floor for different places in the story. "This is the king's forest," or "This is the fire where Rumpelstiltskin danced." Then I bring a child to the place. "And here is Rumpelstiltskin."

When we pretend or dramatize the stories, the children wear drapes or costumes while the teacher leads them through the story in a dream-like way. Sometimes some of the older children will spontaneously speak the words of the character or thing they are pretending to be, and sometimes the teacher just tells the story as the children move through it, often holding the teacher's hand.

Sometimes the story theme finds its way into our circle or play time as well. During playtime, the children will find the same props or make up their own costumes, and then an older child will often direct/tell the story.

As mentioned above, nature stories are also told and curative stories are helpful for the children going through the change. There's nothing like hearing what happened to the little princess when she wouldn't let her sister play with her friends; or what about Mousie-Nibble-Tooth when he hid behind the tree instead of helping to clean up the nest?

As the years have passed, I've noticed that different groups of children have different interests that come forth. Sometimes I've felt that I could perceive a bit of their destiny together. One year the children persistently begged to have a play each day. "Can we pretend the story today?" Their eighth grade Shakespeare play was a wonder to behold. Another year, the children were constantly doing puppet plays. Sometimes during the course of the year, we will invite the parents in to see our plays. The younger children sit with their parents while the older ones play out the story. The preparation beforehand is a wonderful exercise in developing group qualities that the older children have been struggling to cultivate. Sometimes they work out that two children move the same puppet or that, in the play, there are two or three of one character. I try to be available to assist but leave the arranging up to them as much as possible. Of course, a word of suggestion at the right time is often helpful. Sometimes if someone is left out, I will suggest that the child could play the music (kinderharp or tone bars). It's surprising to see how they work together and often come up with solutions that I wouldn't have thought of. All of this is done with the same quality of dream-like play that they also carry into their playtime.

After story time is over, I put out the candle while singing a song. We then stand and say a verse together and then we play games. Games time interfaces with the time that the children are dressing to go home or to our continuing care program. So, while my colleague comes and takes the children one at a time to dress for going home, the rest of us are occupied in focused play together. The parents wait outside the door.

This way makes this transition calmer. Because the children are not usually in the cloakroom area all at the same time, and the parents are waiting outside, we can control this transition with a bit more grace. It is also an opportunity for us to bring to the children some of the old traditional games, which in olden times used to bring neighborhood children together in the spirit of cooperation and fun.

Games Time

These games belong to a rich inheritance that our society is running the risk of losing, and the children love them. To see which games are favored by which children can bring many insights. There are often requests, but I usually rely on my instincts as to what particular game would help to harmonize the events of the day so far.

There are already so many uncontrollable changes in the body, consciousness, emotions, and social realms of the older children that they especially need the security of being able to rely on events happening in the usual order.

There are also other kinds of games that we play at this time. Depending on the energy level of the children and the mood of the group, we will play floor games, finger games, traditional games, obstacle courses, or use the scooter boards or other props.

These games rely on the children's abilities to be able to take turns, to wait, to be in leadership or following roles, and to cooperate for the overall benefit of the group. It can be beneficial for some children to learn how not to be first. Perhaps the hardest lesson learned is waiting for another day if we don't get a turn today. Although the younger children tend to be more accepting, this can be difficult for the older children and especially for an only child. Many productive conversations with parents can ensue and, as a result, the traditional games can be a teaching tool for all of us to show how important these social lessons can be for these children. Valuable skills are developed in the children as they are stretched by these structured play opportunities.

Later in the year, we play skipping games with the skipping rope that we have made from the children's fingerknitting. We know the year is coming to an end when the parents arrive to see us outside, skipping to our jump-rope rhymes.

And this brings us to the end of our kindergarten day. During the final tidy-up at the end of the session, my colleague and I share observations of the joys and challenges of the morning. To record these observations can be very fruitful, especially when one discovers after looking back upon them that there are certain repetitive behaviors happening with a particular child that may signal the six/seven-year change.

As I look back over this article, I am reminded of the importance of our daily and weekly rhythms. If any changes occur in our routine, there is always a ripple effect for the older and younger children. There are already so many uncontrollable changes in the body, consciousness, emotions, and social realms of the older children that they especially need the security of being able to rely on events happening in the usual order. We have found that we can shorten or elongate aspects of our rhythm, but changing the order of things can affect adversely the well-being of our kindergarten family.

When it comes to the weekly rhythm, it is surprising to see how many children gear their week according to which day it is. When they say, "What day is it?" we know they mean, is it porridge day or is it painting day?

Working with the older children on a daily basis can be a challenge. However, a teacher who compassionately appreciates the tremendous upheaval these children are undergoing can contribute much to the immediate well-being of the children and their families and the children's later success in the grade school. We, as teachers, can also experience the joy of taking our place by the child's side as she or he goes through one of life's major transformations. Let's celebrate the emerging butterfly!✦

References

Bryer, Estelle. *Eurythmy for the Young Child: A Guide for Teachers and Parents*. Spring Valley, NY: WECAN, 2005.

Movement Journeys: Enticing the Older Child to Intentional Movement

Nancy Blanning

When planning activities for kindergarten classes, the six- and seven-year-olds have always stood as both an inspiration and a challenge. I knew that if they could be happily enticed into interested participation, then the rest of the group of children would follow them. The needs of this age group in particular have always stood in the background of my thinking. They constantly provoked the questions: Is it true that older children (boys especially) will do what they want and need to do no matter what the teacher says or how he or she tries to redirect them? If so, how can they be given the means to do what they need and want to do in a socially acceptable and pedagogically sound manner? Years of watching and pondering the children have led me to develop movement journeys.

Certain understandings of the "loves" of the children began to emerge out of this phenomenological process. Children love adventures and rich imaginations. At story time we watch them dive into imaginative pictures where there is much movement, all of it in their interior landscape. They love challenges. As their muscles and skeletons mature, their sensory development insists that more complicated, daring movements be tried and mastered. They also love playfulness and humor. Even though they sometimes seem to want a steady diet of unruly silliness, they also long for moments of quiet and reverence in contrast to the expansiveness that impels them. Rich language and rhythmic speech further appeal to what the children crave as they nurture and mature their senses.

As well as their "loves," the children's needs began to become more obvious to me as I contemplated the older child in the kindergarten. What I perceived as the wish of most teachers—to have circle time as the crowning moment of the kindergarten morning—also provoked some further questions. Children in general, and often the older ones in particular, seemed harder and harder to engage in traditional circles. I witnessed many circles where children who did not engage well were either passive and non-imitating or wild and disruptive. Is it possible that the "loves" described above and needs for physical and sensory development were not being met, making it difficult, if not impossible, for some children to participate in the more subtle rhythms of our traditional circle times?

Our culture is becoming more entertainment-oriented and increasingly passive. Productive, purposeful movement that has always come with meaningful work is a rare activity for children now. Active play is harder to encounter in the child's more sedate and car-bound life experience. Safety concerns require children be kept close to home and indoors. A roaming-the-neighborhood childhood of former times is a distant memory for even most adults. Children are more confined and more restrained. The culture encourages them to direct their play toward technology and couch-potato entertainment.

But the need to strengthen, integrate, and coordinate the physical body through movement is undeniable. If it does not happen in guided ways—work, chores, traditional ring games and children's games, for example—an outlet will be found in other ways to satisfy developmental needs. And what we see of the children is too often chaotic, frenetic, stiff, and mechanical. Archetypal, human wholeness strives to manifest itself, but environmental conditions thwart these healthy developments again and again.

The subtleness of the adult's gesture, reverence of mood, and interest in the unseen archetypal world nourishes the imaginative pictures that are flooding into the children.

After much observation and contemplation, some understandings began to awaken in me. And I began to see a way to meet the movement needs of these children. Happily, it seemed possible to join the children's (and teacher's) "loves" and needs through movement and imaginative pictures. Like circle time, movement journeys utilize fun activities to experience polarities, thus creating a kind of breathing. The mood, tempo, volume, and gesture of these journeys pulse rhythmically back and forth from expansive and bold to contracted, contained, and quiet.

These contrasting experiences give opportunities to develop and strengthen the foundational senses of touch, life, self-movement, and balance. (See the article in Section One on "Seeing the Wholeness of the Child" for more on this subject.) Young children long to develop these senses, and we want to assist their unfolding in a healthy way. Traditional circle games blend a wonderful balance of these sensory needs. In the "olden days" before mainstream research, no one knew that "Ring Around the Rosy" and "Circle to the Left, Old Brass Wagon" were helping to mature the senses of self-movement and balance. Children just loved them because they were satisfying and fun. We can take the wisdom of these circle games and elaborate upon them to consciously offer what we see the children needing.

The movement journey may also be seen as an imaginative obstacle course. Chances to climb up and down, balance, jump, hop, spin, skip, gallop, tiptoe, crawl, roll, fly, swim, duckwalk, and otherwise frolic and cavort through imaginative terrain transform this circle time into an adventure. With the six- and seven-year-olds in mind, there exists an element of challenge which inspires their interest.

To prevent these movements from getting too expansive or fast and loud, all the movements are tied together with song, verse, and rhythmic speech. These key elements set and sustain the pace. The speech must be rhythmic in a lively way and the imagination vivid enough to enter into easily. It is remarkable how well the children are carried by the rhythmic speech and song. Held in this way, children in a mixed-age class of eighteen will patiently wait until all have climbed up and down Jack and Jill's hill (ascending and descending balance beams) when they are held by the speech. Adding a hand-gesture element for the children waiting also helps them to stay engaged.

The hand-gesture element has its consciously-chosen place as well. An adventure only remains fun when interspersed with some rest. A chance to sit and express the gestures with arms, hands, even tiny finger movements, affords some respite. These games encourage finer movement right down into the fingertips and help to waken up consciousness as well as dexterity.

Movement journeys are intended to be a support for the circle time, not a replacement. We strive in the kindergarten to address the child's need for verbal and non-verbal archetypes. The subtleness of the adult's gesture, reverence of mood, and interest in the unseen archetypal world nourishes the imaginative pictures that are flooding into the children, reminding them of their origins. Yet, in our time, so many aspects of life seem to deny the children the preparatory steps of coming into the body through purposeful movement. This gap is what the movement journeys offer to fill.

To get the full benefit of a journey, it is ideal to set it up in a separate large space such as a eurythmy room. It can also be adapted to the classroom as circumstances necessitate. If the apparatus is too big or too difficult to arrange in a classroom, it can be set up in the hallway and the class can be guided out to that area by the teacher, including this in the imagination of the journey. The journeys are usually arranged in blocks of four to six weeks, one time weekly, as a special activity, usually in place of circle time that day. I know teachers who also adapt this and use a movement journey every day for a week or two.

It is critical that all movements and all imaginations we bring to the children be filled with liveliness, enthusiasm, and joy, and our full, inner participation. This includes both the large, boisterous movements and the quieter, more reverent times interspersed throughout the imaginations. While these journeys have a therapeutic component, it is important that the movements not be done slavishly, lest the movement become mechanical rather than healing and enlivening. All movements must hold truth and authenticity, so we have to be good observers of our surroundings to represent archetypal gestures well.

It is further hoped that the examples of circles or movement journeys in Section Five will offer inspiration for teachers to create their own original work. Each group of children is different and each teacher has individual gifts to share. Once one has some practice with this idea, the movements and imaginations that will best serve the individual group of children will speak to the teacher. Blending our understanding of developmental movement with rich imaginations leads to a healthy balance. This balance helps alleviate the pitfalls of being too mechanical in our movements or of only living in pictures without careful attention to gesture. The more deeply we penetrate the movements and are true to the image being created, the more the children will be drawn, through their interest, to imitate us. This movement enrichment offers an important opportunity for our children's development that can be a healing therapy for them as well.

The Role of Handwork: Developing Skills and Meeting the Needs of the Older Child in the Kindergarten

Barbara Klocek

Should handwork have a place in the kindergarten? Does it serve the children in some way or does it keep them from play? What is appropriate in the class and why? Does handwork keep the children or teachers focused on product rather than process?

In my kindergarten I have found that there is a place for handwork. It serves the children by providing them with a means for exploring substances, as well as helping them to refine their fine motor skills. The exploration of texture, new materials, and tools unfolds in a mood and process very much like that of creative play. I find that the older children in the class love the challenges the materials give them. The younger children (the four- and young five-year-olds) do not participate in some of these activities, and this allows them more space for their own imaginative play while the older children are engrossed in the handwork.

If the older children are not given challenges, often they become restless and disruptive. By being presented with wood, yarn, wool, needles, and thread, they learn to work with their hands in new ways. I have also found that the children who are not drawn to fine motor skills are often the ones who need practice in this area. We need to balance the breathing tendencies of each child with the question, Does this child need a larger or smaller focus and movement experiences throughout the day, the season, or the year?

Working with the hands on a project unfolding over time develops skills and soul qualities (like patience, for instance). There is a satisfaction in participating in bread making, making our own sandpaper, learning to screw a vice on the table, or to drill a hole for a peg. Carding wool, making a fingerknitted belt or their own puppet requires a focus that becomes strengthened by practice. This serves the children well as preparation for the challenges of first grade.

Just as we seek to create a balance of large/small and slow/quick movements to create a healthy breathing in our circles, so we need to look at our day to see that this breathing is in the activities we bring to the children. I have found the use of handwork brings a much-needed focus to the child who is restless or chaotic. It also brings the joy of creating to the children and begins to build a practice of patience and persistence. The ability to transform wood, wool, paper, yarn, and cloth can reflect the child's own developmental transformation. The children love to play with the materials and experience the alchemy of the changes that the materials and even they themselves experience. So how does this look in the stream of the year in the kindergarten?

In the beginning of the year we are very busy learning how to go through our day, making new friends, and exploring the wonderful kindergarten spaces. Making bread is a favorite weekly activity—wonderfully tactile, from the sifting of flour to the kneading of the dough. We do this as a two-day process, with the mixing the first day, rising of the dough overnight, and then forming and baking the next day. And what a favorite snack it is! In the winter we also make soup one day a week and have many helpers chopping.

In the fall it is traditional in our kindergarten to make swords for Michaelmas. For many years, every child was encouraged to make a sword. The younger children would like to start one but were usually not developmentally able to sustain their interest and attention. I was reluctant to work with only the older children initially because I wanted the class to form as a whole. Yet I have found that the older children love to be acknowledged and given individual tasks. Whether it is in tying shoes or in helping the younger children put on rain gear, the older ones thrive on helping and on having challenging tasks. So for the last three years, only the older children have made swords. Making swords is a process that takes at least two weeks of sanding, rasping, drilling, painting, and oiling the wood. What a relief it has been to work only with the older children who have been "champing at the bit," while the younger children watched with much interest and anticipation. The more eager younger ones were encouraged to work on three swords for the kindergarten during this time, to give them direction and a way to participate in this activity. This allowed for a much more sanguine way of working for these younger ones.

To ensoul the sword in the right way I created a verse for circle time:

I will polish my sword,
so strong, so bright.
I will use it for the right,
not for some silly quarrel or fight,
but to drive away evil I will try,
and protect those who are weaker than I.

During the week of the Michaelmas festival we all dye a golden silk with the marigold petals we have dried. In the story we tell, the children have heard how Michael gave a cape of light "to give you courage, strength, and might." The older children are formally presented with their finished swords as a last activity on our Michaelmas Friday. A note goes home to the parents giving them the verse to help them carry the right mood with the sword. All of the children go home with a golden silk cape and a crown for Michaelmas, the older ones proudly carrying their swords.

I have also found that the children who are not drawn to fine motor skills are often the ones who need practice in this area.

Making crowns is a wonderful activity that happens several times throughout the year. These are simply made and I have heard from parents how they enhance dress-up play at home. In the fall when we are hearing a Native American Indian story, we make Indian crowns. These are made with a strip of felt tied with yarn in the back, on which the children thread six little wooden beads. A few children at a time are with me, while the other children are playing. This allows me to observe the child's eye-hand coordination. With the older children, if there is difficulty with the task I often speak to the parents at our Thanksgiving conference time and ask them to help their child by giving them opportunities at home to refine these skills.

We also decorate crowns again at wintertime, either for Three Kings' or Valentine's Day. They are made of different colored cardstock that I have cut into crowns. How the older children love to cut out hearts or use the hole punch for jewels, glue them on and, when dry, lovingly wear them.

Often for Christmas, we will sew a very simple gift for our parents. I cut out a square for a dream pillow, or a heart for a pocket full of love (stuffed with wool and lavender). I have heard of the opinion that children should not be sewing at such a young age, but rather it is better that they do fingerknitting instead. My experience has taught me that fingerknitting is much more difficult than sewing, and if one is not particular about the stitches, most children who are four-and-a-half and older love to sew. I am often asked to cut out a fish so that the child can sew a present to take home for his kitty.

After Christmas, I take the next six weeks to teach the older children to fingerknit. I have come up with a little verse: "Catch a little fish. Oh, it is so big. Pull its tail, and make it small instead." Most children take to fingerknitting easily and then want to sew their fingerknitting into horse reins, a rug, a basket, and once, a child asked to sew mittens. This is a challenging activity for some children. In order to do fingerknitting children need to have the ability to focus and to pass through an important developmental stage of crossing the midline. Observing this task can help me to see some challenges that certain children may meet when they are in first grade. My observations may be something that I mention to parents if I am concerned.

From mid-February until Easter we all explore wool that comes from the sheep at our farm. I usually do the major washing but will sometimes wash some with the class. We then finger-card the wool and then card it with little inexpensive and sturdy dog brushes that work very well. On our walk day we visit the creek or Crystal Mountain and gather small and medium-sized stones. One day we wash and sort the stones by size and then, after carding a big basketful of wool, we start making balls. In the center of the ball I put a small stone, about nickel- or quarter-size, and around this I wrap the wool we have carded. The children can pick out two colors of colored wool, which I wrap crisscross over the forming ball. I then dip it into warm water in a dishpan and drizzle some mild dish soap over the ball. I show them how to squeeze and roll gently at first and then harder as the wool begins to felt. It generally only takes about five minutes. However some children work much longer and enjoy the sensory touch experience.

Working with the hands on a project unfolding over time develops skills and soul qualities (like patience, for instance).

If there is time before Easter we sometimes make seed babies (after we hear about them in circle time). These are made with slightly larger rocks at the core and a layer of white wool and then colored wool. They are felted by the children, and the next day they have opened and inside there is a little simple baby. I take the seeds home at night, cut them open a crack, take out the stone, and make a very simple needle-felted baby to put inside. We also make little felted rabbits for our Easter baskets (from roving tied in two knots, one larger for the body and one smaller for the head, leaving out the ends for ears with a layer of wool over it). These we felt very gently, stroking the little ears. After a rinse in the warm and cold water the bunnies are named and the children are told that tomorrow their eyes will be open. I take them home and put a little brown or blue yarn through for eyes and needle-felt the eyes a bit for strength. What fun we have with the bunnies until it is time for them to go home in Easter baskets!

I feel very strongly that needle-felting as an activity does not belong in the kindergarten. The gesture is too harsh. Imagine what children, who tend to unite with the adult's gesture, are experiencing with the quick, repetitive, piercing movement of the needle-felter. This can affect their nervous systems and elicit from them nervous gestures as well.

After the spring break the older children have special projects—a needle book and a puppet. First they pick two colors of felt and some colorful thick thread for the needle book. We do a blanket stitch around the edges of the felt and then twizzle two colors of yarn to hold the needle book closed. The twizzle is stitched on the back side of the book and each child receives one needle and six pins to put inside. With this they then begin their puppet. These are simple table puppets and the children can choose whatever character they wish to create. They take time to ponder this. I only say they must be human or angels, not animals. This project takes at least three weeks and I try to have them move through the process at somewhat the same pace. This year I made the heads earlier myself, as this was a challenging step for some of them. When they are all finished we create a puppet show for the younger children in our class. I make up a story for all the characters. One year I had only royalty;

another year there was no royalty at all. Once, six out of thirteen puppets were Michaels. Then the children can bring the puppet and needle book home. This project is met with great enthusiasm as the children come out of free play to make their characters. The choleric ones want to rush right through, but we all work at about the same pace so we are all putting heads, bottoms, hair, and capes on at the same time. What a lesson in patience for some and a lesson in perseverance for others.

This project is such a symbol of the culmination of development at the end of the children's kindergarten years. They come to kindergarten as young children, usually participating inclusively with a "we" consciousness. As they near the end of the first seven years, they become more individualized, creating their own inner images. They choose their character for a puppet, create it, participate in a group puppet show, and proudly take it home with the needle book. This has helped them to be ready for the next step into the first grade.

These ideas are only indications of how one could work. It is most important that the gesture of handwork be a joyful mood of creating rather than something that is product-oriented. It can be a lovely social time, while sitting around and talking and working together…much like a quilting bee. This year a little five-year-old girl told me that she couldn't sew her Daddy's present because her Mother did not allow her to use needles. I said I thought it would be fine if she were sitting beside me. She carefully stitched around the heart. When she finished she danced around the room singing, "I can sew. I can sew." I have experienced many such successes that have filled the children with confidence and dignity. ✦

Little Red-Cap: The Overcoming of Heredity and the Birth of the Individual

Louise deForest

All of us—especially our children—know that there is something powerful in fairy tales; stories told hundreds of years ago are still pertinent today. Fairy tales are the carriers of archetypes that speak to our souls with the same voice regardless of culture, geography, time, and space. We often see the very same fairy tale emerge from Persia, Western Europe, South America, Russia, and the Far East, with only minor changes to reflect the images most appropriate to the particular culture of origin. Fairy tales are vehicles for spiritual truths, expressed in pictures that can guide humanity. As Joan Almon once pointed out, the journey in a fairy tale is always the same: the prince or princess (or simpleton) leaves home in innocence, follows a path, straying from it occasionally, meets challenges and receives gifts, goes through some kind of inner transformation, until finally he or she finds the prince or princess, returns to the father's house, and becomes king or queen. Innocence has changed to consciousness and they live "happily ever after," ruling their kingdom wisely.

Children recognize in these stories a blueprint for life, and if we think of these fairy tales in the light of our own biographies we can see, in an external form, the journeys our souls have taken during our own lifetimes. Fairy tales are our stories as spiritual beings living in physical bodies.

Waldorf teachers, both in the kindergarten and in the lower classes, tell fairy tales to the children in their classes, repeating them often, knowing full well that by so doing we affirm the spiritual truths that the children still live in and long to find as a living reality here on earth. Through the imagination in these stories we help prepare them for the lives that are awaiting them, as well. One of my children loved the story of "The Three Billy Goats Gruff" and asked for it every day for months. I told it, not quite understanding his need until several years later: while still a child, he encountered an enormous obstacle in his path, one that required deep inner changes for him. Then I knew that the story he had so loved had the possibility of helping him overcome the challenge and moving on with his life. We also know that the harder we work to understand these stories, to arrive at the archetypal images and to read the story within the story, the more deeply the children can take these images into their soul lives.

Often adults are uncomfortable with the images in fairy tales—the cut-off toes, the often gruesome deaths of wicked stepmothers, or the perceived maligning of certain types of animals—but children do not identify with the material world as strongly as we adults do. Unlike us, the children do not take these stories literally or personally, and can quickly penetrate to the essential in a story. Children have the imaginative capacity to live so fully in the context of the pictures that no explanation is necessary, and the only comment I have given to my kindergarten children when they ask me if the story is true, is "yes."

The child lives for the first seven years between the poles of heredity and individuality.

The fairy tale "Little Red-Cap," otherwise known as "Little Red Riding Hood," while good for all older kindergarten children, I find especially well suited for the children entering into and going through the developmental phase of the six-to-seven-year-old change—that time when their relationship to themselves and the world around them goes through profound, confusing, and often lonely changes.

Each teacher interprets a fairy tale in his or her own way; what stands out for me may not feel so relevant to someone else, and another teacher may notice a detail that has completely escaped my attention. So the interpretation that follows is by no means the ultimate or only truth but rather my own understanding, with the awareness and delight that there are many other equally valid ways of "translating" this wonderful story.

These stories shine so brightly in their entirety, and the rhythms of the language are so rich, that I always hesitate to dissect them, yet I find that sometimes each word and often each sentence has a gem in it, just waiting for me to dig down far enough to expose it. So forgive me for taking apart this story with you, to proceed haltingly, lifting rocks and looking under leaves to see what lies beneath.

As Rudolf Steiner tells us, one of the many tasks that children have in the first seven years of life is that of adapting the body they have inherited from past generations into the body they need for the particular destiny awaiting them. As soon as the spiritual self finds itself in a physical body, it begins to adapt that body into a more suitable vehicle for the life it intends to live. It's a bit like moving into a new house and remodeling it to fit the needs of those now living in it: expanding, refinishing, tearing down here and adding on there. So the child lives for the first seven years between the poles of heredity and individuality—the past and the future—and it is the child's task to infuse the past with the possibilities of the future.

In the first sentence of "Little Red-Cap," "Once upon a time there was a dear little girl who was loved by everyone who looked at her, but most of all by her grandmother, and there was nothing that she would not have given the child," we see that this story has to do with this past-future polarity. The second sentence confirms this conclusion and takes it even farther, stating that "she gave her a little cap of red velvet, which suited her so well that she would never wear anything else; so she was always called 'Little Red-Cap.' " Not only does the grandmother love the child, she has defined her and the child is known to everyone through the grandmother's gift. She lives entirely in and is carried by the past, the grandmother's gift to her. A name is an important defining presence for us: in my kindergarten class, the children call me Mrs. deForest, but they always want to know what my real name is—my first name. And anyone who has experienced confirmation in the Christian Community Church will have experienced the individuality living in the name of their child. It is significant to me that it is a red cap that gives this child her name: red is the color of the blood (that which carries both the heredity and the I) and the cap encases the head with its open receptacle to the spiritual world, the fontanel.

What now follows is the wonderful wisdom of the mother, who is a harmonizer and mediator between the grandmother and the child, past and future. The mother recognizes that the grandmother is ill and knows that her child can bring her new life. The forces of the past cannot survive without the life-filled impulses of youth. And what does the mother send? Cake and wine—the Holy Communion itself. For the past to live into the future, a transformation is necessary and the being of Christ is invited in.

Unlike Parzival's mother, who, out of a desire to protect her son from his waiting destiny, gives him misleading advice, Little Red-Cap's mother is quite clear and precise with her daughter: "Set out before it gets hot, and when you are going, walk nicely and quietly and do not run off the path, or you may fall and break the bottle, and then your grandmother will get nothing; and when you go into her room, don't forget to say, 'Good morning,' and don't peep into every corner before you do it." She covers all facets of this outing, when to go, where to go, and how to go. And with what innocence and trust Little Red-Cap says to her mother, "I will take great care," as she gives her hand before setting out. How protected this child has been!

The mother does not accompany Little Red-Cap, who must set out on the path with only her mother's warnings to guide and sustain her. The mother knows that the path into the future is increasingly an individual one and that it is now her child's task to overcome obstacles out of her own I. No longer can we rely on the family or tribe (all that we receive through birth) to accompany us; rather, that which leads to the future, the Christ Being, is every individual's challenge and redemption and it is as individuals that we must seek Him.

This is an especially important and significant part of the story for the six- and seven-year-olds who, through their development, are slowly pulling away from their parents. The new urge for independence that we all recognize in the new first-grade-ready child is reflected in the picture of Little Red-Cap setting out alone, and one senses that this is also a picture of the etheric separation between mother and child as the etheric body finishes its physical-formative work. The task of carrying the basket also speaks to me of the older kindergartener who longs to do something meaningful in the world, who begins to feel the call to service, and whose limbs crave movement. Carrying the basket, Little Red-Cap is being asked to focus her will and engage in service through movement. Movement now enters form. Anyone who works with six- and seven-year-olds recognizes immediately the intense need they have for movement, reflecting the changing nature of etheric activity and the intensification of the physical changes the six-year-old experiences. I can almost hear the sigh of relief and open enthusiasm with which the children take up the activity and responsibility of Little Red-Cap and her basket.

Grandmother's home is in the forest—shaded and apart—and an effort of a half hour of walking is needed to arrive there. The forest itself is a place of mystery, an in-between place that, in fairy tales, is often a meeting place of the spiritual and the earthly. Entering into the forest, we enter into the soul realm—full of mystery, possibilities, challenges, and deep wisdom. We can picture the stately trees, full of life, reaching up from roots entrenched in rich soil to the sky above us. In the forest there is an unearthly calm where one feels the presence of elemental beings. One also feels, in the shadows and bushes, the possibility of the unknown, and as human beings, we can often feel vulnerable, out of our familiar realm and afraid. And, sure enough, as soon as she steps into the forest, Little Red-Cap meets the wolf. The wolf, too, is an archetype and one would be mistaken to take the image literally. The wolf symbolizes all that is materialistically insatiable in us—all that is greedy and egotistical and that wants to have something for the sake of having it. He is the perfect picture of the dangers of falling into materialism. However, the wolf is both an opportunity and a formidable challenge, especially for a child who is so innocent that she does not even recognize the enemy. Yet, if she can overcome this resistant force in her path (and she must do this alone, as we all do in the face of the deepest crisis in our lives), she will be on her way to walking the path as a fuller human being.

But in her innocence, Little Red-Cap is quite frank with the wolf, even giving him explicit directions to her grandmother's house: "A good quarter of a league farther on in the wood; her house stands under the three large oak-trees [wisdom], the nut trees [full of the potential for life] are just below; you must surely know it." And immediately we see the insatiable quality of the wolf, who wants to eat both Little Red-Cap and her grandmother, in spite of the knowledge that the grandmother will not be nearly as tasty as the child: "What a tender young creature! What a nice plump mouthful—she will be better to eat than the old woman. I must act craftily, so as to catch both."

From the very beginning we have seen that Little Red-Cap is susceptible to vanity—her little cap suited her so well that she would not wear anything else. And now the wolf tempts her with the joy of sense perceptions: "See, Little Red-Cap, how pretty the flowers are about here—why do you not look around? I believe, too, that you do not hear how sweetly the little birds are singing; you walk gravely along as if you were going to school, while everything else out here in the wood is merry." Don't listen to your mother, don't think about your grandmother; use your eyes and ears and live completely in the beauty of the world—which Little Red-Cap does immediately. Even though she does not recognize her adversary for who he really is, he certainly has recognized her weakness. If we don't overcome our adversary, we run the risk of being overcome by it—and we see that this has happened to Little Red-Cap: "And whenever she had picked one [flower], she fancied that she saw a still prettier one farther on, and ran after it, and so got deeper and deeper into the wood." All thoughts of her grandmother have fled as she becomes greedy for more and more beauty.

Six-year-olds begin to play with good and bad, often quite innocently.

We can recognize the typical six-year-old, vulnerable to new temptations. Suddenly they can experiment with *not* doing as the teacher asks, talking back to parents, becoming a bit sneaky or sly and beginning to tell lies and have real secrets. It's not for nothing that kindergarten teachers often refer to this age as the first adolescence! Six-year-olds begin to play with good and bad, often quite innocently, trying on new behaviors for size and then suddenly, inexplicably, returning to the child we once knew.

Going off the path is also typical six-year-old behavior. What parent among us has not heard the loud and often belligerent assertion, "You're not the boss of me!" While they strike off on their own path, sometimes with enthusiasm, sometimes with fierce independence, children at this age will often push themselves beyond their former capacities, stretching themselves inwardly as a reflection of their outer limb growth. In getting more flowers than she could hold, Little Red-Cap portrays this urge to go beyond, to surpass, to challenge herself—to see what she is made of.

Meanwhile, the wolf runs to the grandmother's house and it's a sign of her weakened state that she offers no resistance at all: "Lift the latch, I am too weak and cannot get up." The wolf enters and swallows the grandmother all in one movement and then, wearing her clothes, gets into bed and draws the curtain. He has swallowed the untransformed forces streaming from the past and all appears lost.

Little Red-Cap suddenly remembers her grandmother and hurries on her way. Here, too, we are reminded that the six-year-old is just waking up to a sense of time and space. Five minutes begin to have meaning (thank goodness!); past, present, and future are becoming contexts in which to store experiences; and the etheric forces are now more free for memory.

She arrives at the cottage, only to be puzzled by the open door. She feels uneasy when she enters, but now she is once again following her mother's instructions to say good morning and not peek into every corner. Indeed, one feels that she might have been helped had she looked around a bit but, having left the path, it is now too late. Little Red-Cap is now afraid. Having fallen asleep in the beauty recently perceived by her senses, Little Red-Cap is not awake enough to identify what is making her uneasy until her last exclamation reveals all: "but Grandmother, what a terrible big mouth you have!" and the wolf devours her. How true to life it is that we often don't wake up enough until it is too late and must suffer the consequences! And how interesting that it is the mouth that changes her consciousness. Six-year-olds are indeed going through a transformation with the changing of the milk teeth, grown from the mother's etheric forces, to producing the densest substance of the body, their own permanent teeth. And when Little Red-Cap does eventually recognize the wolf, we see an important moment in the life of the six- and seven-year-old—the awakening of thought. She has pieced together the clues through her observations and put those clues together with her feeling that something is not right.

Now, combining with the will life that has lived so strongly in the very young child, we see that thought and feeling are added. A huge step indeed!

Luckily, the huntsman comes by and, hearing the loud snoring coming from the grandmother's room, decides to check on her. The huntsman is one who lives in the forest, knows all the paths that cross it and the creatures that live there. He lives in this soul realm, recognizes its beauties and dangers, and strives to maintain harmony and order. He is a conscious being—a guide, a helper, a remover of all the lower, animal-like instincts that hinder one's spiritual growth. He is the one who redirects us to our rightful path, guiding us out of the forest to continue our chosen route. He helps us find our way.

Right away we are told that the wolf is not an unknown to the huntsman: "Do I find you here, you old sinner! I have long sought you!" says the huntsman. But he is not carried away by his first impulse; rather, he considers all possibilities before taking action. As he cuts into the wolf's belly, the metabolic part of us that is so active in the transformation of substances, out comes Little Red-Cap, followed by the grandmother who is now at the point of death. "Ah, how frightened I have been! How dark it was inside the wolf!" says Little Red-Cap, and it is obvious that she has had a real trial. Observing children's confusion, loneliness, and emptiness during the six-year change is a picture indeed of being in the belly of the wolf! All that was once familiar to the young child, all that sustained her is no longer available; the wellspring of imagination no longer bubbles up unbidden, carrying the child with it. This, of course, is a sign of the birth of the etheric body and is a normal, albeit painful, developmental stage. "I'm bored," echoes from house to house where there are six-year-olds, and there is a lack of contentment with all that they do. It can often drive parents (and teachers) to despair and we wonder if we will ever see again the joyful, enthusiastic, cooperative child of a few months ago. If we can, instead, accept that this is the child's moment in the belly of the wolf, we can wait patiently, assured that soon they will re-emerge stronger and wiser.

After her ordeal, Little Red-Cap knows just what to do and she fills the beast's belly with stones, sealing his fate. At last she is awake and able to overcome his influence. What big steps she has made, thanks to such a fearful experience! The wolf, his belly full of stones—the densest and most lifeless of earthly substances—dies the death he deserves and the huntsman carries off his skin.

Now that the evil is overcome, Little Red-Cap turns her attention to her ailing grandmother, who eats the wine and cake and is thereby restored. We all breathe a sigh of relief that all is well now and that, through the power of the Christ Being, the wisdom of the past can continue forward with the life-filled forces of the future. Little Red-Cap, wiser through her experience, can now go into her future with all the experiences of the past. Individuality and heredity have achieved a balance and the individual can now continue in the rightful path of development. ✦

Section Five

Activities and Resources for the Classroom

Question: *How can educators best meet the needs of children from five-and-a-half to seven years old, who usually ask what they should do?*

Dr. Steiner: *Well, in children of that age the feeling for authority is already somewhat present, but the urge to imitate still has the upper hand. That should be the guiding principle for what one does with those children. What I indicated about the picture books with moveable figures applies especially to children of that age; those books work extremely well. It is a good thing to occupy their awakening life of imagination with those types of books.*

From a discussion with English guests held on the 5th of January, 1922, in Dornach.

Mother Goose Movement Journey

Composed and compiled by Nancy Blanning

Preparation and equipment: This journey ideally uses a ***jogging trampoline*** for the imagination of the "old woman tossed up in a basket." Otherwise the children can jump in place as the appropriate lines are spoken. Additionally, a ***hula hoop or rope*** circled on the floor to suggest a well is needed. Two ***beams*** are propped on opposite sides of a jump box or stable bench to be the hill the children climb up and then down with Jack and Jill. If the "Hey Diddle Diddle" option is chosen instead of the "Old Woman in a Basket," one needs a ***rod***, either held off the ground by blocks or by another teacher, for the children to jump over.

Note: The traditional Mother Goose text is written in italics, movement instructions in plain type. Brackets in the spoken verse section indicate transitional material composed by the author of the circle which is not part of the traditional rhyme.

Old Mother Goose

Old Mother Goose	Gesturing with arms as if flying slowly and with strength.
When she wanted to wander,	Mother Goose sitting majestically on the goose's back.
Would ride through the air On a very fine gander.	
Mother Goose had a house, 'Twas built in a wood,	Lifting arms above head to make peaked roof.

An owl by the door *For a porter stood.*	Thumbs and index fingers circling eyes to suggest owl (challenge for older children: hands inverted, palms turned toward the face so other fingers are pointing downward).
She had a son Jack,	Making a little jump on "Jack," hands in Eurythmy /k/ gesture, right foot kicks out and heel brought to floor in time with hands.
A plain-looking lad, *He was not very good,* *Nor yet very bad.*	Tipping head to right side. Tipping head to left side.
She sent him to market, *A live goose he bought;*	Right hand gesturing head of a goose, forearm the long neck.
"Here! Mother," says he, *"It will not go for naught."*	
Jack's goose and her gander *Grew very fond;* *They'd both eat together,* *Or swim in one pond.*	Each hand and arm indicating a goose, bringing arms (geese) together at midline. Gesturing eating, pecking the ground. Arms gliding side-to-side, as if swimming.
Jack found one morning, *As I have been told,* *His goose had laid him* *An egg of pure gold.*	Arms circling to suggest a nest. Cupping hands to indicate an egg.
[But then the son, Jack, *The gold he lost.* *Into the sea it was* *Quickly tossed.]*	Arms in open gesture of "Oh, dear!" Hands open, palms facing upward gesturing tossing forward.
The gold egg in the sea *Was thrown away then—* *When Jack he jumped in* *And got it again.*	Repeat tossing gesture with full arm, as though it is a broad, strong throw. Jumping in place as though picking the egg up.

And Old Mother Goose The goose saddled soon, And, mounting his back, Flew up to the moon.	As at beginning, flying gesture, broad and deliberate, lifting the arms from the shoulders, not elbows or wrists.
[The moon was so high And you'd think so far It shone in the sky Like a bright silver star.]	Gesturing upward as though looking at the moon.

(Option 1: There Was an Old Woman)

[But then an old woman	Walking slowly, gesturing sweeping with slow, deliberate
Came searchingly by	movements, crossing midline of the body.
With a broom in her hand. Now will she sweep the sky?]	
There was an old woman tossed up in a basket Nineteen times as high as the moon;	Each child taking 6-8 jumps on trampoline or jumping in place as high as possible.
Where she was going I couldn't but ask it, For in her hand she carried a broom.	Making sweeping gesture again.
"Old woman, old woman, old woman," quoth I, "O whither, O whither, O whither, so high?"	Standing in place and questioning.
"To brush the cobwebs off the sky!"	As though sweeping the sky.
"Shall I go with thee?" "Ay, by-and-by."	Nodding head in affirmation.

(Option 2: Hey Diddle Diddle)

[The cat, the dog, and the cow came soon
To leap right over the shining moon.]

Hey diddle diddle,	Holding rod for children to jump over.
The cat and the fiddle,	Rhyme is repeated until all have jumped over the rod.
The cow jumped over the moon.	
The little dog laughed	
To see such sport,	
And the dish ran away	
with the spoon.	

(Both options continue:)

[Now the moon has gone to bed.	Tipping head to side, laying it on hands.
The sun has raised	
his shining head.	Circling arms above head.
Out into the light of day	
The village people make	
their way.	
The horse comes trotting,	
throws his shoe.	Trotting in place, kick right foot
Dear, oh, dear!	backward as if to throw shoe behind
What shall we do?]	
"Robert Barnes, fellow fine,	Standing still with open arms
Can you shoe this	
horse of mine?"	with conversational stance.
"Yes, good sir, that I can,	
As well as any other man.	
Here a nail, and there a prod,	Alternately pounding hands in fists,
And now, good sir,	one on top of the other.
your horse is shod."	
Pitty,	Clapping hands together once.
patty,	Clapping hands on thighs.
polt.	Touching knees or toes.
Shoe the wild colt.	Repeat in rhythm of verse.
Here a nail,	Hammering fists as above.
And there a nail,	
Pitty, patty, polt.	Gesturing with clapping hands on each word as above.

This Is the Way the Ladies Ride

This is the way the ladies ride,
Tri, tre, tre, tree! Tri, tre, tre, tree!
This is the way the ladies ride,
Tri, tre, tre, tri-tre-tre tree!

Trotting slowly from leg to leg (emphasizing balance),
knees lifted high,
coming down on toes, heads held high.

This is the way the gentlemen
ride,
Gallop-a-trot, gallop-a-trot!
This is the way the gentlemen
ride,
Gallop-a-gallop-a-trot!

Galloping (tempo a little faster),
coming to a momentary stop on "trot."

This is the way the farmers ride,
Hobbledy-hop, hobbledy-hop!
This is the way the farmers ride,
Hobbledy-hobbledy-hop!

Shifting weight slowly and swaying slightly
from side-to-side with "hobbledy,"
stepping on each syllable.
Jumping with both feet together on "hop,"
stopping forward motion.

[Let us go riding up the hill
To find our friends there,
Jack and Jill.]

(can be spoken or sung to traditional tune)

Jack and Jill went up the hill
To fetch a pail or water.
Jack fell down and broke
his crown
And Jill came tumbling after.

Children walking up one side of
elevated and descending beams and then

down the other as rhyme is repeated
until all children have done so.

Then up Jack got and home
did trot
As fast as he could caper,
To old Dame Dob, who patched
his nob
With vinegar and brown paper.

Skipping to these two lines as seems
reasonable with the group.

Laying hands upon top of head, patting
head with hands.

[At the bottom of the hill
Was the well with water still.]

Ding, Dong, Dell

Ding, dong, dell!
Pussy's in the well!
Who put her in?
Little Tommy Green.
Who pulled her out?
Little Johnny Stout.
What a naughty boy was that
To try to drown poor pussy cat,
Who never did him any harm,
But killed the mice in his
father's barn.

[Pussy ran on home to see
The little piggies, one, two, three.]

A hoop is placed 6-12 inches off the floor, teachers holding it or braced on supports, each child jumping into the "well" on one side and jumping out on the other side. Continue repeating the verse until all children have jumped in and out.

Three Little Pigs

This little piggy went to market.
This little piggy stayed home.
This little piggy had roast beef.
This little piggy had none.
And this little piggy cried,
"Wee, wee, wee" all the way
home.

(children brought to sitting position)

To work on finger isolation and differentiation, choose one:

1. Beginning with thumb, move one finger along with each line, first on right hand, then on left.

2. With palms together, finger tips touching, tap thumb tips together with first line, then index fingers together on second line, and so on.

3. As in #2 above, same position and tapping with each line. However, fold each pair of fingers down, as though to clasp the hands, one pair of fingers at the end of each line so fingers are all folded down by end of verse.

Wee Willie Winkie

[Now here's a sleeping cap
for your head.
Wee Willie Winkie calls us all
to bed.]

Wee Willie Winkie runs through the town,	Two fingers of right hand running across and up left arm to top of head, lingering on head
Upstairs and downstairs in his nightgown,	with "upstairs," then down other side on "downstairs."
Rapping at the window,	Knocking gesture.
Crying through the lock,	Hands to mouth to speak at the lock.
"Are the children in their beds?	Concluding with stretching in sleepy gesture,
For now it's eight o'clock!"	then lying down.

Reproduced with permission from page 107ff of *Movement Journeys and Circle Adventures*, by Nancy Blanning and Laurie Clark, published by the authors. For music accompanying this and the following movement journey, please see this book.

Through the Snow: A Winter Movement Journey

Composed by Nancy Blanning

Preparation and equipment: *Large stones and small branches or logs* set the first part of the path. Children will have to step around and over these objects. Some *tree stumps* of varying heights can be steps up and over the "mountain." Stepping up onto and down from a table can also suffice. A *blue cloth* on the floor suggests a river. *Large, flattened stones* (ideally river stones) placed on the cloth provide the stepping stones across the river. An *elevated beam* propped on a *jump box or secure bench* will create a bridge that climbs upward. A *teeter-totter bridge* or a *plank balanced over a log* will become a teeter-totter for the children to walk over. To roll a snowman, children will do forward rolls on a *gym mat or cushioned carpet*. Finally a *tunnel* created out of cloths and playstands or chairs will complete the journey course.

Horse and rider, come this way. *We'll gallop through the* *snowy day.*	Gallop around the room.
On we gallop, then say "Whoa!" *The snow is deep; we must* *go slow.*	Gesture as though pulling in the reins, come to a stop. Then walk deliberately, picking up feet as though stepping in deep snow.
Sticks and stones through snow *field deep* *Peek up to trip us.* *Watch your feet!*	Have some branches and stones arranged at different heights and distances apart for children to step over and through.

We step along with heavy tread. *To climb a mountain we are led.*	Lead children to part of room where stumps or tables are arranged so as to provide "steps" for climbing up and down a mountain.
Up the mountain, climbing high, *We reach the summit,* *touch the sky.* *Then down the other side we go* *And meet a river down below.*	Climb up mountain and down the other side. Lead children to "river," a blue cloth on the floor with river stones arranged as a stepping-stone path.
To cross the river is our task.	Lead children across the stepping stones.
The water's icy, flowing fast. *The river stones show us this day* *A path across the river way.*	Have an inclined balance beam next, elevated about two feet by a tree stump, jump box, or small table, from which the children will be able to jump down to the floor.
Stepping watchful, slow and neat, *Take care that you don't* *wet your feet.*	
Across the bridge now slowly go. *The other bank is up hill, though.*	Climb up the beam.
Off we jump …	Jump off. Repeat line until all children in group have done this.
… and take some time *To build a warming fire fine.*	Sit down on floor, in a circle so that all have room to criss-cross legs out in front of body.
We'll criss and cross the big *logs so*	Alternate crossing legs, one over the other. Repeat 2-3 times.
The middle logs on next will go.	Alternate crossing arms in front of body, leaning forward, as though placing logs on the fire. Repeat 2-3 times.
And last the tinder of sweet pine *Will help us make a fire fine.*	Repeat crossing gesture with fingers, 2-3 times.
We strike the match	Cross midline with right arm from left to right, as though boldly striking a match.

The flames rise high.	Arms gesture as flames rising.
Bright cinders shoot like stars in sky.	Fingers as shooting stars.
We feel so warm	Rise to standing position in a circle.
We want to dance. *So let our feet* *Begin to prance.*	Alternate tapping toes.

Song: "Circle to the Left, Old Brass Wagon" (Traditional)

Circle to the left, old brass wagon. *Circle to the left, old brass wagon.* *Circle to the left, old brass wagon.* *Now you are my darling.*	Appropriate gestures as suggested by the song.
Circle to the right, old brass wagon. *Circle to the right, old brass wagon.* *Circle to the right, old brass wagon.* *Now you are my darling.*	
Swing, swing, swing, old brass wagon. *Swing, swing, swing, old brass wagon.* *Swing, swing, swing, old brass wagon.* *Now you are my darling.*	Swing in partners if group is old enough to do so. Otherwise, omit this verse.
Jump, jump, jump, brass wagon. *Jump, jump, jump, brass wagon.* *Jump, jump, jump, brass wagon.* *Now you are my darling.*	Jumping in place.
A smooth and sparkling field of snow *Calls us onward; away we go.*	Lead children to teeter-totter bridge.
But first a bridge of rickety-rack *Will slow our going on the track.* *Tipple, topple, rick and rack.*	Walk children across the teeter-totter bridge.

Step right forward, don't look back.	Lead children to floor mat.
The snow is right and perfect now	
To roll a snowman. This is how.	
Roll a snowman. Roll him round.	Guide children singly in doing a forward roll.
Plant him firmly on the ground.	Child jumps firmly, both feet together.
Give a tall, black, shiny hat.	Child presses on his own head to indicate a hat.
And a carrot nose like that.	Both fists brought together in front of nose to make long, "carrot" nose.
Who smells the carrot?	Nose twitching, sniffing.
Snowshoe hare!	Gesture rabbit ears.
He's sniffing here and sniffing there.	Sniffing.
He hops around without a sound.	Bunny hopping, both feet together.
Slips into burrow underground.	Jump down into crouching position.
Into his home we, too, shall creep.	Children crawl or creep on
Hush! Baby rabbits are asleep.	tummy though a tunnel of
We creep out other burrow door	cloths and play stands.
And find the shining snow	
once more.	
Home we'd like to go at last.	Take hands and lead children
Our day of snowy fun is past.	into a circle, sitting on the floor.
So many fun, bright things this day	
We all did see along our way.	
We saw the bunnies sound asleep	Sleeping gesture.
In their rabbit burrow deep.	
A jolly snowman round and fat	"O" gesture in front with arms.
We saw with carrot nose and hat.	
The bridge of rickety and rack	Interlock fingers and tip arms
Led us further on our track.	back and forth like a teeter-totter.
We danced all in a circle line	
In that old brass wagon fine.	

We built a fire warm and sweet *That warmed our face and hands* *and feet.*	Rub hands together, then face.
We walked the bridge across the river, *Walked tippy stones and did not shiver.*	Gesture with hands as though taking steps, one in front of the other.
We climbed a mountain top so high *And felt that we could touch the sky.*	Reaching upward in climbing gesture.
We galloped with the horses gay. *Now we say "Thanks!" for a perfect day.*	Gesture as though holding reins. Nod head on "Thanks!" for emphasis.

Reproduced with permission from page 61ff of *Movement Journeys and Circle Adventures* (see p. 190).

Briar Rose Circle

Janet Kellman
after the story from the Brothers Grimm

This circle written in the mood of the fifth is excellent for the older children in the kindergarten. The mood of the fifth lulls the nerve-sense system and the awakened older children into a more dreamy state. At the same time the polarities—speeding up and slowing down, coming to stillness and then moving into lively activity—address the needs of the more hysterical children. This circle is also good for working with impulse control, so needed by the older children. When the prince kisses the princess and wakes her up and when they have "a lovely wedding feast" often the older boys and girls squeal with delight or cast a furtive glance in the direction of one another. My thanks go to Janet Kellman for her faithfulness to the story line and for her creative genius. Her fine work has brought much enjoyment to many children.   —*Ruth Ker*

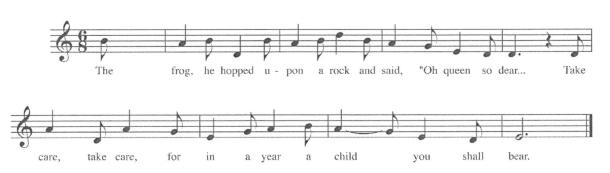

The frog, he hopped u-pon a rock and said, "Oh queen so dear... Take care, take care, for in a year a child you shall bear.

And what the frog did say came true:
The child she came, so fair, so new.

The prin - cess is a love - ly child, a love - ly child a love - ly child.

"We'll have a royal feast!" cried the king.
But only twelve golden plates were there,
So only twelve wise women could come to share their precious gifts.

Tune #1

From all a - round they brought precious gifts they brought pre - cious gifts

brought pre - cious gifts.

But a thirteenth wise woman was left out,
So angrily she came and began to shout.

A spin - dle prick shall bring you death, bring you death,

bring you death. A spin - dle prick shall bring you death, bring you death.

Softly and evenly

One wise wo-man tried to make it good, to so - ften the curse and

save the child.

Sung to Tune #1:

And she shall sleep one hundred years, hundred years, hundred years.

Spoken:

And when she grew older, the princess and the king
From the top of the castle stood watching …

Flames of yel-low, Flames of red, Flames of o-range ri-sing o-ver head.

Flaming and flaming and flaming so high,
Rising higher and higher, way up to the sky.

All the spin-dles burned and gone, Now the child is safe.

But when she was fifteen, and no one was about,
She began to explore the castle, both inside and out.
She came to a tower with a winding staircase,
At the top, a little door, a rusty key, and an old, old face.

Rat-tling round and round and round so mer-ri-ly...

Spin little wheel, little wheel, little wheel,
Spin little wheel, little wheel, little wheel.
(Repeat several times with first slow, then fast spinning motions of the hands and
forearms.)

Prick! Down to the earth she fell,
Fast asleep in a magic spell.
And all the castle went with her too,
The king, the queen and their courtiers too.
The horse in the stable,
The dog in the yard,
The pigeon on the roof,
And the fly on the wall.

Bur-ied so deep in a   fast, deep sleep.   All   a - round   to   sleep, so deep.

One hundred years passed this way.
Not even a leaf was seen to sway.
But all around the castle wide,
A thorny hedge it grew outside.

Sung to Tune #1:

A thorny hedge, it grew around, grew around, grew around. (Repeat)

Spoken:

One hundred years passed this way.
When the time was up, then came a new day!

Ri-ding a-long on a   horse so white, a   brave shi-ning prince   rides through the night.

Up to the hedge he came with his might.
The thorns turned to roses, so shining, so bright.
They easily parted to let the prince in.
He wandered and wandered and wandered around,
Till at last, in the tower, the princess he found.

Sung to Tune #1:

He kissed the princess, and she awoke, she awoke, she awoke. (Repeat)

Spoken:
Then all of the castle woke up too,
The king, the queen and their courtiers too,
The horse in the stable—SHOOK SHOOK SHOOK,
The dog in the yard—wagged his tail,
The pigeons on the roof—"caroo, caroo," (with flying gesture)
The fly on the wall—creep, creep, creep. (fingers of right hand creep up left arm)
When all were awake, no time did it take
For a lovely wedding party to make.

Sung to Tune #1:
They had a happy wedding feast, wedding feast, wedding feast. (Repeat)

This ending can have more complicated movements for older children—crossing legs, skipping, etc.

The Gnomes

Janet Kellman

There is much that has been said lately about the topic of gnomes in the kindergarten classroom. I find that the children themselves have their own imaginations about the gnomes and the fairies, and I find it helpful to connect to the imaginations of the children. Their fantasy reflects their own developing consciousness and may not be based on our adult understandings of what is true to the nature of gnomes and fairies. As the children mature, I have noticed, in my graduates and my own children, that these "childish imaginations" have transformed into new fruits of the soul that enable them to cultivate new understandings of the elementals.   —*Ruth Ker*

Trip, Trip, Trap, Trip, Trip, Trap,
Go we gnomes along the path.
Trip, Trip, Trap, Trip, Trip, Trap,
With heavy sacks upon our backs.

Out of our caverns deep in the ground
Out from the roots which twist all around
Out from the crystals that shine near and far
We gather the light of sun, moon, and star.

Twink-ling shin - ing spark-ling clear, The light filled heav - ens are so

near. Ga-ther-ing cups of their lov-ing light For our star-ry homes in the cry-stals bright.

Deep - a-deep Deep - a-deep In-to the sil-ver-y dew. Deep - a - deep Deep - a-deep

In-to the sil-ver-y dew. Fill-ing sacks with star - light, Fill-ing sacks with moon-

light, Fill - ing sacks with sun - light too. Deep - a - deep. Deep - a deep.

Now we'll go back to our mountain homes
With our sacks of heavenly light.
Yes we are the little gnomes
We work the earth with all our might.

Trip, Trip, Trap, Trip, Trip, Trap,
Go we gnomes along the path.
Trip, Trip, Trap, Trip, Trip, Trap,
With heavy sacks upon our backs.

Back to our caverns deep in the ground
Back where the roots twist all around.
Back where the crystals shine near and far
We've gathered the light of the sun, moon and stars.

Our light-filled caps will guide our way
Down in the roots
Down in the shoots
Down where the crystals stay.

Down in the silver
Down in the gold
Down in the metals, young and old.

Now we'll take our light-filled sacks
Off of our little gnomie backs.
Look! Light has spread all along our tracks.
Now it's time to hammer and hack,
Hammer and hack, hammer and hack.

Crack! Crack! The rock we hack.
Quake! Quake! The mountains shake.
Bang! Bang! Our hammers clang.
In caverns old we seek for gold.

Crack! Crack! The rock we hack.
Quake! Quake! The mountains shake.
Bang! Bang! Our hammers clang.
In caverns old we seek for gold.

No, our work is never done.
We work by stars, moon and sun.
The stones will spread their heavenly light
On the sleeping seeds in the earth tonight.

Open wide your hearts and sacks.
Even open wide your caps.

Star Money

Elisabeth Moore-Haas, adapted by Ruth Ker
after the story from the Brothers Grimm

Once again, this circle in the mood of the fifth is helpful for drawing the children into a dreamier state. I have only slightly adapted this masterful circle. For the first few times we simply sing and move the circle together. Then, one morning the children are surprised to see that we have costumes at circle time. I have costumes for each of the children who pretend to be a star maiden who gives bread, a hat, vest, or shirt. Sometimes one star maiden can be represented by two or three children. Often it is the older children who relish this opportunity, while the younger ones prefer to stay in the context of being invisibly held in the circle. I also have star garlands for each of the "poor" children who, in the story, ask for these things. Then we sing and move the circle and when it comes time for a gift-giving then the poor child or old man and the star maiden step into the circle. The maiden gives her gift to the other child and then the teacher puts a star garland on the maiden's head when "the stars in heaven" see the maiden. When the circle is finished all of the children are wearing golden star crowns. This is just one way to elongate the delightful spell that is often cast by this magical circle. —*Ruth Ker*

A lit - tle mai - den walks, hills up and hills down, she

wan - ders through the fields, whom does she see come? An old man! An

old man!

"I am so hungry, O give me bread!"
"Here, take my bread and give thanks to God."

And the glitt-'ring stars are shin-ing, high a - bove the sky so blue, from a - bove they

all are bow-ing to the lit - tle mai-den true.

And when she went on through the wood, there by the path a

poor child stood.

"I have no cap, the wind is cold!"
"Here, take my cap and give thanks to God."

Repeat second song: *"And the glittering…"*

Repeat third song: *"And when she went on…"*

"I have no coat, the wind is cold!"
"Here, take my coat and give thanks to God."

Repeat second song: *"And the glittering…"*

Repeat third song: *"And when she went on…"*

"I have no skirt, the wind is cold!"
"Here, take my skirt and give thanks to God."

Repeat second song: *"And the glittering…"*

Repeat third song: *"And when she went on…"*

"I have no shirt, the wind is cold!"
"Here, take my shirt and give thanks to God."

Repeat second song: *"And the glittering…"*

Repeat second song: *"And the glittering…"*

The glitt'ring stars, they dance in heaven,
They see the girl so bare and pure;
And weaving her a veil of starlight,
They render her all safe and sure.

The Magic Lake at the End of the World
A Story from Ecuador

Adapted by Barbara Klocek

I have found this is a wonderful story in the spring for the older girls who may be anxious about the transition to first grade. It makes a lovely puppet show and play.

—*Barbara Klocek*

Once upon a time the king of a great land had one son who brought him great joy, but also sorrow. The prince had been born in ill health and as the years passed, no one could find a cure for him. One night the king prayed, "Oh, Great One, I am getting old and will soon leave my people to join you in the heavens. There is no one to look after them but my son, the prince. Please tell me how he can be cured." The king waited for an answer and then heard a voice from the fire that burned always by the altar. "When the prince drinks water from the magic lake at the end of the world, he will be well."

But the king was too old to make the long journey himself, and the prince was too ill, so he proclaimed over his land that whosoever would bring back the water from the lake at the end of the world would be richly rewarded. Many brave men set out to try, but none could find it. In a far valley of that kingdom lived a poor farmer with his wife, two sons and a daughter. One day the older son said, "Let my brother and me search for the healing water. We shall return before the moon is full to help with the harvest." The second son also wanted to go but the father feared for them. Then his wife said, "We must help our king and prince." The father gave his blessing and the sons set out on their journey.

They traveled far and found many lakes, but none where the sky touched the waters. Finally they knew they must return to help their father. Said the brothers, "Let us gather water from every lake. In this way we may receive a reward." When they returned to the palace they told the king that they had brought water from the magic lake. When the prince was given the water he remained as ill as before. The king called for his magician to ask why the prince was not made well. The magician said wisely that this was not the water from the magic lake. The brothers trembled with fright for they knew their falsehood had been discovered. The king angrily threw them into prison and every day they had to drink their false water.

Once again the king pleaded for help from his people. Suma, the little sister of the brothers, was tending her flock of llamas when she heard the royal messenger. She quickly led her llamas home and begged her parents to let her go. "You are too young," said her father. "Besides, look what has befallen your brothers." And her mother added, "We cannot bear to be without our dear Suma."

"But think how sad our king will be if his son dies," replied Suma, "And if I find the lake, perhaps the king will forgive my brothers."

"Dear husband, perhaps it is the will of the gods," said her mother, and they gave her their blessing.

Bravely Suma set off with her pet llama to carry her provisions, a bag of golden corn and a flask of water. The first night she slept, snug and warm against her llama. But during the night she heard the cry of the mountain lion and so in the morning she sent her llama home for safety. The next night she slept in the top branches of a tall tree. In the morning she was aroused by the voices of the gentle birds resting on a nearby branch. They were talking about how she had shared her corn with them yesterday and how she would never be able to find the magic lake. "Let us help her," said one sparrow.

"Oh, yes. Please do!" said Suma.

"We shall help you, for you are a good child. Each of us will give you a special wing feather and you must hold them all together in one hand as a fan. These feathers have magic powers that will carry you wherever you wish to go. They will also protect you from harm." Each bird carefully gave her a special feather. She made a little fan and tied them with a ribbon from her hair. The oldest bird told her how three terrible creatures guarded the magic lake. She should have no fear for she would not be harmed if she held up the magic fan and sang this song:

No fear here. Angel stand near. [1]

Suma gratefully thanked the birds and, holding the fan said, "Please take me to the magic lake at the end of the world." At once, a soft breeze lifted her out of the tree and through

1   Sung on tones A D A—A B G A

the valley. Up she was carried and over the snowy peaks. At last the wind put her down on the shore of a lake touched by the sky. She ran to the water and was about to fill her flask when a large crab said, "Get away from my lake or I will eat you." Trembling only a little, Suma held up the magic fan and sang the song, "No fear here. Angel stand near." At once the crab closed his eyes and fell asleep.

Once more she began to fill her bottle, when a voice came from the water. "Get away from my lake or I shall eat you." She saw a great green alligator in the lake. Quickly she held up the fan and sang and the creature sank to the bottom of the lake, asleep.

As Suma recovered from her fright, she heard a whistling voice, "Get away from my lake or I will eat you." She looked up and saw a flying serpent. Again Suma's fan and song saved her from harm. The serpent drifted to the ground, folded its wings, and began to snore. Suma sat for a moment to quiet herself. Then she realized the danger was past and filled up her flask.

Holding her fan, she whispered, "Please take me to the palace." Swiftly she flew and found herself before the gate. A guard led her to the prince, who was pale and motionless. When Suma gave him a few drinks, he sat up and said joyfully, "How strong I feel."

The king and queen rejoiced. They praised her courage and offered her all the riches of the kingdom. She said that she had only three wishes. The first was that the fan be returned to the birds, and it immediately flew out of the window toward the mountains. The second wish was that her brothers be freed. Immediately the king had them released. The last wish was for a large farm with many llamas for her parents. "It will be so," said the king. "Will you not stay with us in the palace? We will do everything to make you happy."

"Oh, no, thank you," said Suma. "I miss my family and wish to return to them." And so she returned home and lived happily with her parents and brothers and their llamas. ✦

The Pumpkin Child
A Story from Persia

Stories of transformation can be very therapeutic for the older child in the kindergarten, especially since they themselves are going through a mighty time of transition. When we pretend this story together at storytime, the older children, who often like to play "marriage" at free play time, are delighted to participate. I often use this story at Halloween or harvest time. —*Ruth Ker*

Once upon a time there was a good wife who lived with her husband in a small, neat house at the edge of town. She had everything she wanted except one thing. She longed to have a daughter. Year after year, she prayed for a daughter, but year after year, she and her husband remained childless. One day, she said to her husband, "I would like a little girl so much that I wouldn't even care if she looked like a pumpkin."

Not long after she spoke these words, a beautiful girl child was born, with eyes like sapphires and lips like pomegranate seeds. Both the woman and her husband were very happy until, one morning, when the mother went to pick up her child from its cradle, she found a pumpkin there instead. When the husband saw that his daughter had turned into a pumpkin, he ran away from town and never came back. But the good woman felt sorry for the little pumpkin and took care of it and loved it. Year by year, the pumpkin grew bigger and fatter until it became too big to carry. Then it began to roll around the house and out into the street. All the neighbors laughed and mocked the poor wife because she had a pumpkin instead of a child.

Many more years passed, and the good wife continued to take care of her pumpkin child. She dressed it in pretty dresses which she sewed herself. When the pumpkin child was fifteen, the wife decided to send it to school with the other girls of the town so it could learn the arts of needlework and spinning. She gave the pumpkin a little kiss and told it to be good and not to mind if people laughed at it, and then the pumpkin rolled off to school.

The school for young ladies happened to be next door to a rich merchant's house. The merchant's son, Murad, used to delight in watching the young ladies as they spun and sewed in the school courtyard beneath his father's windows. One day, he saw a yellow pumpkin rolling around among the young ladies and he said to himself, "Why is a pumpkin going to a school for young ladies?"

Then, he began to notice that every day at noon, when the young ladies ate their meal under the fig trees, the pumpkin rolled off into a far corner of the garden and disappeared.

So, Murad went up to the roof of his father's house. From there he could see the entire garden. He watched the pumpkin as it rolled away by itself at noontime. After the pumpkin had rolled under a currant bush, so that it was hidden from everyone in the garden, it stopped rolling. The top of the pumpkin flew off and out stepped a young girl as beautiful as the moon on its fourteenth night. She climbed up a grapevine and began to pick grapes and eat them for her meal. When she had eaten her fill, she climbed back down the grapevine and stepped into the pumpkin and the top of the pumpkin flew into place again.

Every day after that, Murad went to the roof at noon and watched the beautiful girl as she emerged from the pumpkin, ate her lunch of grapes, and then returned to the pumpkin. Before a week had passed, Murad had fallen in love with her, not with one beat of his heart but with a hundred beats.

One day, he crept to the edge of his father's roof, which was near the top of the grapevine. When the girl in the pumpkin climbed up the vine, Murad leaned out and grasped her hand. He was just going to ask her to be his bride, when she quickly withdrew her hand, hurried down the grapevine, and disappeared inside the pumpkin. Then she rolled back to join the other young ladies.

Murad was very sad. But he found that the girl's ring had slipped off her middle finger into his hand. He went downstairs and said to his mother, "It is time I were married, Mother. I want a wife who can wear this ring on her middle finger and I will marry no other."

His mother was happy for she had long wanted Murad to be married and start his own life. She gave the ring to faithful Nana, an old servant, and said, "Go to each house in the town and find a young girl whose middle finger fits this ring. Then bring her to our house as a bride for Murad."

So, the gray-haired Nana went from house to house, trying the ring on the middle fingers of all the young girls in town. When people asked her what she was doing, she said, "My mistress, the merchant's wife, has sent me to find a wife for Murad. He wishes to marry the girl, rich or poor, whose middle finger fits this ring."

When the young girls in town heard this news, they were very excited. Some tried to starve themselves so their fingers would grow slender enough to fit the ring. Others tried to stuff themselves with butter and honey so their hands would grow plump enough to fit the ring. But the ring did not fit any of them. Finally, the gray-haired Nana came to the house of the good wife at the edge of town. She knocked and asked, "Is there a young girl living in this house?"

"Don't mock me, don't laugh at me," cried the good wife. "Because I wished too hard for a daughter, I was sent a pumpkin instead."

The servant Nana was amazed and said, "Let me see this pumpkin."

So, the pumpkin came rolling out of the kitchen and Nana started laughing.

"Don't mock me," cried the good wife. "Why do you want to see my pumpkin child?"

Nana said, "My mistress, the merchant's wife, has sent me to find a wife for Murad. He wishes to marry the girl, rich or poor, whose middle finger fits this ring." And Nana held out the ring that Murad's mother had given her.

At this moment, to the amazement of the good wife and Nana, a slender, delicate hand poked out of the side of the pumpkin. When they tried the ring on its middle finger, they saw that the ring fitted exactly. Nana ran back to her mistress in a fright and explained what had happened.

The merchant and his wife were angry. "Our son cannot marry a pumpkin," they said. But Murad answered, "Nana, bring the pumpkin to me."

So, Nana ran back to the good wife's house, and soon the pumpkin came rolling into the merchant's house. Everyone laughed, but Murad said, "The middle finger of this pumpkin's hand fits the ring, and so I shall marry the pumpkin." Murad's mother wept, Murad's father shouted, but Murad insisted. And so the wedding was held, and all the town laughed because the richest and handsomest young man in the town was marrying a fat, yellow pumpkin.

After the wedding, Murad took the pumpkin to a house far away on a hill where he cared for her and never allowed others to laugh at her. Then one night, when Murad was asleep, the top of the pumpkin flew off, and out climbed the young girl who was as beautiful as the moon on its fourteenth night. She kissed Murad gently and he woke up. He cried out, "It is the girl in the pumpkin. How were you released?"

"Your love released me," she said. "If you had not loved me when I was a pumpkin, then I would never have been set free."

And so, Murad and his pumpkin wife lived happily for many years. They kept the pumpkin shell in a corner of their house to remind them of the days when Murad had loved his wife even though everyone else had laughed at her. ✦

The Legend of Babouschka
A Story from Russia

Adapted by Ruth Ker

From 1995 to 1997, I traveled three times to Russia for two- to four-week periods. Visiting different areas of that vast country, I offered courses pertaining to Waldorf early childhood education to kindergarten, daycare and nursery teachers; psychologists, librarians, orphanage employees, doctors and nurses. There are many anecdotes that could be told, but I have to say I learned so much from the striving, tenacity and strength of these fine people. It was a new experience for me to be in a country where the original archetypal stories and the local handwork were still being practiced. Reports from colleagues who are continuing these visits to Russia tell me that this may be quickly changing, so I want to share with you one of the treasures which came my way during my journeys there: the story of Babouschka.

The setting for the story, as imagined by the Russian people whom I met, is in the northern part of the country. Although I did visit Norilsk, a city north of the Arctic Circle which experiences polar night—45 days of total darkness—the translation of this story came from a young university student living in Rostov, a city situated on the Don River near the Sea of Azov. There, I met a small group of educators and medical practitioners who were studying Anthroposophy in English, French, German, and Russian, and were trying to start a Waldorf kindergarten and incorporate some of the Weleda remedies and ideas into their medical practices.

It was telling this story of Babouschka at Epiphany one year in the presence of those intent, shining faces of the kindergarten children that gifted me with the blessed deeper impact of this story. I have only changed a few words from the original translation. I hope that you also find this story of benefit to your work. —*Ruth Ker*

Babouschka lived in a little cabin in the coldest corner of a cold and frosty land. Her tiny little house was sitting right in the place where four roads came together. When Father Frost (King Winter) was in the land, then Brother Wind howled at her windows and piles of deep snow piled around her house and hardly anyone ever came to visit or passed by on those nearby roads. Babouschka's heart yearned for the warmth of summer, the fragrance of the flowers and the song of the birds, and for her friends.

One year Babouschka decided to prepare a party for her friends. "Then I won't be lonely," she thought. "I will invite all of my friends. I will cook and clean and clear a path to my door through the snow!" Babouschka set to work. She swept her floor and dusted her shelves and washed her whole house. Then she began to cook the most delicious things—her good bread and cookies and cakes—and she also went to her storeroom and brought potatoes and apples and jars of cabbage and tomatoes to her kitchen.

As the day of the party grew closer, Babouschka began to clear the snow away and make a path to her house. When she was outside, she thought she could hear in the far-off distance the tinkling of bells. "Oh dear," she thought, "my guests must be arriving early. I still have much work to do. I'm not ready. I must hurry!" So Babouschka quickly went inside and began to set the table for her party.

She was just putting the plates on the table when the first knock happened. Babouschka went to her door and opened it, but the person standing there was someone she did not know. Babouschka was surprised to see that he was wearing a magnificent crown as he bent his head to her and said, "Babouschka, we are following a wondrous star in the sky. A special baby is soon to be born. We think He will be a king and that that shining star will lead us to Him. Come with us, Babouschka, and you too can see the newborn king." Babouschka looked past the king and saw two more kings sitting on camels. She could hear the camel bells ringing as the large beasts stomped their feet. But Babouschka thought of her friends who were coming and she said, "I will go with you later, but now I have to get ready for my party." The king sadly turned and left, and Babouschka closed the door behind him.

"Now, I must take my bread out of the oven and put the candles on the table," thought Babouschka. That is when the second knock happened. Babouschka once again opened the door and peered out into the darkness. She thought she could hear the voices of her friends in the distance, but in front of her out of the darkness appeared another king. His clothes were from a country far away from Babouschka's land, and she thought she could see the light of that star the other king had mentioned shining in his face. Sweet-smelling wisps of smoke floated around the king as he waved a golden censer. He, too, asked Babouschka to go with him to see the newborn king.

Babouschka felt a great stirring in her heart, and she longed to go with the Kings, but she looked around her, saw the warm candles of her house, smelled the fresh bread and said, "I will go another day, but I'm too busy preparing for my party now." Babouschka closed her door again and became very busy sweeping the last bit of her floor.

Then she heard the third knock. "My friends are finally here," she thought. Babouschka ran to the door and threw it open, and was surprised to see yet another king. He was young and Babouschka liked him instantly. His smile was a wise one for his young years, and when he too asked Babouschka to come and follow the star, she knew that she wanted to go very much. "Stay with me tonight and come to my party," she said. "Then I will go with you tomorrow to see this wonderful king." But the wise king sadly shook his head and said, "We must follow the star. You have many things to offer this newborn king, Babouschka. Bring them with you and come with us too." But Babouschka shook her head. She could see that her friends were arriving. As she welcomed them, her gaze followed the Kings as they mounted their camels and set off on path towards that great star that filled the whole night with light.

Babouschka had a wonderful party with her friends. They ate the good bread and most of the food and they danced and they sang.

But when her friends went home the next day, Babouschka thought about those Kings and that Baby and a great yearning began. Babouschka quickly gathered up some presents and some of the food left over from her party and she set out to follow the path of the wise Kings. The footprints of the camels were all covered over with snow, but Babouschka trudged onward looking for that great star. She did not find that star, or that Baby, so Babouschka gave her presents to a poor family who also had a newborn baby.

Babouschka returned home, but all the rest of that long, cold winter, and even when the warm time came, Babouschka prepared to go with the Kings when they visited her again the next year. Babouschka waited for the Kings the next winter, but they did not come. So she set out on her own, taking gifts that she had prepared the whole year before. She searched and searched and again she did not find the Star Child, but she noticed how the children she did find loved the gifts that she brought.

Again Babouschka went home and she followed the longing that was growing in her heart to find that Child of Light. So it came to pass that with every returning year, Babouschka set out to find that Child the three Kings had told her about. Each year, she prepared something for Him and each year she gave her gifts to children who smiled and delighted in her presents. Babouschka came to love the children greatly.

One Christmas, Babouschka had hardly anything left in her house to give. She was old now and had given much to many children and their parents. She had found an old toy and was busy polishing it when she heard a soft cry outside the door. "That sounds like a baby," she thought. "Who would leave a child outside on a cold night like this?"

Babouschka quickly went to her door and opened it. She looked out into the cold, dark night, and there, on her doorstep, she saw a basket. In it was a shining Baby, and when He saw the polished toy in Babouschka's hands He held up his little hands and cooed with delight. Babouschka's heart filled with joy. Then she looked up and saw that there, standing around the Child, was an adoring mother and father, and behind them were the three Kings who had come to her door on that night long ago, and around them were all the children's parents whose hearts Babouschka had lightened. They had all come to Babouschka's hearth … and then, Babouschka knew that nothing had been wasted. She knew that all of her efforts to find the Child of Light had been worthwhile. Her heart was full of love. ✦

Activity Ideas
for Older Children
in the
Kindergarten

Compiled by Nancy Blanning and Ruth Ker

Outdoors: Activities and equipment for older children to play and work with

- Jump rope—child jumps a long rope turned by an adult and then begins to help turn the rope for others. One end of the skipping rope can also be tied to a swivel so that only one turner is required. Also the child jumping a single skipping rope alone is a challenging activity.
- Horse jumps—benches, stumps or obstacles that the children can position for jumping over
- Horse reins devised from strips of leather
- Obstacle courses with balancing, climbing, skipping, crawling, rolling down hills, hopscotch etc.
- Traditional games—What Time Is It, Mr. Wolf? Red Rover, etc.
- Mounds of pea gravel, grassy hills
- Helping others: raking, cleaning, shoveling, trimming bushes, collecting sticks, clearing rocks, gardening, sowing grass seeds, watering, building fires
- Picking up litter from Mother Earth on morning walks

Outdoors: Materials and equipment for playing

- Provision for Earth, Air, Water and Fire experiences
- Stilts
- Saw horses
- Pumps, pails and water barrels for pumping, dipping into, and carrying water
- Straw bales, tree limbs and/or corn stalks tied or draped together to make structures
- Real tools—shovels, rakes, big buckets
- Wheelbarrows, wagons and sturdy gardening tools

- Teeter-totters—safe and low to the ground
- Balance boards
- A-frame ladders
- Big fisherman's ropes for swinging, bouncing, hanging upside down, hauling around
- Cross-cut saw—used with teacher supervision
- Carpentry tools at a work bench
- Fire pit for festival cooking (baked apples and potatoes, bread, pizza)
- Cob oven or chiminera
- Waterplay—tubs, bamboo pole that is hollowed out and used as a waterway to float pinecones, sticks, walnut boats and so on
- Rope "pulley" over tree limb
- Wagons and moving-dollies
- Bows and arrows made from willow sticks or maple saplings
- Large, heavy logs and stumps
- Sand, rocks, sticks, planks, boulders
- Kindling to be chopped with teacher supervision
- Bouncing balls

Indoors: Activities and equipment for older children to play and work with

- Working with wool—shearing, washing, carding. Wool can be dyed in spring, felted into strands, and braided for spring/May crowns or long ropes
- Washing wool—wool passed through three buckets to wash, three buckets to rinse
- Hand- and brush-carding wool (dog combing brushes work well and are inexpensive)
- Rolling yarn into balls
- Four-strand fingerknitting (making hats and/or blankets for the dolls)
- Wet-felting activities—balls, eggs, mice, seed babies, snowmen, etc. (Please note that needle felting is not an appropriate activity for kindergarten children)
- Weaving reed baskets with teacher assistance
- Making knot dolls with a handkerchief for head and body, hemming a doll blanket, and making "nightgowns"
- Making swords
- Making shields
- Pressing leaves or flowers with a wooden leaf press
- Making notecards using pressed leaves/flowers and paintings
- Making stilts by sawing log rounds, boring holes through the bark and fingerknitting ropes to go through the holes
- Making boats from scraps of wood
- Sewing pincushions, doll clothes, blankets
- Sewing napkins for snack time
- Making napkin rings by cutting and sanding pieces of bamboo
- Making candle holders by cutting and sanding log rounds and drilling holes

- Fingerknitting skipping ropes and play ropes
- Making felt, wool or paper crowns
- Sowing wheat berries for Easter grass and harvesting the wheatgrass for drinks or feeding the animals in your environment
- Grinding grains, milling oats
- Making candles—rolling and/or dipping them
- Caring for plants and animals
- Making wool butterflies from tiny bits of dyed wool and pipecleaner
- Making aromatic bath salts with essential oils
- Nature-dyeing silk, wool, and cotton

Indoors: Materials and equipment (other than our usual furnishings)

- Supplies for present wrapping—tissue, small silks
- Supplies for card making and money making
- Large planks for making slides, bridges, etc.
- Available furniture so that the children can make their own obstacle courses
- Scooter boards
- Big wooden boxes—can be pushed, pulled and adapted to being boats, cars, Santa's sleigh, homes for the babies, cargo holds, etc.
- Bowl of grain for sensory games—many examples of small objects in identical pairs can be buried in the bowl of grain and the children have to dig their hands and arms down into the bowl and retrieve the matching objects
- Large wooden box filled with beans that the children can climb into
- Heavy stumps
- Provision for climbing and large movements (loft areas, ladders, permission to climb on top of sturdy play stands)
- Cushions and pillows for jumping into and making sensory "sandwiches." These "sandwiches" are generally made by the teacher in the beginning. The children lie down on a large pillow and another pillow (piece of bread) is put on top of them. While they are saying what kind of sandwich it is, the teacher pushes down on the pillows (spreading mayonnaise, mustard, pickles etc. on top), informing the children underneath about their bodily boundaries by firm pressure. After a few examples the children often will do this for themselves. This is a great way to bring down the noise level in the classroom, and oftentimes the children line up to take turns or incorporate this activity into their play.

Handwork and festival activities:

- Making flower, ivy, willow or large leaf crowns
- Making pinecone birds placed on the ends of saplings
- Making pinecone mice with leather ears and tails
- Making chestnut mice with felt ears and tails
- Making teasel porcupines

- Making God's eyes with streamers
- Making cattails with streamers to take on an autumn parade
- Making Michaelmas shooting stars out of felted wool balls, mordanted with alum, dyed with marigolds and adorned with sparkling streamers
- Apple cider pressing
- Harvesting herbs to boil down with beeswax, oil and lanolin for healing cream
- Harvesting the garden—digging potatoes, pulling carrots, etc.
- Putting the garden to bed for the winter
- Planting bulbs
- Processing grain—scything, threshing, winnowing, and grinding it into flour
- Making a harvest wreath with grain stalks—this can later hang from the ceiling bedecked with gifts of each season: dried apple stars, paper snowflakes, butterflies, dried flowers, Whitsun birds, Easter eggs etc.
- Making jam
- Churning butter
- Peeling apples for pies, applesauce, apple crisp or dried apple rings
- Washing potatoes, carrots and other garden vegetables
- Making leaf kites with large leaves
- Making acorn whistles—find an acorn with no cracks, drill a hole in top with sharp, pointed stone, hollow out nutmeat completely with a sharp, pointed stick
- Floating walnut boats
- Making grass dolls made like wool yarn dolls
- Making corn dolls

Projects for first-grade-ready children

- Sewing a needle book with a button closure and making a pincushion and assembling a sewing basket with safety pins, pins, thread, and needles
- Making a standup puppet and putting on a puppet play with friends
- Basket making with teacher's help
- Making heavy jump ropes with the jump rope stitch
- Making stilts
- Making simple dolls and doll clothes

It's important to reinforce here that the six-year-olds do not need make-work projects. The ideas above are suggestions, but by no means would all of these be part of one kindergarten year. The play of the older children in the kindergarten is still the most important part of their day. Many of the above work activities can be incorporated into the life activities of the kindergarten day and the children can come and go from their play to participate in them. Also it is very acceptable to have activities for the older children that the younger ones will only sample when it is their turn to be the older children in the kindergarten. ✦

Transitional Games, Verses, and Songs

Compiled by Ruth Ker and Barbara Klocek

It is my experience that the older children have endless hours of enjoyment playing traditional games (such as Kling Klang Gloria, Water Water Wallflower, In and Out the Bonnie Bluebells, London Bridge, Oranges and Lemons). We play them as a group every day after storytime and before pick-up time. The children soon organize their own opportunities to play these games both at outside time and during free play time. In my opinion, the traditional games are one of the best resources for the older children. Books of games can be found in many bookstores, especially anthroposophical book outlets. You may see that some of the games and song-games mentioned are not in the mood of the fifth. Nevertheless they carry the children in that same lilting, repetitive and never-ending stream and are often responded to with "let's play it again." —*Ruth Ker*

Seeking games

Little seed goes round and round,
Round and round and round and round,
Little seed goes round and round
And never, ever, ever be found.

Children are seated in a circle. One child has a seed and passes from child to child as if to give them the seed. He drops it in someone's hands. The teacher says, "Sarah, who do you think has the seed?" She guesses and if the child has the seed, Sarah gets to hide it. If the child doesn't have it, he or she gets to guess who does.

This game can also be played substituting the words "little treasure" for little seed. The children then sit in a circle while one of their friends covers her eyes. Then the other children pass the treasure around and hide their hands behind their backs when the verse is over. Then the child who has hidden her eyes opens them and guesses who has the treasure.

❖ ❖

We've lost two children, we've lost two children,
Now tell us who they are.
Come back ——, come back ——,
And tell us who they are.

Children are seated in a circle. Two children go out of the circle and cover their eyes. The teacher chooses two children by gesturing and they hide under a sheet in front of her. We sing the song above and the two children come back and try to guess who it is who is hiding. Usually they cannot guess so the teacher asks if anyone has a hint. They raise their hands and give hints: the color of their hair, their cubby symbols, a little brother's name, and so on. This is a good game for the older children, for they are often able to guess who is missing even without a hint.

❖ ❖

Gnomes (or stars or bunnies) are hiding.
Our eyes are guiding
Us to where they are.

Make up your own tune.

❖ ❖

I spy with my little eye something that is red (green, blue, etc.)

To keep it simple, it is a color on a child. The guesser only needs to name the child.

❖ ❖

Ringline, ringline, you must wander
From the one hand to the other
Ringline, ringline, you must wander
Oh, my lovely ringline

The teacher's ring is put on a fingerknitted rope that is long enough to go all the way around a circle of children. One child is sitting in the middle covering her eyes. As the song is sung (feel free to make up your own tune) the children move the ring along. Then when the song stops, the children clasp their hands on the rope and the child in the middle guesses whose clasped hand contains the ring.

❖ ❖

Doggie, doggie who's got the bone
Someone took it from my home
Open your eyes doggie and see
Who it could possibly be.

Teacher chooses a child to go into the center and places a "bone" (usually a rock or piece of wood) on the child's back. Then another child is chosen to take the "bone" off the hiding child's back. All of the children sitting in the circle then hide their hands behind their back and the "doggie" in the center guesses who has the bone.

❖ ❖

Here is the box and here is the lid
I wonder what inside is hid
It's a ——— without a doubt
Let's take off the lid and let it out

Children and teacher sitting in a circle all touching to make a fenced circle. The children tell the teacher what pretend thing is in the box (horse, butterfly, etc.). Then teacher takes off the pretend lid with her gestures and lets the creature or flower or other being out. Some children will say, "I'm going to make a hole in the ground for my bunny." They then proceed to pretend to dig a little space in front of them. The game proceeds until everyone has a turn and the inside circle is full of ducks in ponds, bunnies in burrows, butterflies and birds in the trees etc.

❖ ❖

Isn't it funny how a bear loves honey?
Yum, yum, yum
Hide your eyes Mr. Bear
And I will find me some.

The children are sitting in a circle with the teacher and the teacher hands the honey pot to a child who then goes into the center of the circle. When Mr. Bear hides his eyes, the teacher points to one of the children who takes the pot and hides it behind his back. All of the children hide their hands and when the bear looks up, she guesses who has the honey pot.

I sent a letter to my love
And on the way I dropped it:
One of you has picked it up
And put it in your pocket.
(Tune: Yankee Doodle)

One child goes around the outside of a circle of sitting children and drops a "letter" behind someone. At the end of the song, the standing child and the receiving child run around the circle in opposite directions and try to sit down in the empty space. Use the traditional tune.

Shoemaker, shoemaker, make me a shoe
Have it ready by half-past two
Shoemaker, shoemaker, tell me please
Who has shoes that are just like these?

One child is standing blindfolded in the middle of the circle while the other children sit in a circle with their feet outstretched. The teacher slowly turns the blindfolded child around and then when the singing stops (please make up your own tune) the teacher guides the child to bend down, touch the shoes of a friend and guess whose shoes they are. If the child cannot guess then the other children give hints.

Marie's in the garden, in the garden is Marie
All the trees and flowers are bigger then she
Guess if you can where Marie can be.

The teacher passes a finger puppet of a little girl to one of the children in the circle while another child has hidden his eyes. When the verse stops the child opens his eyes and guesses which of the children have hidden Marie. Marie gets hidden in pockets, up sleeves, under vests, etc.

Transitional Verses

Please feel free to make up your own gestures.

This is the house with the roof so good,
Here are the walls that are made of wood,
Her are the doors that shut up tight,
Here are the windows that let in the light,
Here are the people that fill it with love,
And here are the angels that guard from above.

❖ ❖ ❖

My name is Christopher Cobbler, I make fine shoes.
I make long shoes, short shoes, tall shoes, flat shoes.
My name is Christopher Cobbler, I make fine shoes.

My name is Betsy Baker, I make fine bread.
I make long bread, round bread, braided bread, bagel bread.
My name is Betsy Baker, I make fine bread.

My name is Tommy Tailor, I make fine stitches.
I make big stitches, tiny stitches, running stitches, blanket stitches.
My name is Tommy Tailor, I make fine stitches.

My name is Bobby Boatmaker, I make fine boats,
I make big boats, small boats, rowing boats, sail boats.
My name is Bobby Boatmaker, I make fine boats.

My name is Farmer Leslie, I care for the farm.
I plant the seeds, I pull the weeds, I feed the animals and keep them warm.
My name is Farmer Leslie, I care for the farm.

And make up your own verses!

Opening Verses and Songs

Gentle fai-ries, Wise elf men, ___ Come join us please do, We

bring gold - en light from our gar-den to you. Our an-gels they guard us by day and by

night, in the sun and the moon and the stars shin-ing bright.

End with (to your own tune):

Light fairies, come to us, bring to us your golden light.
And the light fairies come, bringing light from stars and sun.

❖ ❖ ❖

Down is the earth, up is the sky,
There are my friends, and here am I.

❖ ❖ ❖

Good morning, dear Earth. Good morning, dear Sun.
Good morning, stones and the flowers every one.
Good morning dear beasts, and the birds in the trees.
Good morning to you and good morning to me.

(This verse may be spoken, or make up your own tune. May be sung once standing, once going in a ring)

❖ ❖ ❖

We are guarded from harm
Cared for by angels.
Here we stand,
Loving and strong (bold),
Truthful and good.

❖   ❖   ❖

The front door is shut	clap hands in front of the body
The back door is shut	clap hands behind the body
The big window is closed	place hands together without clapping at chest level (impulse control)
The small window is closed	place hands together without clapping at belly
The basement window is closed	fingertips together at feet
And the tiny window at the top	
is closed	fingertips together over our heads
I am in my house	cross hands over chest, stomp feet

❖   ❖   ❖

The earth is firm beneath my feet
The sun shines bright above
And here I stand so straight and strong
All things to know and love.

Daily Transitional Songs and Verses

To light the morning circle candle:
   When everything is so quiet . . . the light fairies come, bringing light from stars and sun

To end the morning circle:
   I dance with the flowers, I sing with the sun. My warmth I give to everyone.

To put out morning circle candle:
   Here is a spark of Father Sun's light, to keep in our hearts so warm and bright.

Before blessing and snack or lunch:
   Welcome, welcome, welcome to our table.
   Quiet, quiet, we all fold hands together.

Closing of snack or lunch:
   Hands holding together, making our golden chain we say, thank you for our meal.

To be chosen to play the kinderharp at rest time or to begin a game:
  I'm looking to see, who's quiet as can be. (sung to a simple tune)

At the end of rest time:
  Awake the sun is shining bright. The birds are singing in the light.
  Gloria, gloria.

To signal nap time:

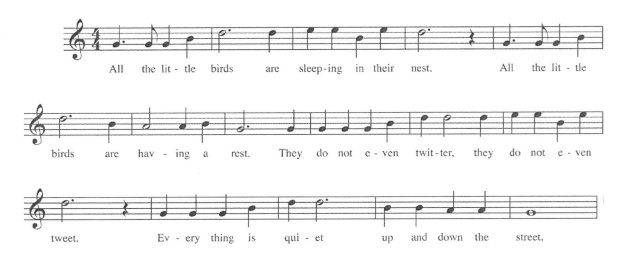

And at the end of the rest we say . . .

  Along comes Momma Bird and taps them on the back
  Come with me, come with me, we've finished up our nap.

      ❖   ❖   ❖

After story:

Ending verses

Angel of God that is guarding me,
Be thou a shining star above me, be thou a clear path before me.
Be thou a good shepherd behind me,
Today, tonight when the stars are shining bright, and forever.

❖   ❖   ❖

Oh lovely Sun, oh lovely Earth, dear friends all gathered here.
Let's all join hands and there may flow,
A stream of warmth and golden glow,
Good-bye.

❖   ❖   ❖

Goodbye now, goodbye now, it's time for us to go back home
Goodbye now, goodbye now, it's time for us to go.
(Sandra and her family) will come to the gate
They will go now, they won't be late
Goodbye now, goodbye now, it's time for them to go.

At festival time, this is useful for a singing verse to help the children and their families to exit the classroom. Often the teachers make a bridge under which the families can exit the circle. Sometimes I say to the waiting children, "I'll know when to ask you because I'll see you sitting so still." This song can bring a peaceful and ordered finish to a festival gathering. Many different tunes have been used; one can be found on page 42 of the second edition of *Spindrift* (Gloucester, UK: Wynstones Press, 1983).

Jump Rope Rhymes

Compiled by Barbara Klocek and Ruth Ker

Ringle rangle rowdy cocka-doodle-doo
Walking in the garden picking berries blue
One for me, one for you
And the grump must have one too
How many berries did he (or she) pick?
1, 2, 3, 4, … [1]

❖   ❖   ❖

Teddy bear, Teddy Bear, turn around
Teddy bear, Teddy Bear, touch the ground
Teddy Bear, Teddy Bear climb the stairs
Teddy Bear, Teddy Bear say your prayers
Teddy Bear, Teddy Bear say goodnight
Teddy Bear, Teddy Bear turn off the light
How many dreams did she (he) have?
1, 2, 3, 4, …

❖   ❖   ❖

---

1   For music see Nancy Foster, *Dancing as we Sing* (Acorn Hill Waldorf Kindergarten and Nursery), 44.

Down by the river, down by the sea
I found a starfish as pretty as can be
How many legs did it have?
1, 2, 3, 4, …

❖   ❖   ❖

Down in the valley where the green grass grows
There sat ———— as pretty as a rose
Along came mother and kissed him (her) on the cheek
How many kisses did he (she) get this week?
1, 2, 3, 4, …

❖   ❖   ❖

Oh see my playmate, come out and play with me
And we'll be jolly friends, climb up my apple tree
Slide down my rainbow into my cellar door
And we'll be jolly friends for ever more
More! Shut the door!
How many friends did she (he) have?
1, 2, 3, 4, …[2]

❖   ❖   ❖

Jack be nimble, Jack be quick
Jack jumped over the candlestick
Careful Jack! Don't burn your clothes.
Just jump right on your tippy-toes.
How many times did Jack jump?
1, 2, 3, 4, …

---

2   The traditional tune of this skipping game, like many others, is not in the mood of the fifth.

Parents as Partners

S peaking out of a real listening and perceiving of the other enables a true encounter to occur, from which new possibilities can arise. The way we listen enables others to speak. In other words, to actively listen means giving others the possibility of saying things that they could not otherwise have said—or could not have said in the same way.

Heinz Zimmermann
Speaking Listening Understanding

Waldorf Education
for the Child and the Parent

Devon Brownsey

I am my child's first teacher, but I could never have fully understood what this means without having teachers of my own.

After the birth of my son, the teacher that I had in my own early childhood years gave me the book *You Are Your Child's First Teacher* by Rahima Baldwin Dancy. I had attended a Waldorf school for a brief time as a child, but had little connection with the philosophy since that time. I found the book interesting, familiar, and thought-provoking, but a world away from my current life and the baby in my arms. I had no intention of sending our children to my old school, because we lived a great distance away.

Now almost four years later I have reconnected with this same Waldorf community, one that I now find I have actually been a part of my entire life. But being a child in a Waldorf school is very different from being a parent in a Waldorf school.

Understanding and applying the Waldorf philosophy to our home life has been a multifaceted process, and at times I have felt completely overwhelmed, not knowing where to begin or how to support the teacher's messages in our home. I have been guided in this journey by many teachers—in parent and child groups, afternoon kindergarten craft circles, and during evening workshops. I now see that my own education in Anthroposophy and Waldorf philosophy is just as important as that of my children—and this realization has made my parenting journey so much more interesting.

When one is a Waldorf teacher who is involved in every facet of a school and its underlying philosophy, it can be easy to forget the journey it took to acquire those understandings. Teachers may even fall into the assumption that parents understand what they are doing and why. But the fact is, regardless of how involved a parent may be, Waldorf teachers draw upon years of training and experience while many parents will only have periodic contact with the philosophy. It can be a mystifying process trying to fit the pieces of the puzzle together, especially when the outside world does not promote many of the same tenets as Waldorf education.

Forming a trusting relationship between teachers and parents is vital to the success of the young child who is entering a Waldorf early childhood education program.

It is my belief that Waldorf philosophy needs to extend beyond the doors of the classroom. Forming a trusting relationship between teachers and parents is vital to the success of the young child who is entering a Waldorf early childhood education program.

My first steps into a Waldorf school as a parent happened when I attended a parent-child morning group with my two-year-old son and my newborn daughter. I had put a lot of pressure on myself and I remember feeling worried for the first few weeks that my child would not live up to my expectations for him to adapt into the program. He didn't want to sit at snack time and I wondered if he would ever listen to the teacher's stories.

Both my son and I learned from this teacher. She did not "teach" me through lectures or direct comments, but through her actions. She gave us readings to take home, gently reminding us to dress our children warmly and give them fewer choices.

Imitation is important not only for the developing child, but also for the developing parent! On some rambunctious mornings, a few of us would joke and say that we had been "channeling" our teacher when we spoke to our children in gentle tones. I truly felt that by thinking of myself as the teacher and modeling her way of being with the children, I would sometimes gain strength. Quieting my voice and imitating her way of conversing helped me to restore order and gain parenting skills.

As the parent and child group fell into the rhythm of our Monday mornings, I felt less pressure on myself and realized that all of the parents and children were working towards the same thing. It was comforting to realize there is no perfect Waldorf child or parent. We were a group of very different people with shared values for our children.

I still attend the parent-child group with my daughter, but my son has since moved into kindercottage (the nursery) by himself. Leading up to his first day there, his new teacher gave me lots of words of wisdom to best set him up for a successful transition … but I still cried into the arms of another mother on his first day. He, on the other hand, embraced the kindercottage with open arms and adjusted easily.

It was through a conversation with my first early childhood teacher that I started to explore other ways to put Waldorf philosophy and education into my life. I had read books, and of course participated in my children's programs, but I wanted more. She told me about an adult lecture series she was leading.

The lectures were attended by many enthusiastic parents. It surprised me that so much of what the teachers were saying resonated with my own life and my own beliefs. It was also an opportunity for the parents to listen and participate and think without the interruptions that inevitably come when the children are present. The thirst for education, guidance, and knowledge was evident as questions poured out and the lecturers tried to stay within the allotted time frame.

I learned a great deal about the philosophy and the Waldorf approach that I had never even thought about until I attended these evening lectures. All the topics really came alive, and concepts such as the twelve senses and the incarnating child were explained to us in ways that were much more effective than simply reading a book.

While I had heard that nothing in Waldorf education is "arbitrary," the concept really came to life for me during that time. Every evening on my drive home from the weekly lecture I felt full—full of inspiration for the next morning with my children, full of happiness for the choices my husband and I had made that brought us to this school, and full of love for the person who had been my first teacher and who was still teaching me twenty years later.

This learning inspired me to become more involved with other parents. I joined the kindergarten's monthly craft afternoon, where we read articles and discussed them with the kindergarten teacher while working on a seasonal craft project for her classroom. Sharing ideas with other parents and working with my hands really showed me the value of stimulating the brain while keeping the hands busy.

Our parent-child teacher has since started another session with parents and children who are all new to the school. She invited me and another mother to attend the first few mornings so that we could bring our experiences and our already-familiarized children to help inaugurate the group. As we gathered at the first snack table, I could feel the frustration of some of the new mothers, as they watched their children refusing to eat the soup and not wanting to stay sitting at the table.

It was at this moment that I could see that I had come full circle and that I had learned so much in the past eighteen months. I reassured the new parents that this was how it was on my first day too. But now, here I was sitting with my child while he asked the teacher for another bowl of our good homemade soup.

Had things really changed that much? The teacher smiled and thanked me for sharing my experience. I could not have come this far without her gentle guidance, support, and teaching.

This experience and the other opportunities that I have sampled have shown me the value of actively pursuing learning in my career as a parent. It is not just the children who need to experience with head, heart, and hands. I am my child's first teacher ... but I still need teachers too. ✦

References

Dancy, Rahima Baldwin. *You Are Your Child's First Teacher*. Berkeley, CA: Celestial Arts, 1989.

Working with Parents: Ideas for Parent Meetings

Ruth Ker and Nancy Blanning
following conversations with Tim Bennett, Louise deForest, and Barbara Klocek

Wise teachers and parents realize that healthy development and happiness arise unconsciously within the child when those around him or her are all working out of the same intentions. The time that parents and teachers spend focusing on the children they share in common and developing a nonjudgmental interest in one another pays off mightily. These efforts build an abundance of warmth between parent, child, and teacher. In turn, this kindling of interest and warmth is what allows difficult topics to be addressed and trust to develop between the key people operative throughout the child's early childhood. Many insights are spawned out of the soul/spiritual substance that is created through this cooperative relationship. How many times have parents and teachers conferred together one day, and the next day the child they were pondering shows them the answer? Something invisible is at work here—spawned out of the efforts that the adults in the child's life have made to reach out for the betterment of the whole. Henning Kohler and others speak about these kinds of events arising out of the link that parents and teachers can cultivate with the child's and their own angels.[1]

We also know that the insights from anthroposophical child-rearing indications and Waldorf pedagogy can provide us with deeper understandings about child development and how to nurture the whole human being. This is something teachers want and need to share with parents, so that we can all work towards the same goals for the children. Yet we see daily that much of our culture contradicts these wholesome ideas. Waldorf schools are truly counter-culture in this regard. Finding ways to share these insights without seeming "old fashioned"

---

1 Henning Kohler, *Working With Anxious, Nervous and Depressed Children*, passim.

or "quaint" is a humbling challenge. In our urgent and passionate desire to protect and support healthy growth, we can also seem dogmatic and intimidating to parents when we do share our views.

The question then arises, "How is it that parents and teachers can best share the essential information?" In "Waldorf Education for the Child, and the Parent" earlier in this section the author, a parent, stresses that there are many ways of making information retainable and many individual styles of learning. Although many of us find it effective to use the lecture format at parent evenings, we must be aware of how much easier and welcoming it is for parents to come to parent talks when the talks are full of warmth and lively examples. It is through these lively examples and true stories that the parents are able to reach into the topic being explained and find commonality with it. The examples allow them to "feel into" the situation. Taking this a step further, many teachers are finding much success when they provide the parents with an experience, where they can do hands-on things or actually momentarily dwell within what is being described by the presenter.

When we discussed the cooperative working of the parent and the teacher at our Older Child in the Kindergarten Research Group retreats, we agreed that we live in a time now where a new task confronts us as educators. The task is to create a new paradigm for our partnering work with parents. We would do well to hear the call to create new ways of involving parents in experiential learning. Perhaps the venue could be a caring circle, a discussion group where parents and teachers bring their own real-life scenarios to the conversation, a study group full of lively examples, or a well-planned parent evening in which the parents are actively involved in examples that teach the principles addressed. In any case, we are challenged to move beyond the top-down model to a more interactive model where the experience of the parents and teachers can co-exist and those involved can drink in more deeply the lessons involved.

As well as providing important basic information, parent meetings are a prime opportunity to strengthen the soul/spiritual substance of the adult social community.

As well as providing important basic information, parent meetings are a prime opportunity to strengthen the soul/spiritual substance of the adult social community. This ultimately benefits each child as an individual and the class as a whole. What we are able to enjoy together in our early childhood class meetings can be carried forward into the grade school, in the form of a class of parents that work well together on many different levels.

The following are some ideas collected from the working-group teachers. These are experiences that they and their colleagues have found effective for parent meetings. One common element apparent within these ideas is that the parents actually are involved in *experiential* learning. Some of these suggestions include a format that does not involve a lecture, and some have an experiential format woven together with lecture material. As we strive to work with the will of the children, so can we also engage the parents' will along with their thinking and feeling.

We live in a time now when humanity as a whole is developing the consciousness soul, and that motivates all of us to want to take things more deeply into the thinking, feeling, and willing parts of our souls. We also encounter each other at different times in our individual biographies. Someone who is learning during the ages of twenty-one to twenty-eight may want to experience the answers with his or her sentient soul, whereas the intellectual soul may be more operative between twenty-eight and thirty-five. The consciousness soul time in our own biographies spans the wide horizon of the years from thirty-five to forty-two. These previous seven-year cycles and their events provide the groundwork for the imaginations, inspirations, and intuitions that arise in the next twenty-one years of our development.[2]

It's important for teachers to really know the ages and likely biographical phases of their audience in order to prepare the most nourishing parent meeting experiences. Preparing for a group of parents who are around twenty-five is very different than preparing for a group who are mostly over forty. There are many books on the life rhythms of biography, like the one cited below, that can be helpful reads for adults who are gathering together in community. Nevertheless, it is best to remember that when experience confirms what we are asking those in our audience to think, they will be able to hold more of a conviction for the idea. They will also be able to retain what they have learned and, if it serves their family, hopefully carry it into their home life.

Suggestions for Parent Meetings

The following are some ideas that we hope will nourish you and your community.

At the first parent meeting, often held before school starts:

- Allow time for the parents to speak about themselves individually—saying their names and occupations, what is their passion or "bliss" for finding joy and rejuvenation in life. Remember to actively take interest in the parents as well as the children. This information sharing can happen as the parents are doing something with their hands to help prepare for the upcoming year. (This interest that teachers extend toward the parents can later expand into the parent-teacher conferences. Then teachers can allow some time to connect to what the parents expressed on that first evening and to ask the parents about themselves and how things are going now.)

- Parents decorate their child's birthday candle for that year and tell how they came to name their child. Later this candle will be used at the child's birthday celebration at school.

- The parents are asked to bring something from nature that represents their children. They can then explain what about this natural item reminds them of their children. All of these items are then assembled in the center of the circle as each parent first speaks about his or

2   Gudrun Burkhard, *Taking Charge—Your Life Patterns and Their Meaning*, 169.

her child, and then places the offering on a table. By so doing, a class sculpture is created. If parents forget to bring something they can be encouraged to find something from within the classroom to add to the sculpture. It is remarkable to see that often the parents' classroom choice is exactly what their children choose as a favorite plaything when they enter school that first day.

- The teacher opens the meeting with an imagination of how each child has intentionally sought out his or her parents as being the perfect ones for their current life on earth. Then the parents are asked to choose two postcards (from a large collection the teacher has assembled)—one to represent the gift the parents already have that they can give to their children, the other to show what new qualities the children are asking of the parents to personally develop. Then the parents have the bonding experience of sharing around the circle their pictures and thoughts around these two topics.

Here are some ways that we could share some of the other important topics at later parent gatherings:

- Schedule a three-, four-, or five-part parenting series. Give the series a lively title. Each meeting could address one topic such as rhythm, warmth, sleep, or other topics particularly relevant to your group. Include within the evening's presentation several ways that the topic can be experienced. Can those attending touch, manipulate, use their bodies in movement, see a picture, etc.? For example, have the room be too cold so that the parents cannot find physical comfort being there. Then ask the parents to pay attention to their reactions and how that affects their behavior and well-being. Then talk about young children not being able to monitor their own warmth organism, show the importance of physical warmth on the formation of the child's organs, and so on. Focusing on one topic alone allows the chance to deepen information and experience so that parents do not feel overwhelmed.

  We want to speak clearly about what is good for the children but in a way that the parents do not feel judged. Carrying this intent into the next parent conferences, we can then make a point of expressing what we admire about their parenting. When affirmed in their parenting practices, often parents will feel freer to discuss their important childrearing questions.

- With the topic of *choices*—As a prelude, when the parents have just arrived at the parent meeting, ask the parents in rapid succession to make all sorts of decisions, with no time to reflect upon them. This can give them the experience of how fatiguing and taxing it is for children to be bombarded with choices. (Thanks to Eugene Schwartz for this idea.) Also ask them how they would feel if they were airplane passengers and the pilot came onto the loudspeaker and asked, "Would you like to fly at 28,000 feet or 35,000 feet?" (Thanks to Dorothy Olsen for this idea.) With respect to leaving the decision to the children as to which school they would like to go to, ask the parents "What city would you like to live in, Timbuktu or Neverland?" Things like this can be woven into an evening's presentation.

- With the topic of *media*—Begin the evening with silence, followed by humming or music, story telling, and then a puppet play. Ask the parents about their experience during and after the puppet play. A presentation can then happen or the evening can simply be concluded by showing a video of *The Lion King* or whatever current video is being portrayed as child-friendly.

  It has also been effective to have a high school teacher, remedial teacher or a teacher of the upper grades speak about his or her experience of seeing children who have been exposed to a lot of media. Having older students who have been protected from media describe their own experience is another option.

  Inviting the parents to a meeting and having loud music blaring in the kindergarten can also portray the experience of how different the environment becomes when invaded by these sounds. Parents have become used to the sacredness of this child-centered space and can feel the violation that is happening.

- On the topic of *toys*—Bring a bag of toys from a thrift shop to a parent evening. Parents feel inside the bag without looking and guess what each item is. Then the toys are taken out and the parents play with them. This can be done by breaking up into small groups. Then the groups can reassemble into the larger group and a lively discussion ensues. It is interesting for all to see what can or cannot be played with and for how long interest can be sustained.

  When experience confirms what we are asking those in our audience to think, they will be able to hold more of a conviction for the idea.

  Another idea is to ask the parents to imagine that they have the consciousness of the young child—filled with the urge to unite with everything. Then pass a Waldorf doll around the circle, asking the parents to unite with this image and to notice how they feel when doing this. Next pass a plastic action figure (spiky collar, green sneering face, muscle-bound—you know the type) around the circle and ask the parents once again to try to unite with this image (you may need to apologize first). Then ask, "Which image would you want your children to carry around within them?"

- To illustrate *the child's need for play and experiential learning rather than intellectual explanations*—Bring to a parent evening some exotic fruits hidden under a cloth in a bowl. These fruits must be unfamiliar to the parents. Then tell the parents that you are going to describe something to them so that they will know it better. Do not show them what is under the cloth in the bowl but proceed to describe the fruits verbally and just assume that the parents will understand what is being described. It is likely that the parents will not be able to picture what they have never seen or experienced before. From this they can have the realization that they *and their children* need to touch and experience things in order to know them. Make the point that many things in this world are unfamiliar to their children and, rather than intellectual explanations, the children need to be given quality and quantities of time to sample appropriate things. And how do they do that? They play at it! (Thank you to Kim Hunter from Salt Spring Island, British Columbia for this idea about the fruits.)

- Practicing *observation and attention*—Do an observation exercise at the beginning of each parent evening, and continue doing this at each meeting for one year. The hope here is that we learn together that slowing down to observe and take in our surroundings actually informs us about important things. This can be critical for our parenting. Often we don't realize how little we take in as we live our preoccupied lives. Here are some observation exercises:

  — Draw something only felt with your hands and not seen.

  — Draw something not seen but which another person describes to you.

  — Describe what the person sitting next to you is wearing without looking at them again. Now describe what they are wearing after looking at them with this task in mind.

  —Observe your child's eating habits—how she eats, food preferences, etc., and then inform the group at the next parent evening about what you observed.

  After some of these experiences, it is explained that observation is a potent tool for teachers and can be for parents as well.

- On the topic of *movement*—Offer experiences of movement, such as a circle time, a movement journey, a playful obstacle course, some circus-type movements. These experiences can help to illustrate to parents that they do not have to put their children in sports or a lot of extracurricular events in order to provide movement and playful experiences for their children. Encourage parents to help or allow their children to create a circus at home so they can see how children would rather do that than play in an organized sport. Through having experiences together, we can create a happening around which valuable conversations can emerge.

- On the topic of *nurturing*—Invite the parents to school one evening. When they arrive they will be surprised to see that the kindergarten table is laid out for a meal. Serve the parents a meal of soup and bread, as the children would have at school, with a candle, the blessing, and a song, all in a mood of calm and warmth.

  After the meal, tell a story to set the mood for bedtime, then describe how children may be put to bed. Better still, if you have a reliable volunteer, have her lay on a mat on the kindergarten floor, light a candle, rub her back or massage her feet with lavender oil, sing to her, and then say, "The angels are waiting for you. Time to go to their house." Blow out the candle and say, "I'll see you at the angel's house. I'll be there too." Have your volunteer say, "Mommy, don't go. I need a drink of water." Then you respond, "Oh, the angels are waiting for you. We'll have some more water in the morning."

Simple domestic chores such as washing dishes, wiping tables, sweeping, or making a bed can be demonstrated with conscious attention to the intent, meaning, and quality of the gesture. Parents can learn to appreciate how inspired children are by purposeful work and how children can become more absorbed and drawn into a task when the movements are slower and focused.

- *Nurturing through artistic activities*—Hold a once-a-month meeting (perhaps in the afternoon, with childcare in another room) and share an artistic activity with the parents. This can be painting, drawing, singing, candle-dipping, felting, story telling, creating a nature table, or a seasonal craft activity.

  This can lead into many questions and further activities, such as plant-dyeing of cloth or wool. Setting up different seasonal scenes for the nature table stimulates questions about the seasonal rhythms, festivals, and the child's experience of the natural world. Often questions arising out of current discipline dilemmas come up at this time and many enthusiastic conversations ensue.

- *Festival experience*—Prepare something for an upcoming festival with the parents. For example, they may come to make lanterns and learn songs in advance of the Martinmas or Lantern festival. While the parents are working with their hands, discussions can happen about the meaning and intention behind the festival. Parents could be asked to recount any other experiences, perhaps childhood memories, they have about this particular festival. The children, during kindergarten time, can then finish in the weeks ahead what the parents started on the night of the parent evening.

  Coming to school on special occasions outside of class time has been very successful when parents and children come together with other families to prepare for festivals, for example to make dipped beeswax candles or lanterns. This can be done in the joyous mood of parents and children playfully creating together. Involving the parents in set-up for the festivals can be a rich and rewarding way for them to sample from the inside out what the meaning of a festival is.

- *Involving fathers*—Hold a meeting for fathers only. Ask them what Waldorf education is like for them and what their questions are. Acknowledge that it is often the wives who choose the children's early childhood education. Fathers can be called on for a work bee—building a compost bin, tool shed, or creating something for the kindergarten. Fathers crave social interaction too and often feel more comfortable when they can be working alongside of someone else. Feeling that they have contributed to their child's education can bond them with the situation and help them to vocalize their questions and areas of interest.

- *Experiences that can weave the social fabric*—All stand in a circle holding hands. A hula hoop hangs over the arms of two people. The group has to collectively pass the hoop around without breaking the circle and without letting go of hands.

  Another idea is to have a big ball of yarn. Everyone sits in a circle and a question is asked. The teacher holding the ball of yarn says something pertaining to the question, holds on to the end of the strand of yarn, and then throws the ball of yarn off to another parent. The parent contributes something, holds on to the yarn, and tosses the ball to another. In this way the comments build and the ball is tossed, developing a picture of the web of ideas within this particular community pertaining to the question or theme that was expressed. An additional aspect of the game could be that everyone has to remember the contribution of the person who passes the yarn to them as well as their own response. Then at the end of the game, when everyone is holding on to their string, they retrace their patterns, throwing the ball of yarn back to the person who gave it to them and speaking out what that other person's contribution was to the theme. This allows a review of the question or theme and also builds rapport amongst the parent group.

  There are many such social games available in books and on the Internet. Parents go away from a parent gathering feeling met and enlivened when they get to have "playful" times with others.

- On the topic of *child development*—Have the parents sit in a circle according to the consecutive ages of their children. That is, if they have a baby, a three-year-old, and a six-year-old, they would sit at the beginning of the round and then they would move over to the place where the parents are sitting who have three-year-olds and then move again when it's time to talk about six-year-olds. Then tell the parents that we are going to create a story together about a child growing up. Each parent will speak in turn about the main character in the story by telling us one thing that is joyful and one thing that is a challenge about who or how their own child is right now. Each parent embellishes the story until it finishes with the parents of the oldest children. (The teacher who offered this exercise said that one evening she did this exercise with a group of parents who had children ranging in ages from three weeks to twenty-eight years. It was like having a course on child development! The parents expressed that it was an opportunity to bond and commiserate with others, and it was energizing to be part of the creative process of information sharing on what otherwise can be a very "dry" topic. The story they created definitely became a secondary part of the process.)

  As mentioned, the above ideas are offered to assist you in strengthening your own inspired approaches. Please enjoy.

Scheduling Parent Meetings

Another consideration is when to hold parent meetings. One suggestion is to hold a monthly (or other rhythmic timing) series of evening meetings. This has worked well when the evenings are stimulating and consistently scheduled so that parents can count on planning them into their routines.

Some teachers found success in scheduling Saturday morning meetings. 10:00 to 11:30 a.m. was the suggested time frame. Childcare was arranged with high school students; $5 per child was the charge. The teacher who suggested this remarked that with these Saturday morning arrangements, couples tended to attend more. On a Saturday morning everyone was more rested and relaxed. These meetings were held in fall, winter, and spring. At the end of the year, parents expressed that they loved this opportunity to be together at the Saturday meetings and would have liked to do the same more regularly.

Friday evening (6:30 to 8:00 p.m.) has also worked well for some. With no school the next day, bedtime can be a little flexible ("We all knew we were compromising something"). Parents brought potluck snacks, and childcare was provided by older children for a modest charge. The evenings were always three-fold:

1. Some experience from the children's day was shared—for example, part of circle time, a puppet play, or the painting activity.

2. The parents worked on something for the class—lantern preparation, preparing materials from which the children would make Valentine post-boxes, or sewing bells on ankle bracelets for May Day. The social time of chatting, in the second part of the evening, was important as well for strengthening class ties.

3. Finally the teachers presented a topic on development, parenting, bridging home and school life, festivals, and so on. The meeting finished promptly by eight o'clock. Finding ways to be succinct and economical with what is said during this last time was important. Sometimes less really is more.

Some teachers have had success holding their parent meetings after kindergarten, or later in the afternoon. Perhaps a conversation with the parents at the beginning of the school year can serve to help decisions to be made that work better for the whole group.

Encouraging Attendance at Parent Meetings

A final consideration is *how can we support a full attendance at parent meetings?* There is nothing more frustrating than low attendance at parent meetings when hours of preparation by the teacher have happened beforehand.

Here is some feedback from a group of parents who were polled on this topic:

- When the teacher looks me in the eye and asks me, "Are you coming to the meeting tonight?" I feel wanted and realize I am important to her.
- Giving me a task to do for the meeting helps me to feel more responsible.
- Make the meetings mandatory.
- Put a sign in your window saying, PARENT MEETING TODAY. PLEASE MAKE SURE YOUR CHILD IS REPRESENTED.
- Tell the parents that there is important information being discussed at the meeting tonight that you don't want them to miss.
- Parents are socially starved. Make sure there is a social element to it.
- Make time so that we can hear other parents' stories and then share creative ways of dealing with our children.
- Refer parents to other vocal parents who advocate going to parent meetings and value what they experienced there.
- Give reminders. Lots of reminders.
- Tell us in a newsletter that the meeting is coming up. Dangle a few carrots as to what will be discussed.
- Make available lists for reliable babysitters or have meetings when babysitting is available at school.
- Make the meetings fun and informative.

The above lists are by no means complete. Please enjoy these suggestions, the fruits of the labor of your colleagues. And, above all, add your own ideas to the list. A great venue for sharing your parent meeting successes is the *Gateways* newsletter published by WECAN. We look forward to reading about what has worked well for you. ✦

References

Burkhard, Gudrun. *Taking Charge—Your Life Patterns and Their Meaning*. Edinburgh: Floris Books, 1997.

Kohler, Henning. *Working with Anxious, Nervous, and Depressed Children*. Fair Oaks, CA: The Association of Waldorf Schools of North America, 2000.

A Bouquet of Wishes in the Rosemary Kindergarten

Tim Bennett

Building a relationship with the children's parents is a big part of our work in the kindergarten. Over the years I have come up with a few ways that can help the parents feel that they are a part of the life of the kindergarten during our year together.

Parents are included at the beginning of each day. At nine o'clock, we gather outside together for a brief morning circle. Parents, children, and younger siblings all take hands in our circle as we welcome the day. I lead everyone in an opening seasonal song and then we speak our morning verse:

> Our hearts open wide.
> Light streams deep inside.
> Stars, moon and sun shine down on everyone.
> On earth we now stand, giving all our hands.
> Good morning, dear friends.

I sing, "Ring a ring a Rosemary day, welcome, welcome, nature walk day and oatmeal day" (or whatever day it happens to be). Then we get ready to leave on our nature walk, and the parents and little siblings go off on their day, leaving their children in my care. This transition works well, and the parents tell me that they love this circle time together. They leave the kindergarten feeling refreshed and renewed for their day in the world.

Another aspect of my work with the parents is the parent evenings, which I have five times a year. I start the year by giving the parents a question to think about: what do you wish or hope for your child in the kindergarten this year? We share the answers to this question at our first parent evening of the year. This first meeting creates a "bouquet of good wishes" to begin the year. I always feel that during the first weeks of school, we glide along on those spoken good intentions. At the last parent evening of the year, we return to those wishes and see what has happened. I can always see much change in the children, as the parents' wishes have often been realized.

The last parent evening is also the time when we turn our attention to the children who are moving on to first grade. I take time to honor each child. I do so by speaking about each child in relationship to a plant or flower that symbolizes various aspects of the child. I describe the child through speaking about the qualities of the plant or flower. For example, a rosemary plant may be brought to symbolize a strong child who is a clear and wakeful thinker. The numerous, little blue flowers of the rosemary may bespeak her good intentions and blossoming ideas. She may like to join in with others' games, as the rosemary leaf can join the bread dough to make a special loaf. After this, I talk about how the child has grown and changed over the year, sharing short (often humorous) anecdotes about the child. Then, I open it up to the parents and we spend five to ten minutes building up a picture of the child from their various impressions. As we speak about each child, I place the flower into a vase that is our centerpiece for the evening. As the evening progresses, the bouquet grows in size and beauty. In reflecting on each child, the parents get a sense of each child's strivings and his gifts. I find it is a wonderful rite of passage for the parents, as they are also transitioning to the first grade.

These first and last parent evenings are the two pillars that hold my parent work together. Acknowledging the striving of the parents and the growth of their children makes for a warm and lively way of meeting each other as adults. It is a time when the arts of teaching and parenting and the art of being social can weave golden threads into the cloth of mutuality we hold together as we embrace and honor the children who brought us together.   ✦

Meetings with Parents on the Topic of Discipline

Louise deForest

Among the challenges facing parents today, none is more difficult than setting and enforcing limits, creating and holding boundaries, and guiding children with loving discipline. Many parents, feeling that their own parents were too strict, give their children free rein. Others, knowing their children to be creative, bright beings, follow their child's lead, feeling that to do otherwise would infringe on the child's freedom and creativity. Still other parents, spending little time with their children during the day, don't want any unpleasantness in the little time they do spend together and therefore avoid any kind of conflict with their children. All of these situations are unhealthy ones for the child and the parent.

The young child instinctively expects guidance and when it is not forthcoming, the child tends to feel insecure and frightened. Growing up without guidance, without boundaries, often translates into being left alone to flounder in a world that the child is not experienced enough to understand. Constantly being consulted by adults about what the child wants is not only bewildering, but can create an egotist, unprepared for the world awaiting him or her. Many parents believe that choices strengthen their child but, on the contrary, too many choices can undermine the child.

Because parents are so close to their children they have many valuable observations to offer teachers. Parents can also benefit from the teacher's objectivity. I always hasten to reassure parents that being a teacher is ever so much easier than being a parent. Guiding a class with clarity, firmness, and consistency is what we do every day and there is much we can share with parents, either in our parent-teacher conferences, phone conversations, or class meetings.

Our class meetings are a wonderful opportunity to build community among the parents in the class and can serve as a forum to share ideas, questions, and thoughts. It is also an opportunity for us to share our expertise, giving parents the support and guidance that we often wish we had experienced ourselves when we were parenting young children. But how can we bring a topic as complex and as personal as discipline? Can we offer our thoughts in such a way that we empower others with deeper understandings? Can we inspire understandings that can guide parents under a myriad of situations with their children? The following are a few of the ways I have worked with this topic in my class meetings. These are, of course, not menus to be followed exactly, but rather some ideas that may inspire you to create endless possibilities of experiences and conversations with the parents in your class.

One meeting, for example, may start out with me asking the parents to divide up into pairs, separating couples (it is best to do this part way through the school year when the parents already know and feel comfortable with each other). Choosing a partner myself, I then show the parents how to do a form of wrestling. Yes, that's right, wrestling! Facing each other, my partner and I put our right feet together in front of us, sides touching, and we touch our four hands in front of us, palm to palm. The purpose of the game is to move in such a way that the other person is forced off balance and must move their right foot. The left foot can move but the hands and the right foot of each one must always be in contact. It is not the type of wrestling that is aggressive or fast; on the contrary, each one slowly follows the subtle pressure of the hands of the other. First one person takes the lead, applying pressure with both hands and bending forward or backward, up or down, to force the other off balance. As soon as you feel yourself losing balance, you then take the lead and, exerting pressure with both hands, try to force the other to lose balance, using the same type of movements. And so it goes, listening with the hands and taking turns leading or following as your sense of balance calls for it. You can squat down and swivel from side to side, just so long as the right feet are always immobile. Try it at home with your family to get a sense of how this exercise works. Once they have been shown how to do it, the pairs wrestle for five to ten minutes, then change partners and do it again for another five minutes or so. Much laughing and many strange positions follow, and it is usually a very fun exercise.

A large part of discipline consists of careful, wakeful listening.

When we have finished, we sit in a circle and I ask what the experience was like for them. Believing as I do that a large part of discipline consists of careful, wakeful listening, I ask them about whether they were able to "hear" the other's intentions and to communicate, physically, who was leading. What was the experience like, I ask them, when it was unclear who was leading? What was it like to have no resistance meet your hands? What if the touch of the other was overbearing? Could you make yourself heard? Can you identify, I wonder, what made you lose your balance? As you can imagine, the conversation and the discoveries parents make are most interesting; quickly they come to the conclusion that without meeting resistance, they lose their balance, and that too much resistance makes them feel helpless. Getting mixed messages from your partner leads to feeling very insecure and frustrated. We then speak about these experiences in the context of discipline, and it is through their discoveries that they themselves come to the conclusion that meeting resistance helps them discover where they are; that clear communication and consistency gives security, and so on. They can also get a sense of what their own style is as they find themselves overpowering or shrinking from their partner. Getting in touch with our own styles is another interesting conversation.

One of my goals in my parent evenings is to lead the parents to discover what they already know and allow them to uncover their own common sense and wisdom. This is in keeping with the age in which we all live: the consciousness soul age. In this time, no longer are we, as individuals, willing to take someone else's word for it. It is only through individual questioning and the striving of our own efforts that we truly know something. I try to make my class meetings experiential in nature, setting up certain possibilities and then guiding the parents in a conversation that may uncover the knowledge that lives within them. I always feel that a really successful class meeting is one in which, partway through, I could quietly walk out the door and never be missed.

The experience to be avoided in our class meetings is when parents leave feeling that they have done everything wrong with their children. My goal in my meetings is to have parents leave feeling more confident in themselves as parents and proud of all the good things they have done for their children. For those of us who host evening meetings, we welcome parents at a time of day when we are all tired. So let's make our class meetings dynamic, artistic, and fun, so that we can all leave feeling enlivened by our time together. As a parent in a Waldorf school for fourteen years, I have experienced some wonderful, thought-provoking meetings, and I have sat through my share of dull, boring ones, too.

Another way of working with the question of discipline is to ask parents what the first word that comes to mind is when they hear the word "discipline." I write down what they say without commenting on it (often even they are surprised by what comes out of their mouths!) I then ask them to break into groups of three or four people (again trying to keep couples in different groups) and ask them to think of a person they knew when they were quite young, before seven. I ask them not to choose their parents—though it could be another family member, such as an uncle or a grandparent—and it should be someone with whom they felt completely at ease and true to themselves. I ask them to describe this person to each other, focusing more on the attributes of that person and less on the relationship they had with them. Each person has about five minutes to speak. I am not part of these groups but stay in the room going from group to group helping them to stick to the topic. Again, this is a wonderful way for parents to get to know each other and to build a community within the class. When each person has had the opportunity to speak, we all join the circle again and I ask everyone to speak about the common threads in the descriptions of these people from our past. Every time I have done this, the comments have been the same: someone who has time for the child, who is generally quiet and never lecturing or moralizing, who loves them with no ulterior motives, and who accepts them just as they are. Very often it is a grandparent or an older neighbor, and often people mention that, as children, they would do things with this person: bake cookies, go fishing, walk in the woods, thread their sewing needles, and so on. After everyone has had time to contribute to the picture of this type of person, I then ask them if these attributes they have all mentioned are still important to them now that they are adults. Taking it further, I then ask how do these attributes live in them as parents? This always leads to an interesting discussion, especially when I read back to them their words associated with the word "discipline." We can then go on to talk about the root of the word "discipline"—disciple—and how that can fit into a rightful understanding of discipline. Slowly we begin to uncover an understanding of discipline as an inner attitude as well as a manifestation of outer deeds. We can also go on to speak about our own relationship to discipline. I often share with the parents my own struggles with self-discipline, citing the wonderful lesson taught to me by my youngest son.

At the time when my son was a young teen, and a very rebellious one, we had an experience together that was a teaching moment for me. I can't remember what it was that set me off with him. I do, however, remember working up a real head of steam and saying things that I knew I shouldn't say to him, but being unable to stop myself. At first he was contrite and a bit abashed, but as the harangue continued, with me yelling at him and wagging my finger in his face, his body posture changed. He relaxed and sat back with a rather smug, superior look on his face. He was no longer listening; instead he was watching me, in awe of just how out of control I was. I do remember uttering the words, at the top of my lungs, that it was about time, young man, he learn some responsibility and some discipline. His sudden laugh stopped me short. "If you could only see yourself now, Mom," he quietly said, and walked away shaking his head, disappointed with yet another adult who cannot practice what she preaches.

When I tell the parents this story we all have a good laugh at the image of our children sitting back and watching the show. But then we can go on to have a discussion about the inner work we as parents and teachers must do as our children grow and change, adapting our boundaries as our children's ages change. I share with them the image that serves me so well, both at home and in the classroom, of being the rock for my children, always there, always available to provide resistance, always solid and still and grounded. Or of the farmer who periodically walks his or her fields, kicking the fence posts to see if they can still be counted on. We are those fence posts and our children push at them to find out if they can still be trusted. Are they solid? Can I lean on this one and be secure? Often we can then speak about our willingness to sometimes be disliked by our children and what that means for them and for us. We struggle to clarify the boundaries between who we are and the experiences that have formed us, and who our children are. "What are your children asking you to develop?" I often ask, and we go on to talk about parenting as a schooling for us in mindfulness, observation, flexibility, and deepening understanding. We talk about our task of not just embracing the act of parenting but transforming it into the art of parenting.

Gudrun Davy, in her wonderful articles in the first *Lifeways* book (which I recommend all parents read), likens the journey through parenting to three stages: for the first seven years it is like being in a small boat, taking a long journey. Sometimes the waters are calm, but often they are choppy and we are alone, guiding ourselves and our small children with no land in sight and no signposts along the way. The second stage (from seven to fourteen) she compares to a journey through a rich countryside of trees, rivers, forest, villages, and cities. We are once again on dry land but now, through our children, we move into a broader social landscape. Suddenly we find ourselves centrally responsible for directing a large and complex drama with, as Gudrun points out, an extensive and varied cast and an elaborate plot unfolding from day to day. And the last stage of parenting is compared to climbing into the high mountains, a journey fraught with dangers and challenges but also full of excitement as our horizons broaden and the world spreads before our feet. Here the going is steeper and when we have finally conquered one peak, a still higher one looms in the distance. The joys arise when we look up and get glimpses of a high, ideal world, raying down on us with sudden moments of bright sunshine.

> My goal in my meetings is to have parents leave feeling more confident in themselves as parents.

It is important to share these impressions from those wise elders who have gone before us in their parenting. When our children are small it is hard for us to realize that we are preparing the foundation for their future life. We can feel as if it will always be sleepless nights, battles over food and brushing teeth, and constant surveillance to ensure physical and emotional safety. But if we can look at our efforts to discipline our little children as the laying down of the framework of their future self-discipline during the teenage years, it can give us the perspective we need to strengthen our resolve to hold those boundaries as an act of love for our children.

I wish you great joy and fulfillment in your preparations for meeting parents. Teachers have much to gain by sharing the wisdom that our work with early childhood bestows. Joining wholeheartedly with parents as colleagues in this ever-challenging, ever-wondrous journey towards becoming truly human benefits parent, child, and teacher. ✦

References

Davy, Gudrun and Bons Voors. *Lifeways: Working with Family Questions*. Stroud, UK: Hawthorn Press, 1983.

Working with the Will of the Young Child— Giving Tools to Our Parents

Nancy Blanning

For too long in the kindergarten, I would find myself in the act of verbal "dueling" with particular children, especially the six-year-olds. Two children stand out in my memory as special teachers for me because they were experts in this art of "teacher ambush." Firmly resolving to not get entangled in convoluted conversations with these very articulate and intellectually awake children, I would find myself ensnared time and again. Observation of what was happening in the behavior of the children and, more importantly, *in the speech habits of the teacher*, revealed deep truths confirmed by anthroposophical understandings. Recalling these truths helped me to understand which responses to the children were more workable, and eventually this research was distilled into practical suggestions to share with parents. The following notes about the resulting presentation to parents and the separate parent handout are meant to be a resource for you if you should decide to use them.

As mentioned, out of this research was born a parent presentation: "How to get your child to do what you want without talking yourself to death." With this admittedly provocative but truthful title, the presentation was well-attended and well-received. Because the advice was practical, parents could confirm whether the suggestions worked or not through their own experience.

Our Waldorf parents are asked to trust our insights in so many areas where the results won't be observable for many years to come, so it is wonderful to offer them something concrete and immediately useful. For teachers, review of these principles can bring to greater consciousness why we intuitively work with the child's will as we do. We can then better observe our own behavior to refine and strengthen our interactions with the children. The essential point of this presentation is to give parents the possibility for self-observation and self-development through having a clearer picture of the nature of young children.

Adults can adjust their approach to take into account the child's developmental stage rather than impose an inappropriate and unfair expectation on the child that will meet with disappointment. So much cultural influence tells us that we should speak to children about everything, with detailed, logical explanations. Sometimes the children do respond in a reasonable way, fooling the adult into thinking that the young child is a logical being. But the insights of Rudolf Steiner reveal that young children live in the will, in imitation, not in conceptual thinking. They do what they see. They are movers and doers. Through doing, they explore the world and educate themselves about its realities. Through movement, children establish healthy control of the body, integrate their senses, and develop useful habit patterns to guide their future growth. In normal, healthy development, purposeful body movement always precedes speech development. When there is deviation from this order, our teachers' attention is immediately alerted. When we speak in an intellectual, direction-giving way, this actually has a paralyzing effect on the child. All the forces of will seem to rush to the head, freezing the limbs into immobility. When the child needs to move—put on shoes and coat, pick up the lunchbox, and walk to the door to leave for school—giving directions or commands can actually create the opposite of what we want. We have to activate the will through different avenues:

- Help the child literally to begin moving

- Use the power of imitation

- Use stories and imaginative images

Years in the kindergarten taught me that the easiest way to get a child to come to the teacher was to slip my hand into the child's and draw them in the direction I wanted. Almost always the child grasps the teacher's hand and follows—especially if the child's thinking has not already been first awakened by a verbal direction.

So the first principle to share with parents is: Get the child moving before you speak. If the task is to walk to the door, slip your hand into the child's and start walking toward the door. If getting on a coat or shoes is needed, offer the right sleeve to the child's arm, beginning to slide the sleeve onto the arm. If opposition has not been awakened, the child will almost always continue the movement, offering her left arm to the coat. Gesturing the shoe toward the foot is often all that is needed to get the child into the movement of putting on the shoe. Once the movement has begun, the blockage seems to dissolve and the child is free to follow. A handout sheet given to the parents suggests:

- Help the child to begin to move, literally, before you speak. Or, if you must speak, say something like "It is time for coats now," making a general matter-of-fact statement instead of giving a command.

Parents are usually skeptical about the simplicity of this. However, after trying out the technique, they are amazed to experience that this is almost always successful. Over time, the actual physical assistance is gradually reduced until just holding up the coat is invitation for the child to begin. Eventually saying, "Coat time," will be enough, once the healthy movement habit-pattern has imprinted itself. Through this sequence, the child develops independence and self-reliance.

The child's deeply imitative nature is a second aid in engaging his will. With the young child, the adult has to remember: If I want the child to "do," I must "do" first. A very young child cannot help imitating what the adult does. If it is time to clean up the toys from the floor, the child will imitate the adult doing so and automatically join in the process. If these patterns are established when a child is young, it is easier to guide the child when he or she becomes an older kindergarten child. The kindergarten teacher employs this wisdom all the time by initiating clean-up time, always setting the imitative example that can then be followed by handing the child a piece of wood or a cloth to put away.

A third powerful aid is *using imaginations and stories* to inspire the child into movement. Here speech is employed quite differently. Using the example of getting the coat on, a story could begin: "Little bear looked outside, eager to go to his friend's house to play. They were going to build a big snowman, but it was too cold for even little bear's fur. He needed more…" It is a rare child who is not instantly engaged in a story or imagination. As the story is told, the coat is offered as above, getting the child to begin movement. Once the coat is on, the story continues: "Once he had on his winter clothes, he could go out the door to play. On the way he saw…" and child and parent go out the door to the waiting car to go to school while the story continues.

This very familiar kindergarten activity may not be as obvious to a parent as it is to the teacher. Additionally, parents often feel embarrassed and sure that their story will be inadequate. Parents can be urged to "just try and see what happens." Teachers know the children are not literary critics who will reject stories. They are grateful that the adult is making the effort to create something for them, and the loving effort behind the story is what they experience. This assumption was borne out recently by a story told to me by a parent in our school. She had expected that her effort to create a story for her kindergarten son would fail. To the contrary, the simple, inexperienced stories she created got them to school harmoniously for two years. Her son, now seven-and-a-half and in first grade, said to her the other day, "Do you remember Little Bear, who used to help us get to school? Could you tell me about him again?"

There is a threshold time with the older kindergarten child when these subtle actions will not be as effective. The six-year-olds are appropriately moving from imitation to authority.

They want to feel more deliberately engaged and purposeful. The dreamy imitation that has guided their actions to this point is transforming into more awakened intention. Offering an imitative model of what we wish to have done is still powerful and necessary, but not enough in and of itself. The children know that they are not equal to the adult, but they want their emerging maturity to be recognized. When they can feel that they are working side-by-side with the adult, their cooperation is more easily offered. Perhaps the play dishes are scattered on the floor. A simple, "What a jumble these plates are! Here's one for you. I'll help, too," is often enough to get things started.

Choosing the right kind of task to offer to the six-year-old is also important. They are reaching a point where they seek more complexity and challenge. They want to do things that are "hard" enough but not overwhelming for their developmental stage. In the classroom they may be eager to pour the juice or tea at snack or to deliver the bowls of porridge around the table. After seeing the teacher set up a puppet play several times or create an obstacle course for movement time, they enjoy the challenge of arranging these things themselves. They may refuse to put wood pieces in a basket ("That's baby stuff!") but happily and enthusiastically create a "bucket brigade" (with the teacher's initial modeling and inspiration) by passing the wood pieces person-to-person to get the objects across the room into the proper place. The older children like to contribute to the community if they are asked to do the right kind of thing in a way that engages their imaginations and displays their growing competence.

There are other elements parents can cultivate in home life that will support the success of these and other parenting efforts. These include:

• Rhythmic routines that help to carry the child, so no tiring decisions have to be made about what comes next or when.

• Form and order—coat, shoes, lunch box, etc., always put away in the same place so they will be found in the same place when needed the next day.

• Pre-arranging and pre-thinking how things will go so there is order and predictability in routine. Lunches prepared the night before, clothes laid out in advance for the morning, and so on, enhance the possibility of success in otherwise probable rough spots.

A final point to consider is that of whether we offer choices to young children. As teachers, we know that doing so, as modern culture advises, can be inappropriate developmentally and exhausting for young children. Additionally, adults have a tendency to pose something as a yes-or-no question when there truly is not a choice in the matter. Picture the parent picking up her child from school with, "Shall we go home now?" meaning, "It's time to leave." The child may (and probably will) respond, "No." Opposition has been awakened and the battle begins. A suggestion to the parent is:

- Don't offer something as a choice unless it really is one. Rather, state objectively and imaginatively what needs to happen next. As an example, suppose that dinner time is approaching. "Would you like to help set the table?" will usually not get the job done. Once a child has been shown where the forks go, handing the utensils to the child with, "Forks are ready to go on the table," will often be enough.

This attitude of not offering unnecessary choices to children is an important guideline. But as the children mature, one can take a slightly different tack with the six/seven-year-old. This may be the time to offer a little bit of "choice." At dinner time, the conversation might begin, "Tonight we have a restaurant. Are you going to be a cook in the kitchen to peel the carrots or the waiter who sets the table?" Once the imagination is set, a reminder of, "The waiter always makes sure the table is beautiful so people will want to come to his table," can keep the activity inspired. Letting the older child select a task from specific options can engage willing cooperation.

It behooves us as teachers and parents to look objectively at our own use of speech. We want to make sure we are employing our understanding of the young child to its greatest effectiveness. We want our speech to be clear, enlivened, enthusiastic, pictorial, and imaginative. We want what we say to be meaningful and interesting to the children. Our culture is so penetrated with bombarding noise and meaningless talk that the children and we, ourselves, often withdraw our focused attention. In reaction to this situation, we can run the risk of speaking too little, of becoming too silent. This we do not want, for speech is one of the greatest gifts that connect us as a human social and spiritual community.

We also do not want to be speaking constantly about meaningless trivia. We need to make sure that what we say to the children is worth listening to, that our guidance through movement and speech awakens and engages their will into healthy activity. As we cultivate and strengthen these practices through meaningful speech and movement, the fruits of our experience become wisdom-filled. Teachers have much to share with those who accompany us on this educational path—the dear parents of the children we serve. ✦

Suggested Reading

Konig, Karl. *The First Three Years of the Child*. Edinburgh: Floris Books, 1997.

Mellon, Nancy. *Storytelling with Children*. Stroud, UK: Hawthorn Press, 2000. This is especially suitable to recommend to parents.

Blythe, Sally Goddard. *The Well Balanced Child: Movement and Early Learning*. Stroud, UK: Hawthorn Press, 2006. Ms. Blythe gives a wonderful picture of supporting healthy development overall. Her discussion of music, hearing, and neurological development awakens an appreciation for the importance of the quality of sound.

A handout for parents follows on the next page.

How to Get a Young Child to Do What You Want Without Talking Yourself to Death

—Or—

Working with the Will of the Young Child

Nancy Blanning

Young children may seem logical and reasonable to us, but this really is not their primary mode of being. They live in their limbs, in movement, in forces of will.

When you really want a child to move into action, speaking to him or her can actually freeze the child into immobility. All the child's forces have to rush up to the head for thinking and nothing is left over for immediate movement.

Help your child to begin to move, literally, before you speak—take him by the hand or arm. Or if you must speak, say something like, "It is time for coats now," making a general statement instead of a command, while at the same time offering the coat.

Instead of reasoning with your child, try to tell an impromptu story about a similar situation. It is a rare child who is not instantly captivated by a story. As you tell the story, literally start a movement involving your child's limbs (e.g., put arms into the sleeves of the coat, hand her one block to put away in the basket as you do likewise to model what you want the child to do, etc.).

Do not ask your child a question unless it is really a choice. For example, when it is time to leave, many parents get into hot water by asking, "Are you ready to go?" instead of stating, "It is time to leave now."

Limit the choices you give your child. Unless your child is exceptionally aware of clothes choices, food preferences, and so on, children are usually grateful to be spared making a choice. You choose the clothes, or set the meal in front of the child with "Here's breakfast." Think of yourself in a situation where you have to make a lot of choices; it can be exhausting. It is even more so for a little child.

Set the "form" ahead of time. This means place the clothes for tomorrow out the night before, ready to be put on in the morning without having to make decisions about it—by either you or your child. Know what you will prepare for breakfast the next morning without asking what the family wants.

Remember that each adult responsibility you take care of for your child allows his or her energy to be available for growing. We do a child a great service by pre-thinking and pre-planning how things will happen—by creating a "form"—which will support both the child and ourselves, so there is order and predictability in our lives.

Please do not misunderstand that a parent should become a servant for the child. As parents, we are guides and teachers of the ways of the world. We want our children to do as much for themselves as they can, such as dressing, feeding, and simple chores. But we do need to create an environment in which the child can be successful, where there is a starting point, middle, and end, rather than leaving the child alone to figure it out.

The image of the child as our "apprentice" is helpful. In any trade or craft, the apprentice is always shown how to do a task, from the simplest beginning step. Then the task is built up step by step. Each time we give our children concrete, practical experience in how to physically do something, we are escorting them along the pathway to becoming a "master craftsman."

These suggestions will help in many situations, but not all.

There will be times when you have to do battle. So choose your battles. Do not engage in a struggle of wills with your child unless you are committed to winning—not for your sake, but for the child's. This means you must be on home ground where time is not an issue. The supermarket is not the place to choose to battle.

Before drawing battle lines, see if you can transform the task at hand by creating a story, making the task into a game, or by offering assistance. "These books are all scattered on the floor. They'll be happier up on the shelf. Here's one for you and I'll help, too." Or, "I bet I can pick up this pile of books faster than you can. Let's race." Or, "I'll close my eyes and see if those books can jump back to their shelf without a sound." A story could begin with, "Did I ever tell you about the time a big windstorm came into little bear's bedroom and blew everything topsy-turvy?"

If you are in a battle with an older child, state clearly to your child what must happen in objective and matter-of-fact terms. "The dirty clothes need to be put in the hamper. We can wait until that is done." Then leave. If your child also leaves the site of the task, guide him or her back and restate the above. Try to do so calmly without accusation or anger.

Remember, you, as the parent, are the child's loving authority. Do not be afraid to claim that role. Your guidance will strengthen, not suppress, your child's will. The child is reassured by a warm, confident adult who knows how things work in the world and who can show him or her the way.   ✦

Handouts
for
Parents

Susan R. Johnson, MD

The following articles by Dr. Susan Johnson have been included as handout resources that are helpful to give to parents. The six/seven-year-old change in the life of the child is often a challenging time for parents and teachers, so articles on parenting can be comforting and informative. Also, the birth of the etheric is often assisted by fevers, which can be complicated by other symptoms such as earaches. Dr. Johnson has kindly given her permission for these to be photocopied.

Part One: How Can We Help the Young Child Through this Transition?

The Importance of Warmth
The Importance of Breakfast
The Importance of Sleep
The Meaning of Illness
Fever
The Earache

Part Two: Helpful Hints for Parenting

Parenting a Young Child—What my Formal Education Never Taught Me
Confronting our Shadow
Product vs. Process

The Importance of Warmth

Susan R. Johnson, MD, FAAP, Raphael House

As a pediatrician, I actually was taught that you could tell if a baby or child was warm enough by touching their skin. If she felt warm, then she was wearing enough clothes, and if she felt cool or her skin was mottled (bluish-pink), then she needed more clothes. It was simple. I was also a parent who had her two-year-old child outside in the rain wearing only a diaper while playing in the puddles. I actually thought he was okay because he felt warm!

Warmth is probably one of the greatest gifts we can give our children, not only the warmth of love, but the physical warmth of their bodies. Children are developing their bodies especially during the first seven years of their lives. An infant or a young child will always feel warm unless they are on the verge of hypothermia because they have an accelerated metabolic rate. If we don't provide them with the layers of cotton and wool to insulate their bodies, then they must use some of their potential "growth" energy to heat their bodies. This same energy would be better utilized in further developing their brain, heart, liver, lungs, and other organs. In addition, being cold decreases our immunity. We are all more susceptible to the germs and viruses that are always around us when we are wet and cold. When our body has to expend extra energy to keep warm, then less energy is available to "fight" off infections.

So the question becomes, how do we get our children to wear jackets? One can develop the habit of always having a child put on a hat and coat when he goes outside during cool weather. One can also try telling the child that she will actually run faster and have much more energy to play if she wears a coat. If children don't wear coats, then their bodies have to expend a lot of energy just warming up, and they will have less energy to build muscles and less energy to play. Finally, the type of clothing our children wear also makes a big difference. Polyester pajamas don't breathe and children will often wake up sweating. Even polyester jackets will not insulate a child from the cold as well as layers of cotton, silk, or wool. When the child sweats while wearing polyester, that sweat is trapped against his body and he eventually becomes chilled.

So why do children rarely complain that they are cold? Children often are not connected with their bodies enough before the age of seven to even acknowledge or communicate that they are cold. They live in the moment and are so excited and stimulated by all that they see that they don't have the capacity to sense the coldness of their bodies. This is why children often will play in a swimming pool or ocean until they are literally "blue," denying that they are cold or that they need to come out of the water. So as parents, we have to help our children develop their sense of warmth. By helping a child develop this sense of warmth, we are actually strengthening his immunity and laying the foundation for a healthy body and healthy organs in his adult life. ◆

The Importance of Breakfast

Susan R. Johnson, MD, FAAP and Patricia McPhee, RN, BSN, Raphael House

I have always heard from my own parents that breakfast was the most important meal of the day. Yet as a teenager, I often skipped breakfast or had the infamous "chocolate instant breakfast" or "pop-tarts." I thought I was doing just fine. I really didn't learn the importance of eating breakfast until my twelve-week surgery rotation in medical school. It was 7:00 a.m., and I was assisting in surgery and literally passed out while holding a retractor. After I had partially recovered in the corner of the operating room, the chief resident in surgery came over to me and whispered an invaluable piece of "survival" advice—eat a good, nutritious breakfast every morning! Needless to say, I have been eating a good, nutritious breakfast ever since that day.

I still struggle trying to get my son out of bed early enough so that he can eat a good breakfast before he goes to school. I know that getting my six-year-old to bed early (7:00 to 7:30 p.m.) allows him to wake up more easily and gives us time to have a sit-down breakfast. I also learned, from my training in Switzerland, that if your child has any tendency towards overactivity or irritability, then it is critical for the child not to consume sugar in the morning. Most cold cereals these days are made with lots of sugar (or honey). One has to read the labels carefully to find a cereal without a lot of sugar, colored dyes, or preservatives. A breakfast with some protein, especially a grain like oatmeal (or a seven grain cooked cereal) is great, but even something like soup, waffles (again watch the sugar content) with unsweetened applesauce, cottage cheese, or leftovers from dinner can be good, too. Hardboiled eggs are actually a lot harder to digest than scrambled eggs.

Eating a good nutritious breakfast is also essential for adults. There are studies, with adults, that show that if they consume all their daily intake of calories in the morning, they lose weight. If they consume the same amount of calories in the evening, they gain weight. Our metabolism is designed for a hearty breakfast, a hearty lunch and a light supper ("breakfast like a king, lunch like a prince, and supper like a pauper"). The enzymes and other substances in our body that help digest our food are at their peak activity in the morning and early afternoon. Our liver, which processes our food and thus has a relationship to our energy level, likes to start going to sleep in the late afternoon and early evening. By afternoon, the liver wants to start storing up energy for the next day (anabolic activity) rather than metabolizing food (catabolic activity). A light supper consisting of easily digested carbohydrates and/or soups is much better tolerated than a dinner high in proteins or fats (which often leads to indigestion at night and difficulty sleeping).

Caffeine in coffee and chocolate is also hard on the body because it directly stimulates the pancreas to secrete insulin. The insulin causes an uptake of sugar from your bloodstream and leads to feelings of hunger, irritability, and a craving for sugar. This is why one often feels hungry twenty minutes to an hour after drinking a diet cola or a cup of coffee, especially on an empty stomach. With regard to weight loss, drinking diet drinks is one of the most counterproductive ways to lose weight because they actually make you crave sweets and promote low blood sugar or hypoglycemia. In addition, there are lots of concerns about the sugar substitutes in all diet drinks. They mimic brain neurotransmitters and have been linked to adverse behaviors and neurological symptoms, like headaches, in both children and adults.

The following are some facts about grains from a lecture by Gerhard Schmidt, MD. Wheat has the highest content of protein compared to all other grains. It typically is easy to digest but has a protein called gluten that is sometimes more difficult for children to manage. Rice has the lowest protein content, lowest content of fat and the highest content of carbohydrate (77%). This is why rice is a good food when one is sick or recovering from an illness because it is so easy to digest and it is healthier to consume foods low in protein and fat when febrile. Rice is a good grain for all stomach diseases. Ryes have a high value of protein. Rye crisp bread is one of the easiest breads to digest. It also has more fiber substance than wheat. Oats are great, and as a grain they have the richest content of vegetable-based fat. This is why a bowl of oatmeal fills you up for the entire morning. Oat grains mixed with unsweetened applesauce also are gentle on the stomach and digestion. If you are feeling depressed, then a bowl of oatmeal each morning is supposed to help you feel better. Barley is rich in silica and in iron. Millet is rich in sulfur. Millet also contains silica and fluoride. It is considered the grain of beauty because it purifies the skin. A treatment for teenagers with acne is porridge cooked with millet every morning for three months.

Finally, two quotations from Dr. Schmidt:

"In refined white flour, we have an example of unnourishing nourishment."

"Our not finding our way—our being lost—is also a problem of daily nutrition."

So set your alarms and raise your spoons for the feast of breakfast!   ✦

The Importance of Sleep

Susan R. Johnson, MD, FAAP, Raphael House

I still struggle getting my almost seven-year-old son asleep by 8:00. It seems there is a magic window. If we eat by 5:00 and I start slowing down his activities by 6:00, then there is a good chance that he will fall asleep soon after reading stories at 7:30. If I don't have dinner ready until 6:00 or 7:00 and slowdown doesn't begin until 8:00 or 8:30 then my son seems to get a second wind that keeps him awake and active until 10:00 or 10:30 at night. The next day is difficult for him. It is hard for him to get up, eat breakfast, and get to school on time. He is tired and more irritable the entire day. What is happening?

If you go to see an anthroposophical physician with these complaints, then chances are your child will end up with a remedy for the liver. Often Hepatodoron (made from the leaves of the vine, Vitus vinifera, and the wild strawberry, Fragaria vesca) is given. It seems that the liver is involved in our ability to have a good night's sleep. It regulates our energy level for the next day and relates to our overall feelings of contentment or depression. The liver follows the cycle of the sun. Around 6:00 in the evening it wants to go to sleep and starts to store up the sugars (glycogen) to be used for the next day. It doesn't want to process any big meals (especially ones high in protein or fat after 3 p.m.).

When our children (and we) stay up late at night, we affect the liver's metabolism. It can no longer simply store sugar. Our body, by being awake and active, needs sugar in the bloodstream and so we force the liver to reverse its process and break down glycogen to provide this sugar. We get a second wind, a burst of sugar in our bloodstream, and yet we are really depleting our energy for the next day. Our liver can't store up the glycogen it needs for the next day and so the next day we have a liver that is depleted of glycogen. Our body then requires us to release stress hormones from our adrenal glands to keep us functioning. These hormones act to provide more sugar in the blood, but they also accelerate our heart rate, increase our blood pressure, and suppress our immunity (we get colds more easily). You can tell when stress hormones are acting since one also develops cold hands and cold feet during the day from the vasoconstriction of the blood vessels to the hands and feet.

The combination of stress hormones and too little glycogen in the liver makes us develop a craving for sugar. When we eat something really sweet (like candy or cookies), especially on an empty stomach, the excess load of sugar overstimulates our pancreas to produce too much of another hormone, insulin. Too much insulin causes our cells to take up or absorb too much sugar so that there isn't much sugar left in our blood. We become hypoglycemic, with a low blood sugar. We feel tired, irritable and lightheaded and, for children, their body movements become more impulsive and overactive (less purposeful). Being hypoglycemic makes us crave sugar again and the whole process repeats itself throughout the entire day.

Some children and adults are more sensitive to these changes than others. Their pancreas may release more insulin in response to sugar. Some children and adults release more stress hormones in response to sleep deprivation, but this physiologic response occurs in all of us. For children that are already very active and have difficulties paying attention in school, going to bed early and cutting down on sugar really can help the child and family function better.

It is said that any sleep you get before midnight is restorative and counts double, and therefore it is far better to go to bed early (7:00 to 8:00 for a young school-age child and 9:00 to 10:00 for an adult) and wake up early to get your work done. Maybe this is the truth in that saying by Benjamin Franklin: Early to bed, early to rise, makes (one) healthy, wealthy, and wise. ✦

The Meaning of Illness

Susan R. Johnson, MD, FAAP, Raphael House

In anthroposophical medicine our spirit (our higher self) is always considered to be healthy. It is our soul that first becomes ill. If we do not pay attention to our soul, then we start to lose our vitality (our etheric body becomes weak) and then our physical body becomes ill. Dr. Philip Incao, an anthroposophical physician who practices in Denver, Colorado, spoke this summer at the Artemisia Conference held at Rudolf Steiner College. He described a picture of health and illness that comes from a Dutch anthroposophical physician.

Imagine health as a beautiful sunny day with a brillant blue sky and no clouds in sight. The earth is covered by a layer of green fields, plants, and trees springing up from a firm ground composed of minerals. The sun is our spirit, the sky is our soul, the green living layer is our vitality (etheric body), and the mineralized earth is our physical body. We come to this earth with the purpose of purifying our soul. There are always clouds that form in our soul: those issues in life (our needs, wants, and desires) that we are trying to work through and transform. At any given time, if our spirit is strong enough, then like the sun we can often dissolve the clouds that come our way. Sometimes too many clouds form at the same time or a cloud grows too quickly and becomes too large, obscuring the sun's light. If we don't pay attention to the messages from our soul, the clouds can grow and merge into a huge thunderstorm and eventually pour down to earth as rain. After the rain, the sky will become clear again, but all the rain may have flooded the earth. If our etheric body is not strong enough to withstand the rainstorm, then our physical body can become ill. Hereditary factors, destiny and karma can all affect the physical body we have in this life, but there are things we can do to strengthen our etheric body to help us resist becoming ill during these rainstorms of our soul life.

The etheric body is formed during the first seven years of our life. Routines and daily rhythms (especially around mealtimes, bedtimes, morning times, and holiday celebrations) all strengthen the etheric. Adequate sleep (usually around eleven hours for young children and teenagers), adequate clothing (so hands and feet stay warm), and proper nutrition (that follows the cycle of our liver, consuming fats and proteins before 3 p.m., eating a hearty breakfast and hearty lunch with nutritious snacks, and followed by a light dinner) all help our organs grow in a healthy way and strengthen our immune system. Minimizing the stressors in our culture (television, videos, computers, caffeine, sleep deprivation, prolonged car rides, and always hurrying from one place to another) can strengthen our etheric body. These stressors overstimulate our nervous systems and cause us all to release stress hormones that weaken our immune system and our vitality.

Nature is one of the greatest healers. Taking a long walk through a park lined with trees, in a quiet forest, or by water nourishes us. When my spirit and vitality needs strengthening, I hike in the mountains and sit under a redwood tree by a small flowing stream. When my soul feels in torment and too many thoughts and worries are flooding my consciousness, then I sit by a rushing waterfall or walk along the ocean and listen to the crashing waves. Finally, one of the greatest gifts we can give to ourselves and our children is to slow down and remember that "less is often the best." ✦

Fever

Susan R. Johnson, MD, FAAP, Raphael House

The anthroposophical approach to fever is different from that which I was taught during my residency. In anthroposophical medicine, a fever is seen as good because it actually strengthens the child's immune system and helps a child get further into her physical body. Once it is determined that the child does not have a serious illness like strep throat, pneumonia, or meningitis, then one supports the fever process in the child. (For a febrile child less than two years of age, it is important to see a physician or nurse practitioner first to ensure that the child doesn't have these illnesses.) Instead of letting a child "cool off" by running around barefoot in a T-shirt, I learned that it was important to encourage rest in a peaceful environment (without television and radio) and to keep the child's whole body warm during a fever. It is recommended that children be dressed in natural fibers with three layers on the top and two layers on the bottom, in addition to wool socks. The goal is to keep the warmth distributed throughout the body so that the child's forehead, hands, feet, and abdomen are the same temperature.

It is also important to give children lots of warm fluids (like linden tea, warm water with lemon juice, or warmed diluted fruit juices) and avoid anything cold (like popsicles). Somehow, if part of the body is cold, then the body tries to compensate by generating more heat, and this can cause the temperature to rise faster and higher. A rapid rise in temperature, especially in the first twenty-four hours of an illness, is linked to febrile seizures.

It is important to avoid eating proteins (eggs, meat, milk) and fats when one has a fever. These foods are harder to digest, and proteins actually generate heat when they are metabolized and, therefore, can cause the fever to go higher. Vegetable broth, rice, applesauce, bananas, and toast are carbohydrates and are easier foods to digest. Sugary foods, chocolate, and caffeinated drinks make children more irritable and are a stress to their metabolism.

As a parent, one of my first exposures to anthroposophical medicine was when my child had a cold and a fever of 104 degrees. He didn't have a sore throat, cough, or any difficulty breathing and his lungs were clear to auscultation. He also didn't have any vomiting, or a stiff neck, so there weren't any signs of meningitis. It was late at night, and I was up in the mountains and at least thirty minutes away from any hospital or urgent care. Well, my son started having auditory hallucinations with his fever. I gave him a lukewarm bath. The bath worked temporarily (for five to ten minutes), but he would get chilled and shiver, and then the fever rose higher than ever. After two more tepid baths, which didn't work, I then called a friend who was an anthroposophical physician. I was told to feel my son's feet. If they were warm (and not cold) then I could apply a "lemon wrap." If the feet were cold, I would need to warm them first using blankets or a covered hot water bottle before applying the lemon wrap.

To make a lemon wrap, you take a lemon, squeeze it into a pan and add one-half to one cup of water and heat it to almost boiling. I was then instructed to soak a pair of my cotton socks in this hot lemon juice (reportedly tepid or warm lemon juice also works), wring the socks out well, and put the hot socks on both of my child's feet (pulling the socks up over his calves). I then placed a pair of my wool socks over the cotton socks so his feet and legs would not get chilled and covered him with a blanket. All I could think of while doing this was the headlines in the morning newspaper: "Son dies of a febrile seizure while mother, who is a pediatrician, applies lemon juice to his calves."

Well, the headlines didn't turn out like that. My son's fever immediately came down to 102 and the hallucinations stopped, all in ten minutes. I left the lemon wrap on his legs for a total of twenty minutes and then removed it. Lemon wraps are usually only needed when a child is restless and uncomfortable with a fever greater than 102 degrees. Usually one would apply no more than three lemon wraps in a twenty-four hour period while carefully observing the child for any signs of a more serious illness. A lemon wrap does not cause a large drop in temperature, but, rather, it works by pulling the inflammation away from the head.

The rest of the night, my son remained comfortable and only had a low-grade fever of 99 to 100 degrees. The fever continued to subside on its own until it returned to normal by the next afternoon. I couldn't believe I had actually managed his fever without Tylenol. He seemed much more comfortable. He didn't have the alternating periods of chills and sweats. In addition, the fever brought to him a developmental burst. His personality had softened. He was kinder and gentler to other children, and he could do things at school, like coloring and painting, with a much greater ease. I had also grown closer to him because I really was there with him during his illness. ✦

The Earache

Susan R. Johnson, MD, FAAP, Raphael House

Last week my son flew to Southern California to visit my parents for eight days. When I talked with him the next day, I noticed he had come down with a cold. My father then called me a few nights later to tell me that my son was crying and complaining that his ear hurt. He had no other symptoms except for a stuffy nose. In the past, my son has had fluid in his ear, but he had never complained that his ear actually hurt. My father asked me if he should give him some Tylenol or something else to treat the ear. My father had looked in his ear and thought the pain was coming from the inner ear and not the outer ear canal.

I then swallowed a few times and replied, "No, Dad. I don't want you to give him any Tylenol or even antibiotics. This may sound strange to you, but I would like you to go down to the grocery store and buy an onion (white or yellow, but not red). I then would like you to cut the onion in half and put half of the onion in the oven for five to ten minutes at 200 to 250 degrees just to warm it but not to dry it out. I then want my son to hold the onion over his ear for ten to fifteen minutes."

I heard a contemplative silence at the other end of the phone line. I then explained that I didn't know how the onion worked but I thought there must be some aromatic chemical that is given off that anesthesizes the ear drum. I told him that I had heard in my medical course in Switzerland that onions were routinely used to stop ear pain, and I personally knew two friends who had diced an onion and made an onion bag with cheesecloth and placed it over their children's ears to relieve ear pain. He then asked me to repeat my instructions and went off to the grocery store.

I called home the next morning and discovered that the earache had resolved. My son had held the onion over his ear for ten minutes the night before and the pain had stopped. He then slept peacefully until morning and awoke without any ear pain. Was it the onion that had stopped the ear pain, or was it a placebo effect or a coincidence, and the ear pain just stopped at the same time the onion was applied? These were the questions I left my family to wrestle with that morning as I cheerfully talked to my son and then hung up the phone. ◆

Parenting a Young Child—What My Formal Education Never Taught Me

Susan R. Johnson, MD, FAAP, Raphael House

As a pediatrician with subspecialty training in child behavior and development, I thought I knew everything there was to know about children and being a parent. Then I became a parent, and I humbly realized that I knew very little about either one. So here are some parenting experiences (and babysitting survival tips) that my education never taught me about raising a young child:

1) Young children, especially children less than seven years of age, are not capable of delaying gratification. Children live in the present, and what children see or what they hear about they want now. They don't have the cognitive capacity to resist temptation or delay gratification. For example, I bought a "special" advent calendar for my son when he was four years old. On December 1, I let him open the first window. I then returned the calendar to a special place in the kitchen and briefly left the room. Well, you guessed it. All twenty-four days before Christmas were consumed in a matter of minutes. Since this time, I have learned to be more quiet and not verbalize all my ideas and plans in front of my young child who would subsequently want to do everything I mentioned—NOW!

2) If we are confused about a limit or boundary then we confuse our child. Children push until they find our boundary. I never had any arguments about wearing seat belts in the car, though I frequently had arguments about going to bed. My son quickly learned that he could continually ask for water at bedtime (how could I deprive a thirsty child), ask for a snack after he was in bed (how could I send him to bed hungry), ask lots of questions about everything in the whole wide world (how could I not satisfy his intellectual curiosity), and the list went on and on. I am still learning this lesson. Somehow my learning doesn't seem to always transfer from one situation to another. It takes me a long time to sort out and prioritize my own values and thoughts so that I present clearer boundaries to him.

3) Young children, especially those less than seven years of age, really can read our thoughts and are barometers for our own soul moods. I was taught that nobody can read your mind. Maybe babies could sense our anxiety by the rapid beat of our heart or breathing rate, but that was as far as perception went. For a toddler, if one didn't say it, then the thought didn't really exist. In other words, I could be really angry at my child and my child wouldn't know it unless I actually said I was angry or showed the anger by the tone in my voice or the expression on my face.

I then went to my first parenting workshop at a neighboring Waldorf school. My son was three years old at the time, and I was looking around for a kindergarten. I attended a lecture on parenting the young child and heard from the speaker about the importance of holding good thoughts because a young child had the ability to sense thoughts. I remember coming home that night not really believing this idea, but I liked the parenting image I was given at the talk: If you are the parent of a teenager or a toddler, then hold the image of a stone in a stream. You have to hold steady like the stone and let the water of emotions flow around you without dislodging you, carrying you away, or knocking you off balance. I woke up very early that next morning and meditated on this picture. My son then woke up and walked downstairs and climbed up into my lap. I hugged him but said nothing. He then looked at me and said, "Mommy, let's play firefighter by the stone in the stream." (My son had never used the words stone or stream in his whole life.)

I have learned that thoughts are as powerful as actions. It is not only what we do, what we say, or how we move (our gestures) that matter. It is also what we think. We can influence each other in so many ways that go beyond our hearing, sight, and motor movements. What we do for our children, what we tell our children, how we move in front of our children, and the thoughts we think all matter. The thoughts we hold about ourselves also have a lot of power. We can be our own worst enemies sometimes. If we don't believe something will work out for us, then it usually doesn't. What we fear the most often comes to us. There is a power to positive thinking. This is why so many Olympic athletes hire sports psychologists to teach them the skills of positive thinking and visualizing a perfect performance.

4) Whatever you tell a child not to do, they will then proceed to do it. Young children hear the verb, the action word, and not the rest of the sentence. I remember my son's preschool teacher calling out to him "Don't jump into the puddle with your tennis shoes on." You can guess who jumped into the puddle. My friend who loves and works with animals says it goes deeper than that. It is the picture you hold in your thoughts that instructs the child. Children have the ability to read the pictures in our mind. If we say "Don't run out in the middle of the street," then we create the picture in our mind of a child running out into the street. Chances are that this picture is transferred and the child dutifully runs out into the street. If instead, we say and hold the picture "Stay on the sidewalk," then chances are the child will stay on the sidewalk.

5) When making a request of a child, saying "You may … " closes the door to negotiation. "You may …" works far better then "Would you please … " or "Don't you think it is time to … ." If there is no choice, then don't give one. In addition, children like to see what happens if they don't do what their parents ask. Giving too many choices draws the attention of the child prematurely to itself and can make a young child more self-centered. It also weakens their will. They stand frozen trying to figure out what choices to make or what to do.

As I struggle in my parenting I try to remember that it is the striving that counts. No one is perfect. We all make mistakes and mistakes are part of being human. It is the way we learn and grow. ✦

Confronting Our Shadow

Susan R. Johnson, MD, FAAP, Raphael House

Parenting is one of the most awe-inspiring, noble, and challenging professions. Yet being a parent gets so little support and appreciation from our culture. It was much easier for me to go through medical school, a pediatric residency, a fellowship, and work as a pediatrician, than to be a parent. I can't remember ever being so depleted and exhausted as I have been these past seven and a half years parenting a child. I think some of the exhaustion comes from the developmental work that I needed to do (and am still doing) on myself, when faced with this bright-eyed, intuitive, energetic, developing boy. Raising a child provided me with the opportunity to relive my own childhood. I am discovering that all my unresolved feelings and thoughts, that were long ago repressed, now have come bursting forth to the surface.

A few months ago, I spent a weekend participating in a Natural Learning Rhythms workshop for parents that was organized by a group in Nevada City called Encompass. Many of the thoughts and ideas about childhood were similar to what I recently had learned during my Waldorf teacher training and anthroposophical medical course. During the workshop, I learned that each age group has its own wisdoms, nourishing "foods," and poisons or threats to development. For example, children in the first seven to eight years of life live in their body and their senses. They are sponges for all that they see, hear, smell, taste, and touch. They are doers who are trying to integrate their sense of hearing, sense of vision, sense of balance, sense of movement, and many other subtle senses.

Children in this age group also have an incredible capacity to perceive our soul moods. It is not the words we say that teach children of this age group; rather, it is who we are on the inside. It is the tone of our voice, our attitudes, our gestures, our mood of soul, and our ability to remain present in the moment (and not be scattered and overwhelmed by thoughts of past failures and future worries). Children absorb who we are and what is around them into the deepest core of their being. Therefore, we must ask ourselves if we are worthy of their imitation, and if the environment that surrounds our children (what they see and hear) also is worthy of being imitated.

From the parenting workshop, I learned that the newborn-to-eight-year-old child is trying to discover his or her own strengths, determine his or her own boundaries, and come into his or her own body. These are the wisdoms of this age group. The nourishing foods for this age group include loving touch, security, warmth, flexibility, and nourishment of body, soul, and spirit. Children of this age group need clear rules and boundaries, lots of predictable routines and daily rhythms, good nutrition, lots of sleep, and not too many choices (actions and examples speak louder than words). To threaten children, either physically or verbally, is a poison because it causes them to withdraw physically and etherically (in the realm of their life forces) and also at a soul and spiritual level. This undermines their ability to discover their strengths, to explore their boundaries, and fully enter into their bodies.

An important idea I learned from the workshop was that all children, and especially teenagers, act as mirrors of their environment and our culture. Children show us our shadow, and teenagers show us both our shadow as parents and the shadow of our culture. In other words, sometimes the characteristics that we as parents refuse to acknowledge in ourselves, or in our society, can be seen in our children. If we were not allowed to show anger in our childhood, then often our children demonstrate lots of anger and ignite our own. If we were taught to be afraid of anger in our childhood, then our child can control us with outbursts of anger when he or she wants something.

Our relationship to our children, just like our other intimate relationships with family members and friends, continually reveals our shadow, and therefore provides each of us the opportunity to transform and heal our soul. ✦

Product vs. Process

Susan R. Johnson, MD, FAAP, Raphael House

What an identity crisis being a parent can be. Here I was brought up in a culture where the final product and not the process was mostly what was valued. During medical school and my pediatric residency, it didn't matter if I didn't get any sleep, didn't eat right, didn't see my own family, and was downright grumpy to my friends, as long as I completed my goals (saw my patients, prepared my clinic talks, and finished my research papers). In other words, I was living a life where "the end always justified the means."

Having a child finally taught me that "the end" doesn't justify "the means." When I first started to bake with my child, I was so focused on the product, the end result. I was overly concerned with how accurately the flour or baking powder was measured. I wanted to end up with "perfect" muffins. Yet, my child wanted to experience the joy of feeling the texture of the flour and just mixing everything together. I was so worried about the future (i.e. whether the muffins would turn out) that the experience of baking together was not an enjoyable one for either of us. The muffins turned out, but after that experience my son was not interested in baking with me anymore. The same held true with going for a walk. Before having a child, I had always had a destination when I took a walk or a hike. I thought you had to arrive at the destination to "have a successful walk." Here was my child wanting to stop every few feet to observe a rock, a bug, or pick up a stick. A whole hour would go by and we had only walked one block. I was frustrated and my child would pick up my frustration though he probably didn't understand it. For a while, until I learned how to live more in the present, going on a walk together was not an enjoyable experience.

It also mattered if I didn't take care of myself (skipped meals, didn't get enough sleep, drank too much caffeine, or held unresolved anger). It greatly affected the relationship with my child. Especially during their first seven years, children absorb our soul moods and our gestures. Even in the older child, our moods and our gestures serve as their teachers and role models. The mood of our soul is in every one of our gestures and these gestures imprint on our child. If I am doing one activity, like grating a carrot and I am thinking about something upsetting that happened earlier in the day or on the news (i.e. the past) it affects the way I grate that carrot. I will grate that carrot in a jerky, angry, and chaotic way. How confusing for a child to be watching the gesture of grating a carrot and absorbing the jerky movements of my arms and absorbing my facial expressions that have nothing to do with the actual act of grating a carrot.

One lecturer I recently heard wondered if the increased anxiety and nervousness in our children's movements today could be related to our lack of presence in the activities we are doing in front of them. We are all under stress and there seems to be so little time to get everything done. Yet time, and how we spend it, is a spiritual matter. There is a tendency to constantly dwell on the past or worry about the future when we are with our children. Children live in the moment, and if we spend enough time with them they will remind us how to live in the present as well.

Finally, there is a saying that goes, "It is not so much what we say that children remember; it is how we make them feel when they are with us." The greatest gift we can give our children and each other is our presence.   ✦

Notes
on the
Contributors

The WECAN Working Group on the Older Child

Tim Bennett

Tim Bennett, born in England, came to America when he was ten years old. Living in the Pacific Northwest, he took full advantage of experiencing the wilderness around him, camping, skiing and hiking. He graduated from the University of Washington with a BFA in Fine Arts, concentrating on ceramics and painting. Through art, he came to working with children. After assisting for three years in the Waldorf kindergartens of the Seattle Waldorf School, he became a lead teacher. He has been teaching kindergarten since 1990. Tim also graduated in the first class of Spacial Dynamics taught in the USA, back in1994. His interest in young children and movement led him to meet Helle Heckmann and visit her school in Copenhagen. His own kindergarten incorporated a love of nature and joy in movement.

Nancy Blanning

Nancy has taught within Waldorf education for twenty-five years as a lead kindergarten teacher and presently serves as a therapeutic and remedial teacher at the Denver Waldorf School. Her special focus is on developing movement enrichment for young children. With her colleague, Laurie Clark, she has co-authored the book *Movement Journeys and Circle Adventures*. She also does consulting work with Waldorf schools in North America, teacher training and mentoring. She is a member of the WECAN board.

Louise deForest

Louise is the mother of four children ranging in age from 40 to 23. She has also been a Waldorf kindergarten teacher for many years and is now the Pedagogical Director of the Early Childhood program at the Rudolf Steiner Waldorf School in Manhattan. Adult education has always been a deep interest and Louise has taught classes at Sunbridge College for many years, offered an ongoing course for parents called Bringing Waldorf

Education Home, and, with Jennifer Brooks-Quinn, given monthly support to homeschooling families, as well as offering parent consultations and traveling to mentor and evaluate teachers and early childhood programs nationally and internationally. While continuing this work, Louise is also a WECAN board member, a regional representative of WECAN in Mexico, one of the representatives from North America to IASWECE and leader of the Waldorf early childhood teacher training in Cuernavaca, Mexico. In her "free" time, Louise enjoys travel (three of her four children live in other countries!), handwork, gardening, and canoeing on the lake behind her house.

Ruth Ker

Ruth is a mother of two children, aged 27 and 21, who have been educated in the Waldorf school that she has pioneered on Vancouver Island, in Duncan, British Columbia, Canada. She has been a teacher of early childhood education for over thirty years, first in mainstream education and then at Sunrise Waldorf School. Ruth is presently in the mixed-age kindergarten classroom with her beloved six-year-olds, is a member of the WECAN board, and a teacher trainer and mentor for the early childhood teacher training program of the West Coast Institute for Studies in Anthroposophy. Ruth was also a facilitator for the retreats attended by the Older Child Working Group and lovingly tended the birth of this book. In her spare time Ruth likes to garden and do wilderness hikes.

Barbara Klocek

Barbara Klocek has been teaching a mixed-age kindergarten for many years at the Sacramento Waldorf School. During that time she has also worked professionally as an artist and art therapist. Her love of art early in her life led her to a Master of Fine Arts degree from Temple University. Her three sons, now grown, were educated at the Waldorf School and that experience inspired her to become a Waldorf teacher. She completed her teacher training studies at Rudolf Steiner College. She has offered many workshops for kindergarten teachers at Rudolf Steiner College, as well as teaching art nationally and internationally. Her other interests include music, gardening, and nature.

Other Contributors

Melissa Borden

Melissa Borden is a kindergarten teacher at the Seattle Waldorf School, where she has taught for 20 years. She, her husband, and their three children spend the summers in south central Alaska, where they have a commercial salmon fishing business.

Devon Brownsey

Devon Brownsey is a pioneer alumna of Sunrise Waldorf School and is presently attending the parent-child classes at her alma mater with her daughter, while her son attends the Nursery there. Devon is a professional photographer and full-time mother.

Laurie Clark

Laurie Clark lives in Colorado with her husband, Tom, who is also a Waldorf teacher. They have three daughters and one granddaughter. She is entering her 26th year as a Waldorf kindergarten teacher and currently works at the Denver Waldorf School. She is also a conference presenter, a teacher trainer, and a kindergarten mentor. Recently she coauthored a book with Nancy Blanning entitled *Movement Journeys and Circle Adventures*.

Susan R. Johnson, MD

Dr. Johnson works as a behavioral and developmental pediatrician for Waldorf schools, writes parent newsletters about preventative health, and gives community lectures. She has a private practice in behavioral and developmental pediatrics at Raphael House in Fair Oaks, CA, where she sees children two through eighteen years of age with their parents for developmental, behavioral and learning concerns.

Janet Kellman

Janet Kellman has been involved in Waldorf education for over thirty years. She and her husband were members of the founding circle of Live Oak Waldorf School in Applegate, California. She served as a kindergarten teacher, she was Director of Early Childhood Teacher Education Program at Rudolf Steiner College for twelve years, and is currently with the Nursery Preschool, as well as the Parent and Child Baby classes at Live Oak. She is a former Board member of WECAN, an avid gardener and thoroughly enjoys the blessings of three grandchildren.

Elisabeth Moore-Haas

Elisabeth Moore-Haas was a kindergarten teacher in Switzerland and is the founder and director of the kindergarten training seminar in Bern, Switzerland. She taught in early childhood education programs in North America as a visiting faculty member for many years.

Helge Ruof, MD

Helge Ruof studied Medicine at the University Witten/Herdecke which was funded by Dr. Gerhard Kienle and a group of anthroposophical medical doctors. Her internship and residency were at the University Hospital in Basel, Switzerland. She received Board Certification in Pediatrics in 2004.

Jörg Ruof, MD

Jörg Ruof received his MD at the University Witten/Herdecke, Germany and his training in Internal Medicine & Rheumatology at Hanover Medical School, Germany. For several years he has worked in various functions in the Pharmaceutical Industry. Helge & Jörg currently live in Basel with their two children.

References

Section 1
Rudolf Steiner, *The Roots of Education*. London: Rudolf Steiner Press, London, 1982, page 61.

Section 2
Rudolf Steiner, *Waldorf Education and Anthroposophy 2*. Hudson, NY: Anthroposophic Press, 1996, page 212. From a lecture given in London on August 30, 1924.

Section 3
Freya Jaffke, ed., *On the Play of the Child: Indications by Rudolf Steiner for Working with Young Children*. Spring Valley, NY: WECAN, 2004, pages 18-19. Extract from a lecture given on June 10, 1920, not available in complete form in English.

Section 4
Rudolf Steiner, *The Essentials of Education*. Hudson, NY: Anthroposophic Press, 1997, page 40.

Section 5
Freya Jaffke, ed., *On the Play of the Child: Indications by Rudolf Steiner for Working with Young Children*. Spring Valley, NY: WECAN, 2004, page 41. From a discussion with English guests held on the 5th of January, 1922 in Dornach, quoted in *Kunst und Handarbeit* (Art and Handwork), by Hedwig Hauck.

Section 6
Heinz Zimmermann, *Speaking, Listening, Understanding*. Hudson, NY: Lindisfarne Press, 1996, page 43.